THE CORRESPONDENCE OF POPE GREGORY VII

Records of Western Civilization

THE CORRESPONDENCE OF
POPE GREGORY VII

SELECTED LETTERS FROM THE REGISTRUM

TRANSLATED WITH AN INTRODUCTION BY

EPHRAIM EMERTON

COLUMBIA UNIVERSITY PRESS
New York

Columbia University Press
New York   Chichester, West Sussex
Copyright © 1932, 1960, 1990 Columbia University Press

Library of Congress Cataloging-in-Publication Data

Catholic Church. Pope (1073–1085 : Gregory VII)
[Registrum. English. Selections]
The correspondence of Pope Gregory VII :
selected letters from the Registrum /
translated with an introduction by Ephraim Emerton.
p.   cm.—(Records of western civilization)
Originally published 1932.
Includes bibliographical references and index.
ISBN 978-0-231-00599-9.
ISBN 978-0-231-09627-0 (pbk.)
1. Catholic Church.
Pope (1073–1085 : Gregory VII)—Correspondence.
2. Papacy—History—To 1309—Sources.
3. Europe—Church history—Middle Ages, 600–1500—Sources.
I. Gregory VII, Pope, ca. 1015–1085.
II. Emerton, Ephraim, 1851–1935.
III. Title.
IV. Series.
BX1187.A4   1990
282'.092—dc20
90-37584
CIP

Casebound editions of Columbia University Press books are printed on
permanent and durable acid-free paper

Printed in the United States of America

PREFACE

The immediate motive to the publication of this volume was furnished by the appearance, in the year 1923, of a new edition of Pope Gregory's *Registrum* by Professor Erich Caspar of the University of Freiburg. My own interest in the Hildebrandine period was of long standing, and I was glad to improve the leisure offered by release from teaching to attempt a translation of some of the more important letters. The work grew under my hand, and the prompt and generous response of the Columbia University Press to my suggestion of publication encouraged me to proceed until the selections, though still far from complete, came to include enough to give a significant impression of the man and his work.

I am greatly indebted to my younger colleagues, especially to Professor Charles H. McIlwain and Professor George La Piana, for their kindly interest and assistance.

E. E.

HARVARD UNIVERSITY
January 11, 1932

INTRODUCTION

The papacy of Gregory VII, extending from April 22, 1073, to May 25, 1085, covers one of the most momentous periods of European history. Within this short term of twelve years was enacted a drama of politico-religious conflict the echoes of which may be heard through the changing battle cries of parties down the centuries to the present moment. The recent compact between Fascist Italy and the Vatican is a companion piece to the fateful bargain of Canossa. For the issue of that far-away struggle was one that must persist so long as organized religion holds a place in the allegiance of man. It must persist and it must call for settlement with an insistence proportioned to the interest in religious matters taken by great numbers of men at a given time. In our own day religious interest is notoriously going through a period of depression. It is, so we are quick to say, crowded out by the intense pressure of an age primarily concerned with material welfare and with what seems to be material progress.

It costs us a considerable effort to set ourselves back into a time when religious considerations were uppermost in the consciousness of all right-minded persons. More than this, religion in the eleventh century meant only the creed and the forms of the Roman Catholic Church. Whatever varied from these carried its own condemnation as more or less well-defined heresy. On this point there was no real difference of opinion. The bold defiance of enlightened minds in the fourteenth century in defense of frankly heretical ideas was utterly foreign to the eleventh. Heresies there were indeed then, as there always had been and doubtless always will be; but they were not of such a nature as to attract a wide or influential following. Manichaean dualism, with its extravagant subtleties, was calculated rather to shock and repel than to win the allegiance of devout minds.

The real foes of the Roman institution were certain social and political tendencies not yet worked out into permanent forms but gradually defining themselves with increasing distinctness. The first of these tendencies was the growing spirit of nationalism. In the break-up of the Carolingian empire racial distinctions were the most obvious cohesive force. Through the ninth and tenth centuries a Germany, a France and an Italy were emerging as nuclei around which smaller local groups were gathering. The larger units found their interest in attaching the smaller to their schemes for ever wider development, and the smaller saw their advantage in securing from the larger some protection against the aggression of their neighbors. The eleventh century brought a still wider extension of these political creations. In Spain, England, Denmark, Bohemia, Hungary, arose powerful ruling houses enforcing upon their more or less unwilling subjects such rights of sovereignty as they could from time to time maintain.

The problem before all these greater centers of political power was the same: so to capture and hold the loyalty of their subject members that they could utilize them for their support at home and their service in arms abroad. In the earlier stages the relation of the sovereign, king, duke or what not, to his subjects was vague and indeterminate. He was one among them, not always the most powerful or the most capable, and he was liable to be overthrown by any combination that might seem to promise a new partition of rights and revenues. It was to be a long and bitter struggle, but already the foundations of permanent social organizations had been laid. The sense of national coherence was being felt with ever increasing force. The king was beginning to be thought of as the symbol of a unity which had its rights as against other units of corporate life. If the king would do his duty as the guardian of peace within and the leader of the nation's strength without, then the members would live up to their side of the bargain and furnish him with the needed revenues and the needed arms.

The second menace to the domination of the catholic ideal came from within the Church itself. It involved the whole question of the relation of churchmen to the economic structure of the new mediaeval society. "The Church must live." That was the starting point for the economic argument in the case of the religious corporation as it was for the individual. But how were the means of livelihood to be provided for the countless religious establishments of the western world? The answer to that question had been given in the amazing record of pious foundations from the time of Charles the Great down. In every corner of Europe endowments for religious purposes had been maintained with jealous care by the corporations to whose hands they were entrusted. The basis of these endowments was land and the revenues derived from the profitable working of the land. In other words, the Church became the economic equal, the rival, and often the successful rival, of the lay cultivator. The holder of church property was also a landlord and was on the way to become a lord of the land.

It was a long and slow development, and the processes of it were so silent and obscure that its dangers did not become evident until it had reached such a portentous height as to attract the attention of social students and reformers. Looked at from the side of power, it marked a decisive victory of the organized Church. On the other hand, it had become evident by the eleventh century that the line between the religious and the secular had become obscured almost to the vanishing point. If, as I began by saying, the world accepted the formal guidance of the church establishment, the Church, certainly as far as its economic interests were concerned, had adopted to a perilous degree the standards of secular life. Its high officials stood in all respects in the same relation to their subjects as did the great lay lords. They formed with these the high aristocracy in every country. They shared with these the duty of military service toward the shadowy monarchy which was the symbol of national unity.

It was rapidly becoming a critical question where the ultimate control of these very intricate relations was to lie. What was to be the status of the Church on its economic and political side? Was it to be the superior or the equal or the subject of the lay authority? The answer to this question was working itself out mainly along three lines: first, the appointments to clerical office; second, the right of conferring the final sanction upon appointments of the highest church functionaries; and third, the sharp separation of the clerical from the secular mode of life.

The arguments on the two sides, complicated as they were in detail, may be quite simply stated. The lay powers saw with alarm the gradual slipping away from their control of great masses of landed property from which they had derived a great part of their support in men and money. They saw these revenues being diverted to the support of a large and increasing class of men whose primary interests were of a non-social character. They claimed a right of sovereignty over these lands, and therefore they claimed also the right to have a voice in the selection of men to fill the important clerical offices. Unless they could in some way control these appointments there was a very real danger that they would lose one of the most valuable sources of their power.

Church office had by this time become an exceedingly desirable function. Its honors and emoluments made it the object of ambitions far removed from religious considerations. To secure such prizes was worth elaborate planning and lavish outlay of money, and hence arose that form of corrupt practice which has been branded forever with the name of the arch-corruptionist Simon Magus, who sought to purchase the gift of God for money. The word "Simony" covered every form of commercialism in clerical matters. As to the right procedure in clerical appointments, there was no question whatever. The bishop was to be elected *clero et populo*, by the clergy and people of the diocese. The abbot was to be chosen by the chapter of the House. In fact, however, the pressure of outside interests was so great that the result of an election was seldom reached by any such simple process. Bishops and abbots were politically and economically the peers of princes and were actuated by similar motives. Simony, the purchase of high clerical office, was eating into the very life of the Church as a religious institution.

Closely associated with the war against Simony was the combat against Lay Investiture. So important was this aspect of the reform movement that it has given its name to the whole long struggle from the first general proclamation of 1075 to the Concordat of Worms in 1122. Investiture was the crowning act in the electoral process of the higher clergy. After the candidate had been selected by the canonical choice of clergy and people, he must be "invested" by some higher authority with the right to perform the functions of his office. It was a procedure similar to our "inauguration" of elected officials by some organ of government duly authorized for the purpose. The burning question of the eleventh century was: What was the higher authority which could lawfully confer this final sanction upon the newly elected bishop or abbot? In practice it had largely fallen into the hands of lay rulers — kings, princes or local lords — but not without protest from zealous partisans of clerical right. To these it was a scandal that clerical office should be dependent in any way upon the approval of the lay authorities. To this objection the answer was made that the bishop was not merely a clerical person. He was also a great landholder with all the obligations which feudal landholding entailed. If these lands were not to slip away from the control of the political ruler, it was of the first importance that their holder should be a man upon whom he could count for support in all his undertakings. The same considerations which determined the ruler's attitude toward the choice of the candidate guided him also in his decision whether he would or would not confirm the election by conferring the investiture.

The issue was thus clearly drawn. Each side was fully aware of its far-reaching importance and was prepared to stake its all upon the outcome of the inevitable conflict.

The third menace to the dominance of the Church was, or seemed to be, of a different character. The enemy in this case was the most deep-seated instinct of humanity, the natural desire of the normal man to propagate his kind and to protect his offspring by the sanctions of a normal family life. At first and for a long time the Christian priesthood had followed the natural course, had taken wives, reared children and provided for their future like the ordinary layman. It is well to remind ourselves that such has continued to be the practice of the Eastern Church. In the West several circumstances combined to create a different attitude toward the whole question of the social obligations of the clergy. The Augustinian theology, with its fateful separation of the human body and the human soul, gave added force to the idea of the essential sinfulness of the physical world. Monasticism, taking form in the midst of the disintegration of the ancient Roman and early mediaeval society, was the standing illustration of the superior sanctity of the celibate life. Comparison with the secular clergy, involved as these were in the cares of this world, must inevitably be greatly to the disadvantage of the latter.

So it was that, notably from the time of Gregory I (d. 604), himself a monk, church authority came to insist more and more strongly upon the celibacy of the secular as well as of the regular clergy. Here also the motive was not exclusively a religious nor even a moral one. If clergymen were to be fathers of families, it was obvious that the revenues by which they were supported would be diverted from their original purpose as religious foundations and would become endowments for the maintenance of sons and the dowering of daughters. Or again, if, as seemed altogether possible, benefices were to be passed on from father to son, there was a very real danger that the priestly order might become an hereditary caste, a Levitical hierarchy resting upon community of blood and independent of all superior control.

By the eleventh century the doctrine of sacerdotal celibacy had become fairly established in the theory of church polity. It was curiously assisted by the prevalence in many regions of the type of heresy already mentioned. Manichaeism, wherever it was found, served to keep alive that tradition of antagonism between body and spirit which we have seen to lie at the root of all ascetic teaching. This unholy alliance between acknowledged heresy and the highest orthodoxy forms one of the most curious chapters in the history of the Gregorian crusade.

On the other hand, there still survived in many parts of Europe the ancient theory which regarded the priestly order as part and parcel of the Christian community, subject to the same human instincts and none the less true servants of God because they lived the normal human life as lawful husbands and fathers of families. Probably nowhere would a married bishop have been anything but a scandal to the community; but the lower clergy, coming closer to the common man, sharing his temptations and understanding his mental processes, were not restrained by fear of losing their influence. Indeed their hold upon their parishioners may well have been strengthened by this nearer approach to the common ways of living.

By the middle of the eleventh century these various forms of departure from the strictest interpretations of the canon law were becoming more and more acutely felt at the center of the church administration. The Papacy, under the fostering care of the early Salian kings in Germany, had begun to show a zeal for reform which, but for its unhappy political complications, might have had great results. The Alsatian pope Leo IX (d. 1054) began an aggressive campaign against the twin evils of Simony and clerical marriage. He carried the war personally into France and Germany, held largely attended synods at Reims and Mainz, made bold proclamations, but could produce no lasting effect. Almost at the moment of his most imposing demonstration there was born in Germany a king who for a long half-century was to be the storm center of every form of organized opposition to all that this reforming pope represented. The Salian Henry IV stands out as the

champion of national right quite as distinctly as his greater opponent stands for the extremest form of papal sovereignty.

The third quarter of the eleventh century saw the further working out of the same antagonisms. On the papal side we find an
unbroken continuity of policy, notably during the pontificates of
Nicholas II (1058-1061) and Alexander II (1061-1073). The establishment of the electoral college of cardinals in 1059 secured for
all time a constitutional basis for the exclusively clerical control of
the papal office. The acquisition of the new Norman duchy in
southern Italy as a vassal state gave to the Papacy a backing
against all territorial aggression from the north. The principles of
the reform campaign of Leo IX were reasserted by his successors
with hardly diminished emphasis but without that persistent enforcement which was essential to their success.

In this interval also the affairs of Germany had been moving
toward the inevitable catastrophe. The boy-king, ruler in name
alone, was handed about by a succession of regencies, no one of
which could be thought of as truly representing the nation as a
whole. His majority in 1065 brought no solution to the provincial
rivalries coming down from Carolingian times and long to be the
hopeless obstacles to national unity within and efficiency abroad.

Such, in briefest outline, were the conditions of European public
life at the accession of Gregory VII. The problem was clearly indicated. The religious consciousness of Europe was awakened to the
necessity of action. It remained only to bring the whole force of
this awakened conscience under the direction of a commanding
personality, and this happened with the elevation of that extraordinary man Hildebrand to the chair of St. Peter. There can be no
doubt that the influence of Hildebrand as a high official of the
Roman administration had long been exercised with profound effect upon the policy of his predecessors in the Papacy. We shall
have frequent occasion to notice in his correspondence references to
his activities in carrying out the reform measures of Nicholas II
and Alexander II. From the beginnings of Leo IX in 1049 there is
a continuity in the papal policy that could hardly have been secured
without some watchful individual guidance.

The tumultuous "election" of Hildebrand, in open violation of
the electoral law of 1059 which was in all probability his own cre-
ation, was thus nothing more than the natural expression of a

general feeling that he was, above all others, the man of the hour.
There was no significant protest against the irregularity of his
election, and at once began the series of striking proclamations
which form the material of the present volume. Beginning with
formal notifications of his selection to "bear the burden of apostolic office," they go on rapidly to declare the threefold program of
reform outlined above. Hitherto the work of Hildebrand had been
to give form and direction to the action of others. Now he was free to
step out into the open, to have a polity of his own. The keynote
of this new stage in the progress of reform is found in the word
"freedom." If the Church were to take the lead in the social life
of Europe, it must first be free. It must be free from the social
entanglements of a married clergy, free from the commercialism
involved in the purchase and sale of benefices and free also from
the political servitude consequent upon the investiture of clergymen
by laymen of whatever rank. Nationality in church affairs must be
combated by the principle of universality.

The *Registrum* of Gregory's letters was the first even approxi-
mately complete collection of the correspondence of a pope since
that of his sainted predecessor, Gregory I, nearly five centuries
earlier. Brought together into one volume, they were preserved
with pious care, were frequently copied and excerpted and after
the invention of printing were repeatedly edited by scholars of
reputation. Quite recently renewed interest in them has been
aroused by several important publications.

Until now scholars have depended for their knowledge of the
Registrum upon the edition of Philip Jaffé in volume II of his
Bibliotheca rerum Germanicarum published in 1865. That edition
was based upon an examination of the Vatican manuscript by Wilhelm v. Giesebrecht, the historian of Germany's imperial period.
Jaffé himself had not seen the manuscript and was, therefore, dependent upon the printed texts. In his work as editor he aimed to
give an intelligible reading and to this end allowed himself considerable freedom in corrections and additions. After his time no
important progress was made toward a more critical examination
of the Vatican codex. Jaffé accepted the conclusion of Giesebrecht
that the *Registrum* was a compilation made near the close of Gregory's papacy or perhaps shortly after his death. It was made up,
according to this theory, of selections from a more extensive body
of material which has been lost. A chief argument of Jaffé was the

paucity of letters in the most crowded years of the great struggle — only twenty-one in the third and twenty-eight in the fourth. That Gregory VII should not have followed the long prevailing papal custom of keeping a full inventory of all his important pronouncements seemed to Jaffé quite inconceivable. He believed, therefore, that this collection, which he called *Registrum minus*, was made, surely with Gregory's approval, by some other person. Later scholars, such as Paul Ewald and Scheffer-Boichorst, followed the main conclusions of Jaffé, until in the year 1911 an Austrian scholar, Wilhelm Peitz, S. J., presented to the Vienna Academy of Sciences an article of 350 pages with the title, "The Original Register of Gregory VII in the Vatican Archives." The purpose of this study was to show that this Register was not, as Jaffé and his successors had supposed, a compilation made towards the close of Gregory's life, but a continuous record made as each document or group of documents was issued. Peitz had long suspected that the accepted idea of the *Registrum* was not supported by the facts. He made, therefore, a prolonged examination of the Vatican codex and found his expectations abundantly confirmed. The results are given in the *Proceedings of the Vienna Academy*, vol. 165 (1910-1911). It was evident that the weak point in Jaffé's equipment for his editorial task was his lack of acquaintance with the manuscript upon which in the last resort every argument must be based. Peitz undertook to remedy this deficiency by making a minute study of the handwriting, employing all the means which the science of palaeography could supply. He was able especially to profit by the progress in knowledge of the methods of the papal chancery which had been developed in the last half century.

A great part of Peitz's monograph is occupied with the proofs of his documentary analysis. As to the main facts of the composition of the *Registrum*, there was no room for very great differences of opinion. It was composed of nine books, of which the first seven were in strict chronological order, one book for each of the first seven years of Gregory's papacy. This carried the collection down to the year 1080-1081. The eighth book begins with the same chronological system, but then shows many instances of disarrangement, letters often being placed before those of earlier date. In the ninth book, covering the period from the spring of 1081 to the end of 1083, there is no pretense of strict sequence in time. These differences of arrangement have been variously explained. Did they indicate some radical change in the administration of the papal chancery? Or a new hand in the bureau of copyists? Or can they be explained by the outward circumstances of the papal government? Certainly these were very troublous years. In the spring of 1081 King Henry IV came down into Italy with a considerable force of northerners augmented by contingents from all the anti-Gregorian elements of the Italian populations. The rallying point of this imperial demonstration was Ravenna, whose archbishop Wibert had been set up as antipope by an assembly of German and Lombard bishops at Brixen in Tyrol in 1080. King Henry was received with enthusiasm in Lombardy and the Romagna, and overcame what resistance there was in Tuscany. It was, however, to be three years before he could break down the opposition of the city of Rome. In the spring of 1084, accompanied by his antipope, he entered the Eternal City and seemed to have reached the highest goal of his ambition by his coronation as emperor at the hands of Clement III. Then came the recovery of the rebellious city by the Normans and the withdrawal of Gregory under their protection to Salerno, where he died, May 15, 1085, exiled but undaunted to the end.

It can hardly seem strange that under these extremely disturbing conditions the systematic recording of papal documents should have been seriously interrupted. The fundamental thesis of Fr. Peitz that the *Registrum* was compiled by successive entries made at the time, or immediately after the time of issuance, is rather confirmed than otherwise by the seeming contradiction of the last two books. The entries were made in order as long as possible. When outward conditions made this impossible, then they took place as chance dictated. If, as was formerly supposed, the *Registrum* had been compiled by a later editor, it seems hardly possible that he should not have followed a consistent plan throughout. Especially would this seem to be true if such an editor had had before him a larger collection, the *Registrum majus* of Jaffé, from which to make a selection.

But, after all, the *Registrum* is a selection, as scholars have realized from the beginning. Besides the letters there given are numerous others scattered through contemporary chronicles or in the archives of churches and monasteries. Jaffé gave fifty-one of these under the title *Epistolae collectae*. Now why were certain letters recorded in the *Registrum* and others allowed to go out without record? It cannot have been on account of relative importance; for many of the outside letters are among the most emphatic and most characteristic declarations of the Gregorian policy, while many of those in the *Registrum* are of comparatively trifling nature. Various answers have been given to this question. It has been supposed that in some cases no copies of letters dispatched were preserved; but no reason for such omission could be discovered or invented. Fr. Peitz calls attention to a remark of Giraldus Cambrensis that only *causae magis arduae* were entered in papal Registers; but what did that mean? One's first thought would be that it meant "only the more important cases," but it is perfectly evident that this did not apply to the case in hand. The cases covered by the letters *in* Gregory's *Registrum* were, as we have said, no more important than those in the outside letters. Peitz therefore suggests that the word *arduae* should be rendered by "difficult" or "intricate," that is, cases which could not be settled by a single proclamation, but were likely to lead to further action. In such a case, he thinks, we have in the *Registrum* the key-document, so to speak, recorded for future reference. He supports this theory by the remark that in every case of a group of documents relating to a single subject, the one given in the *Registrum* invariably marks the development of the case into some new phase. I cannot think that this explanation goes very far toward solving the problem, and I have not found elsewhere any really satisfactory solution.

Rather more rewarding are the arguments for the originality of the Vatican codex grounded upon indications of the personality of Gregory himself. These have been studied by Dr. Otto Blaul, at first in his Strasbourg doctoral dissertation in 1911 and afterward in greater detail in an article by him in the *Archiv für Urkundenforschung* for 1912. It is, of course, not to be supposed for a moment that Gregory wrote any of these documents with his own hand, though the possibility of an occasional exception is not quite excluded. The actual writing was done by official scribes attached to the papal chancery. Discussion is possible therefore only as to the method of composition. How far were Gregory's letters his own work? As one reads them in sequence, long and short, weighty or comparatively insignificant, and addressed to every kind of person, one is, I think, impressed by the continuous evidence of personality. No doubt there were certain formulas, so well established by long usage that a trained official, given the subject matter, could compose

the needed letter without much, if any, supervision. There was
a formula for the address, for the arrangement of the material and
for the conclusion, but even so we perceive the touch of personal
feeling. For example, in the formula of the address, the same words
occur with monotonous regularity: "Gregory, bishop, servant of
those who serve God, to . . ., greeting and the apostolic benediction." But even this conventional greeting is given with a certain
reserve. Again and again some phrase is added to show that the
divine blessing is conditional upon the absolute subjection of the
person addressed to God, to St. Peter, to the Roman Church and
to their earthly representative, the pope himself. For example,
"To Tedaldus, a clerk of Milan, greeting and the apostolic benediction, if he shall be obedient" (III, 8, p. 259) ; "To all those citizens
of Ravenna, both of high and low estate, who reverence St. Peter
and his son Apollinaris, martyr and bishop, as Christians should,
greeting and the apostolic benediction" (VI, 10, p. 411) ; "To
King Henry, greeting and the apostolic benediction, but with the
understanding that he obeys the Apostolic See as becomes a Christian
king" (III, 10, p. 263).

Another interesting glimpse into the personal side of the Gregorian letters is given by the use of the first person singular. In
accordance with the long established custom of the papal chancery
Gregory usually employs the royal "we" and "us," but occasion-
ally, under the stress of unusual emotion, as it would appear, he
slips into the more human "I" and "me." For example, in a
letter to Archbishop Wibert of Ravenna, four days after his accession to the Papacy, he writes:

We doubt not that rumor has outrun *our* letter and has informed you
and many others of the decease of *our* lord Pope Alexander. His death
was a great blow to *me*, and all *my* inward parts were shaken to their
depths. For at first the Roman populace, contrary to their custom, placed
the control of affairs in *our* hands so quietly that it was evidently done by
the special providence of God. But then, suddenly, while our late master
was being borne to his burial a great tumult and shouting of the people
arose, and they rushed upon *me* like madmen and dragged *me* away by
force to the place of apostolic rule. . . .

The use of the singular continues through the letter until the final
paragraph, when the formal "we" appears again. One can feel the
profoundly sincere emotion of the man breaking through the con-

ventional dignity of the ruler and again passing over into the formalities of public office.

This distinction is especially noticeable in all Gregory's dealings with the two women whose friendship was absolutely indispensable to his policy. The lands of the Countess — whom Gregory sometimes addresses as Duke [*sic*] — Beatrice of Tuscany and her more famous daughter Matilda formed alternately a highway and a barrier between Rome and the turbulent communes of Lombardy. The tone of the papal letters to these women is a mixture of paternal affection and almost pathetic appeals for aid, with unbending insistence upon obedience to the apostolic authority. In a peculiarly affectionate letter of February, 1074, to Matilda, exhorting her to pious observances, he employs the first person singular throughout. In another, of a more political character, he uses the royal plural except at one point, where he sharply reproves the good ladies for interfering with his plans. There he slips at once into the "I" language. Again, some months later, speaking as head of a government, he begins in the plural; then he inserts a report of his restoration to health, using the singular; but returning to public affairs, he again takes up the plural.

All this, it will readily be seen, contributes to the impression of contemporaneousness. The entries in the *Registrum* were probably made as the documents were issued, but Fr. Peitz's minute study of the make-up of the volume shows a certain grouping. This might be according to the subject treated or, as Peitz ingeniously suggests, according to the locality of the persons addressed. In that case a bundle of letters would be made up and dispatched by one trusty messenger in a certain direction, while another bundle would be sent to another quarter, and so on. The originals would then be filed in the *Registrum* in corresponding groups, and this registration might take place some time after the dispatch of the letters.

A suggestion may possibly be found in a phrase repeatedly used at the close of an epistle. After a statement of the business in hand, the pope adds in substance: "Besides what we have written, there are many details about which the bearer is authorized to give you full explanation." The carrying of written messages was a very risky affair, as frequent references in this correspondence show; so that a large discretion within certain well-defined limits was necessarily allowed to the trusty legates who were the personal representatives of the pope. The choice of his agents was a matter of especial care to Gregory VII, and he held them to a very strict responsibility. May we not find in these well-known facts at least a hint in explanation of the dearth of recorded letters over considerable periods? Their place may well have been taken by these confidential servants of the papal policy.

While the investigations of Fr. Peitz and Dr. Blaul were in progress, other scholars were busying themselves with the same topic. Professor Erich Caspar, now of Freiburg, made two visits to Italy in 1911 and 1914 for the special purpose of checking up the results of Peitz's research. He became convinced that these results were in the main sound, but that they needed amplifying and correcting in certain details. In an article in the *Neues Archiv* for 1913 he defended this position.

Another and far more important result of Caspar's studies was the conviction that a new edition of the *Registrum* was a prime necessity for further research. The edition of Jaffé, admirable as it was in its day, was antiquated, and the time seemed ripe for utilizing all the work of study and criticism that had been done in the interval of half a century. Further, Jaffé's introduction, as well as all his notes and comments, was in Latin. Caspar discarded this pedantic affectation and used the language in which he could best express himself and which would be most readily understood by present-day scholars. This new edition, begun in 1913, was interrupted by the war and did not appear in complete form until 1923. It is in most respects a model of editorial skill and completeness. Of especial interest is the use made by Caspar of what he calls the parallel transmission in distinction from the legacy of the *Registrum* itself. Peitz had made a further distinction here between archival and literary material, but Caspar, wisely I think, combines the two under the phrase: "receiver transmission." Wherever a letter is found either in an archive or in an historical narrative he makes a careful comparison of its form with that which it has in the original at Rome. In fact he makes it clear that these are quite as much "originals" as those entered in the *Registrum*.

Another of Caspar's contributions is seen in his study of the second oldest manuscript of the *Registrum* preserved in the Library of Troyes in France. This manuscript had long been known and used, but never before carefully collated with that at Rome. A comparison showed that the French copy varied in many details and that these variants corresponded to passages where the Roman entry showed evident traces of erasure or of later correction or substitution — so that the conclusion seemed inevitable that this French copy had been made before the emendations of the Roman original. In some respects, therefore, the text of Troyes was nearer the original form than the original itself as it exists today.

To say that Caspar accepts without qualification every detail of Peitz's analysis would be going too far. On the whole, however, he adopts the conclusions of his predecessor, and when he has occasion to compare Peitz with Jaffé it is almost invariably to the disadvantage of the latter.

A word as to my own method in the present work. Translation is at best rather a thankless task. It is often said, with a considerable measure of truth, that those who really care about the matter can and will use the original, and others need not be considered at all. Those who make this objection are likely to add that a really good translation is an impossibility. Every writer can express in his own language and in his own way shades of meaning which no other person can quite accurately reproduce. Granting all this and admitting that a good translation is a counsel of perfection, the fact remains that the majority of students and readers of history are glad to be spared the time and labor of working back to the original sources for their knowledge of a given period or of a commanding personality. It is for such students that the present translation is intended. The criticism just cited is especially justified in the case of a great masterpiece of literature; but here we have not to deal with any such precious heritage. The letters of Gregory VII are far from being literary treasures. They are written in a school Latin, fairly correct or at least systematically incorrect in its structure. They employ frequently recurring formulas, as the business in hand brings up often repeated situations. The range of words and phrases is limited to the needs of the case. There is very little attempt at philosophical generalization. The appeal is always to authority, and all authorities are given nearly equal weight. The Bible, old and new, the Fathers of the Church, the decrees of popes and councils, the edicts of emperors in so far as they favor the rights of the Church, all are used to support the claim to power which is the primary object of Gregory's every utterance.

The work of translation is thus comparatively simple. The present version aims to give as nearly as possible what Gregory VII said. It seeks to hold a middle ground between literalness and paraphrase, with a leaning toward the former rather than toward the latter. In the choice of words it tries to employ the familiar rather than the novel, the short rather than the long, but even so it would not be bound by any rigid rule.

It would evidently be aside from the purpose of this introduction to attempt any extended appreciation of the contents of this extraordinary record. The key to it is found in the famous dying words of its author: "I have loved justice and hated iniquity; therefore I die in exile." The use of the word *justitia* was only the last utterance of a word so familiar to Gregory that it stood in his mind for the guiding purpose of his public life. So frequently does it occur in his letters that it has been made the subject of more than one special treatment. It is one of two Gregorian catchwords almost equally difficult to translate — *justitia* and *superbia*. The antithesis between these two words runs through the whole of Gregory's literary output. Under *justitia* he includes every possible derivative from the original meaning of "righteousness." His highest aim in life is to bring about the reign of righteousness on earth. In that purpose I believe he was absolutely sincere. But what was this righteousness, whose servant he claimed to be? It was the will of God. But how was this divine will to be realized? Simply and solely through the divinely established Church acting through its divinely ordained Head, St. Peter and his successor, the bishop of Rome. Whatever was favorable to the Roman church system came within the definition of *justitia*. Whatever opposed the dictation of that Church was the outcome of *superbia* — pride, insolence, audacity, the kingdom of Antichrist. All other obligations were forgotten in the tremendous sweep of this magnificent conception. It had the simplicity which a conquering idea must have. It lent itself with amazing success to the reform program of the Gregorian party.

The record lives before us in these letters. We see here the whole process, the dominating spirit at the center, the mechanism of responsible officials, sent out into every corner with minute instructions for the specific case in hand, but always with reference to the general principles underlying the whole unified system. Unrelenting severity, tempered always with mercy toward the offender if only he will confess his wrong, return to his senses [*resipiscere*] and profess obedience to that *justitia* which is the same thing as

God and St. Peter, the Holy Roman Church and its present Head.

In making the choice of letters for translation, I have been guided primarily by the desire to make the selection as nearly as possible representative of the various interests of the Gregorian policy. We have to remember that Gregory entered upon his primacy after a quarter of a century of active participation in papal affairs. The consequence was that he was able to begin at once upon a campaign of action. There is little indication of a development in his ideas during the years of his papacy. All his lines of activity are closely marked from the beginning and are brought out in his correspondence as specific cases come before him for decision. Nothing is too small for his personal attention. The property rights of obscure clergymen in a remote parish in Flanders are defended with the same zealous persistence which he shows in facing the opposition of kings.

The reader becomes aware from the outset of a certain nervous dread on Gregory's part lest the circumstances of his election should be used against him to weaken the authority of his utterances. Again and again he refers to this, not by way of apology, but in order to make clear that the election truly expressed the canonical choice by the clergy and approval by "the people." This being established, he goes on to declare the three articles of the reform program outlined above and to build up the mechanism for their enforcement. The success of his campaign depended largely upon the choice of agents, and on the whole he was exceptionally fortunate in his selection. His personal acquaintance with the personnel of the Roman administration enabled him to choose as his representatives men whom he could trust to carry out an aggressive policy in countries where local sentiment and vested interests of many kinds were in opposition to his plans. These are the *legati* to whom many letters are addressed. There are also many references to them in letters which Gregory wrote to the rulers to whom they were accredited. We are not to think of these, however, as permanent resident ambassadors of the Holy See. They were *legati* in the strict Roman sense, deputies sent on specific missions. They were expected to perform their function with reasonable dispatch and to report in person or by special messenger at the earliest convenient date. Several times we find letters sharply reminding them of this requirement and suggesting a natural fear that they might be influenced by local pressure to a criminal laxity in their ungrateful task. On the other hand, we have convincing evidence of loyalty and unyielding courage under hardships that must have tried their patience and fortitude to the last degree and which prove that their master's confidence was not misplaced. There are two interesting hints as to the peculiar responsibilities of the papal agents. One is the phrase referred to above, coming not infrequently at the close of a letter and stating that the writer would have written at greater length were it not that the bearer is a person enjoying his full confidence and able to supply any omissions in the text. Another bit of evidence is in the closing sentence of a few letters, to the effect that the writer was unwilling to affix a leaden seal lest, if the missive should fall into the hands of "evildoers," some falsification of the seal might take place. The seal was intended as a guarantee of the genuineness of the document, and its absence would therefore throw an additional responsibility upon the messenger and expose him so much the more to the hostility of the opposing party.

If we were to choose one word to characterize the entire policy of Gregory, it would be "centralization." Local administration there must be, and the mechanism for this was provided by the episcopal system which by this time had become firmly established throughout the western world. Bishops were the recognized heads of church provinces and were in theory equal in powers and privileges. Gregory constantly refers to them as brothers and colleagues [*coepiscopi*] and addresses them in terms of fraternal courtesy. He does not interfere with them in the internal affairs of their diocese, but, on the other hand, he never lets them forget that they owe to him — "or rather to St. Peter" — absolute and unquestioning obedience in all the larger relations of the clerical life. Again and again, after laying down the law in the specific instance, he urges them to come to Rome, *ad limina apostolorum*, if possible, to attend the synods held there usually during the Lenten season, and thus to keep themselves in constant touch with the dominant central power by which they were at once upheld and kept in check.

Other illustrations of the centralizing process are seen in the dealings with certain foundations, churches or monasteries, as standing in a special relation to Rome. One perceives here the germs of those exceptional situations — "exemptions" and "reservations" of many kinds from the ordinary episcopal jurisdiction — which in the course of time added their irritations to those other sources of discontent which were to culminate in the Protestant

Revolution. On the whole, however, it is evident that Gregory's purpose was to strengthen the authority of bishops, always reserving the final sanction of the Apostolic See. Upon the vexed question of the rival claims of bishoprics and monasteries he speaks in no uncertain terms. Within the diocese the episcopal authority was supreme. The monastery had its own well-defined rights of property and of control over its own membership, but beyond these limits it was subject to the overlordship of the bishop. He in turn was bound to protect the monastery with all his resources of men and revenue. That this ideal relation was very difficult to maintain in practice is a commonplace of the mediaeval story and is abundantly proved in these pages.

We have already noted the obstacle which more than any other was working against papal centralization, namely, that other centralizing movement which we described as the rise of nationality. Just in proportion as the national powers could gather the resources of their several territories into effective political units, they were bound to resist any larger unifying process. Centralization within meant decentralization without. This irrepressible conflict is seen especially in all Gregory's dealings with the rulers of the European states. His vision of Europe was of a vast commonwealth of peoples, each governing itself under its own traditional forms, but all subordinated to the higher jurisdiction of one divinely ordained Church. His correspondence reaches out to the remotest members of the Christian family. The kings of England, France, Spain, Sweden, Denmark and Hungary, the dukes of Bohemia and Poland, are all drawn into the circle of his influence.

Above all, Germany was the object of his especial solicitude. A boy-king, surrounded by a horde of land-hungry princes both lay and clerical, heir to a kingdom which had no roots in the loyalty of its nominal subjects, was a tempting mark for the policy of an ambitious pope. And not only was this youth the accepted head of the German kingdom; he was also the presumptive successor in the line of "Roman" emperors. Only the sanction of the Papacy was lacking to place him on this pinnacle of earthly honor. Control of the empire was the dramatic culmination of the papal claims. It is no exaggeration to say that the highest object of Gregory's ambition from the start was to secure his own recognition as arbiter in the affairs of Germany. The campaign must, of course, be fought upon moral issues, and these were provided by the several articles

of the clerical reform program; but the ideal purity of the moral
conflict was clouded by the practical political considerations. If
offenders against the papal requirements were to be punished by
ecclesiastical censure, and if persons under this censure were to be
excluded from all participation in civic and social life, and if a
ruler still continued to keep up his relations with these "excommunicated" persons, then he became, *ipso facto, particeps criminis*,
and all those of his subjects who, in the Gregorian language, "pre-
ferred God and St. Peter and the Holy Roman Church to the things
that are of men" were absolved from their allegiance to him. That
is the logic of Gregory's policy toward King Henry IV as it is
defined in his numerous letters to the king himself, to his subjects
both loyal and rebellious and to papal supporters everywhere. The
natural effect was to create in Germany a party of malcontents with
local grievances of their own, racial and economic, tied together by
a common hostility to the king and a common expectation of support from the papal power.

It would require a superhuman degree of charity for the impar-
tial historian to suppose that these discontents were not actively
fomented by the Gregorian policy. They offered to the pope the
opportunity, for which he had long waited, to cross the Alps in
person and to sit as judge between the contending parties. His
letters show the confident expectation that the German princes
would send a sufficient escort to meet him half way and give him
safe-conduct to some suitable place — perhaps Augsburg — where
his judgment seat could be established. They reflect also his bitter
disappointment at the failure of his plans. Accepting, as I incline
to do, the entire sincerity of his repeated protestations of impar-
tiality and his single desire to see the affairs of Germany settled
once for all in the hands of a king who would "prefer the things
of God above those of man," the evidence of the letters themselves
makes clear that it was not so much the settlement of the immediate
question at issue as it was the far-reaching precedent that was his
real object. An established right of popes to arbitrate between the
candidates in the elective monarchy of the empire was a goal for
which hardly any sacrifice was too great.

Beyond the Alps also the far-reaching significance of the papal
scheme was apparent. Each of the contending parties would welcome the papal support, but neither party was willing to commit

itself to any such theory of a *right* to decide between them. The expected escort was not forthcoming; the king slipped away from his retirement without any serious opposition and with Lombard help forced the hand of the pope at Canossa. The letters of this critical time reflect the deep disappointment and chagrin of Gregory, but show also his undaunted spirit and his determination to carry on the fight to the bitter end.

During the last years of his primacy we note, alternating with bold defiance of his opponents, a growing sense of failure. Through his correspondence with his more intimate and trusted friends there runs a continuous lament that all the world is turning against him. It is as if a vast conspiracy were drawing a net around him. Over and over again he wishes he might escape the burdens of this life, but soon rises once more to renewed energy.

The most dramatic illustration of this inner conflict is, perhaps, to be found in Gregory's dealings with the idea of a crusade. Disquieting reports of dire distress were coming from the Christians of the East, and the fighting spirit of Gregory was roused. In several letters he bewails the lack of readiness among Christian princes to forget their petty grievances and unite in one glorious effort to bring deliverance to their oppressed brethren. He is confident that many thousands of fighting men are ready for the great adventure, and he is prepared to place himself at their head and to sacrifice his life, if need be, in this holy cause. Nothing came of it, for the time was not yet ripe; but one sees how this splendid dream fitted in with Gregory's conception of leadership. His was the plight of many a temporal ruler before and since, who has seen in the plan of a foreign war an escape from a rebellious people. If he could rouse the nations of Europe to this holy cause, he might well hope that his added prestige would break down the opposition that seemed likely to overwhelm him.

As to Gregory's relation to purely doctrinal problems, it must be said that these were to him a matter of secondary consideration. There can be no question of his entire orthodoxy in matters of faith. He accepted the tradition of the fathers in doctrine as in organization, but he was no fanatical persecutor. It is significant that when the heresy of Berengar of Tours touching the central doctrine of transubstantiation began to assume dangerous proportions, it was he who was chosen by Pope Leo IX in 1054 to go up into France to investigate and if possible to harmonize the existing differences. His treatment of the case was eminently fair and was so far successful that Berengar was brought to make a modified recantation of his opinions, followed in 1059 at Rome by a sweeping declaration of the orthodox doctrine. After Hildebrand had become pope he repeated this recantation at the Lenten synod of 1079 in the most formal and solemn manner. He was sent back to France under papal protection, and strict warning was sent to all concerned not to molest him in any way. Indeed so conciliatory was Gregory's attitude throughout this critical controversy that his enemies made it a pretext for insinuations against the soundness of his faith. A similar indifference to doctrinal divergence is seen in his relations with that curious popular movement in Lombardy known as the *Pataria*. Of Manichaean origin, this peculiar form of heresy emphasized especially the sinfulness of the flesh and consequently the comparative virtue of celibacy. It was heresy, but it was an ally not to be despised in the warfare against sacerdotal marriage and against that *superbia* of the Milanese clergy which was one of the greatest obstacles to Gregory's political and reformatory plans. The word heresy meant for him not so much speculative error as opposition to his far-reaching ambitions. The "heresy of Simony," one of his favorite phrases, illustrates this convenient transfer of meaning. The offense of Simony lay in its violation of a rule regulating a purely functional process of church administration. It involved a question of faith only in so far as the good Christian was bound to believe that every part of the ecclesiastical structure was divinely ordained. To describe it as "heresy," therefore, was technically unwarranted. The value of the word for Gregory was that it enabled him to attack Simony with the weapon against which his enemies had no defense, the excommunication, the "sword of the divine justice."

These are the principal points of interest which have governed my selection of letters for translation. In addition to those from the *Registrum*, I have taken from the *Epistolae collectae* of Jaffé some of the most important and have placed them with the others in regular sequence. The chronological arrangement seemed likely to be more convenient than any grouping by topics.

No attempt has been made to give a complete bibliography, but a list of the more important and serviceable publications within the special field is given.

To comment exhaustively upon each individual letter would mean nothing less than to write a history of the Age of Hildebrand, a splendid task still awaiting the labor of an historian who shall be able to rise above the furious contentions of the time and to see them as a dramatic chapter in the story of human liberty.

THE CORRESPONDENCE OF POPE GREGORY VII
Records of Western Civilization

—what suprises you
—who is writing & why?

holy shit
your hands are
shockingly soft.

eyes: gray-hazel
grayzel
alarming power

THE FIRST BOOK

Official Record of the Election of Gregory VII [*]
April 22, 1073.

In the Reign of our Lord Jesus Christ, in the year of his merciful incarnation one thousand and seventy-three, the eleventh Indiction, the tenth day of the Kalends of May, and the second day of the week, and the day of the burial of our lord Pope Alexander II of happy memory, in order that the Apostolic See might not long mourn the loss of a suitable pastor, We, the cardinal clerks of the Holy Roman Catholic and Apostolic Church, acolytes, subdeacons, deacons and presbyters, in the presence of venerable bishops and abbots supported by [their] priests and monks, and amid the acclamations of vast crowds of both sexes and of various ranks, assembled in the church of St. Peter *ad Vincula*, do choose for our pastor and supreme pontiff a man of piety, eminent for learning both sacred and profane, famed for his love of justice and equity, strong in adversity, moderate in prosperity, and, according to the words of the Apostle, of good character, of pure life, modest, sober, chaste, given to hospitality, ruling well his own house, brought up and taught in noble fashion from childhood in the bosom of this Mother Church and for his merits raised to the honor of the archidiaconate — namely Archdeacon Hildebrand, whom we choose to be and to be called now and forever, Gregory, Pope and *Apostolicus*.

"Do you agree?" "We agree!"

"Do you desire him?" "We desire him!"

"Do you approve him?" "We approve him!"

Done at Rome, the tenth of the Kalends of May and the eleventh Indiction.

To Desiderius, Abbot of Monte Cassino, Informing Him of Gregory's Election
Book I, 1, p. 3. April 23, 1073.

Gregory, Roman pontiff-elect, to Desiderius, abbot of the monastery of St. Benedict at Monte Cassino, greeting in Christ Jesus.

---

[*] Given on the first page of the *Registrum*, but without number.

Our lord Pope Alexander is dead. His death was a heavy blow
to me, and all my inward parts were stirred to their depths. For
after he had died, the Roman people, contrary to their custom,
placed the conduct of affairs in my hands so quietly that it was
evidently done by a special act of divine grace. And so, taking
counsel, we decided that after a three days' fast and after public
funeral services and the prayers of many persons, accompanied by
works of charity, we would determine what it would be best to do
about the choice of a Roman pontiff.

But then, suddenly, while our lord the pope was being carried to
his burial in the church of Our Savior, a great tumult and shouting of the people arose, and they rushed upon me like madmen, so
that I might say with the prophet: "I am come into deep waters
where the floods overflow me. I am weary with my crying; my
throat is dried." And also: "Fear and trembling are come upon
me and darkness hath encompassed me about."

But, as I am confined to my bed completely tired out and cannot
properly choose my words, I will not tell the story of my anxieties.
I will only ask you in the name of Almighty God to beg the brethren and sons who are under your charge and to call upon them,
out of your affection for me, to pray God in my behalf, so that
prayer, which should have kept me free from danger, may at least
protect me now that I am in danger. And do you yourself not fail
to come to us as soon as ever you can; for you know how greatly
the Church of Rome needs you and how much it depends upon
your good judgment. Give our greetings to our lady, the empress
Agnes, and to Rainald, the venerable bishop of Como, and exhort
them in our name to show toward us all the loyalty they have
for us.

Note Referring to Five Other Notifications of the Election

Book I, 4, p. 7. April 28, 1073.

Gregory, Roman pontiff-elect, to Duke [*sic*] Beatrice; Hugo,
abbot of Cluny; Manasses, archbishop of Rheims; Swen, king of
Denmark; and the abbot of Marseilles. [These notices are all alike,
except that toward the end the several letters differ from each
other to conform with the differences of place and person.]

To WIBERT OF RAVENNA, ADVISING HIM OF GREGORY'S ELECTION
AND SOLICITING HIS LOYAL SUPPORT

Book I, 3, p. 5. April 26, 1073.

Gregory, Roman pontiff-elect to Wibert, archbishop of Ravenna,
greeting in Christ Jesus.

We doubt not that rumor has outrun our letter and has informed
you and many others of the death of our lord Pope Alexander.
His death was a great blow to me, and all my inward parts were
shaken to their depths. For at first the Roman populace, contrary
to their custom, placed the control of affairs in our hands so
quietly that it was evidently done by the special providence of God.

Wherefore, having taken advice, we came to this decision: that
after a three days' fast and after the public funeral services and
the prayers of many persons, accompanied by works of charity, we
would declare by God's help what should seem best to be done
about the choice of a Roman pontiff. But then, suddenly, while our
late master the pope was being borne to his burial in the church
of Our Savior, a great tumult and shouting of the people arose
and they rushed upon me like madmen, leaving me neither time nor
opportunity to speak or to take counsel, and dragged me by force
to the place of apostolic rule, to which I am far from being equal.
So that I may say with the prophet: "I am come into deep waters
where the floods overflow me. I am weary with my crying; my
throat is dried." And again: "Fearfulness and trembling are come
upon me, and horror hath overwhelmed me." But now I am wearied
with many and heavy cares, so that I cannot well dictate, and so I
pass over the story of my misfortunes.

I beg you, by Almighty God, to show me especially in this crisis
the charity which you have promised to the Church of Rome and
also, as you must remember, to me in particular, as circumstances
and the nature of things may demand — to show this now to me,
not indeed for any merit of mine, but for love of the Apostles. I
beg you also to exhort your suffragans and the sons of your church
to pray God on my behalf that he may give me strength to bear
this burden imposed upon me against my will and with great re-
luctance on my part; that he may reach forth his hand and, though
he has willed that I should not rest in a haven of safety, he may
at least not desert me now that I am cast into such great peril. For,

as I love you with genuine affection, I demand of you the same and whatever good offices belong with it.

You can have no doubt whatever that we should desire to bind together the Church of Rome and that over which you under God's will preside, by every bond of affection, so far as our mutual honor permits, so that perfect peace and harmony may unite our hearts forever. As, therefore, we have urged upon your good judgment, know that it is our will and pleasure that by frequent interchange of messengers we may enjoy mutual comfort and consolation.

INSTRUCTIONS AND ADMONITIONS TO THE PAPAL LEGATES IN FRANCE
Book I, 6, p. 8.   April 30, 1073.

Gregory, Roman pontiff-elect, to Gerald, bishop of Ostia, and Rainbald, subdeacon, legates in France, greeting in the Lord Jesus Christ.

The report of the death of our lord Pope Alexander, who rendered up his soul to God on the twenty-first day of April, and the news of our promotion have doubtless reached you. But, wishing you to understand them in every detail, we have thought no one better fitted to give you a trustworthy account than this beloved son of ours, a cardinal priest of the Holy Roman Church, who was present on both occasions. And so we earnestly entreat Your Affection, after you have learned the simple truth from him in regard to both events, to have prayers offered to God that he may receive the soul of the departed to the joys of eternal blessedness and may lend us the aid of his mercy to bear the burden imposed upon us.

But, since the need of the time and the fitness of things seemed to demand that this our colleague, Hugo Candidus, should be sent into that country, we desire to urge Your Prudence so to persuade Hugo, abbot of Cluny, and the whole congregation of the brethren toward peace and harmony with him, that with God's help no enmity or shadow of dissension shall remain in their minds. For he, the abbot, has thrown aside his own opinions and returned to our heart and our judgment and has joined himself to us in a common understanding, will and endeavor. We have recognized that the offenses once charged against him during the life of our lord the pope were the fault of others rather than of himself.*

---

* At the Lenten synod of 1073 Abbot Hugo had been accused by the monks of Cluny of the guilt of Simony.

Further, you should have remembered that in letters of the lord
Pope Alexander and also in our legation you were begged and commanded to support the cause of Count Evulus of Roucy with
your own efforts and through the aforesaid abbot. Also when you
had learned the agreement concerning the land of Spain made with
us in the writing which we gave him, you were to arrange that,
with the approval of the abbot, men should be sent over there who
would know how to correct the errors of doctrine among the Christian inhabitants and who would be competent to inquire into the
rights of St. Peter in accordance with the agreement, if the affair
should go well. If this has been done, well and good. But if for any
reason it has hitherto been neglected, or even if the agreement is
not yet thoroughly understood by certain other chiefs, who, we
have understood, were about to go over into those parts independ-
ently of Evulus, we desire that Cardinal Hugo shall go over and,
with the approval of yourselves and of the abbot, shall exact from
all parties, in the name of St. Peter, an equitable compact and
[collect] what is due. Do you also, in our name, beg the abbot to
send with him as his companions men by whose advice and aid he
may enter upon his journey and upon his task with security — the
[papal] legation, however, always taking the principal place. Outside of Spain we have given him no authority to undertake any
transaction in church affairs without your approval, as long as you
shall be in France.

We are very much surprised at your delay in returning here,
especially since, after you had been ordered to return and while we
were long expecting you, you have not given us so much as a hint
of reasons for your tardiness. Wherefore we enjoin upon you to
return to us as soon as you possibly can, so that we may understand
what you have accomplished and, with God's help, may come to a
more intelligent decision as to further action. Further, we desire
you to remind the aforementioned abbot and in our name conjure
him now, when it is especially needed, to show with unwearied loyalty the affection which he has hitherto had for us. May he strive
so much the more earnestly to aid our infirmity by his prayers
and those of his most holy congregation as he knows how heavily
our weakness is weighed down by its accumulated burden.

6 — THE FIRST BOOK

To the Barons of France, Who Were Preparing an Expedition against the Moors in Spain *
Book I, 7, p. 11. April 30, 1073.

Gregory, Roman pontiff-elect, to all the barons who are minded to make an expedition into the land of Spain, greeting for evermore in our Lord Jesus Christ.

We are sure that it is no secret to you that the kingdom of Spain was from ancient times subject to St. Peter in full sovereignty [*proprii juris*], and up to the present time, though long inhabited by pagans, nevertheless, since the law of justice remains inviolate, it belongs of right to no mortal, but solely to the Apostolic See. For whatever has once by divine act passed lawfully into possession of the Church may indeed in the course of time be diverted from its *use* but never so long as God lives from its lawful *right* thereto without a legal grant. Therefore Count Evulus of Roucy, whose fame is, we believe, well known among you, wishes to enter into that country and rescue it from the hands of pagans. He has received a grant from the Apostolic See to this effect: that he should hold in the name of St. Peter those lands from which he could drive the pagans by his own exertions and with the help of others, under the conditions of an agreement made between us.

In this enterprise whoever among you shall wish to join him, with every regard for the honor of St. Peter, let him so govern himself that he may surely receive from him [St. Peter] both protection in peril and the due reward of his loyalty. But if any shall prepare separately from the count and with their own resources to invade any part of that territory, it is incumbent upon them to have in their minds a righteous motive for their expedition, determining beforehand and firmly resolving in their hearts that after the land is taken they will not commit the same offenses against St. Peter which those who now occupy it do in their ignorance of God. For we wish you every one to understand that unless you determine to attack that kingdom under a just agreement to uphold the rights of St. Peter, we would rather lay our interdict upon your attempt to go thither than that our holy and universal Mother Church should suffer the same wrongs from her own children as from her enemies, to the injury not merely of her property but of her sons.

* This letter is the earliest specific evidence for the claim of the Roman See to sovereignty over the land of Spain.

What is the goal of the pope??

To this end we have sent into that country our beloved son Hugo, cardinal priest of the Holy Roman Church, to whom we have committed the more open and complete declaration of our purpose and decisions and the execution thereof in our stead.

To Duke Godfrey of Lorraine, Accepting Congratulations and Urging Support, Especially in His Relations with Henry IV

Book I, 9, p. 13.   May 6, 1073.

Gregory, Roman pontiff-elect, to Duke Godfrey, greeting in the Lord Jesus Christ.

The pleasure at our promotion which your letter shows is most welcome to us, not because of any enjoyment of the fact itself, but because we have no doubt that it springs from a sincere affection and a loyal spirit. For our elevation, which gives to you and to others of our adherents a godly opinion of us and a real satisfaction, produces in ourself the bitterness of pain within and the torment of extreme anxiety.

For we perceive what cares surround us, what a load the burden we have assumed presses upon us, so that when the consciousness of our own weakness begins to trouble our soul we desire rather the repose of death in Christ than to live in the midst of such dangers. The very thought of the duties entrusted to us weighs upon us so that were we not supported by confidence, first in God and then in the prayers of spiritually minded men, our heart would fail us under the burden of our responsibilities.

human life/govt is a fallen thing

Because of sin almost the whole world is so set in malice against us that all, and especially those who hold the highest places in the Church, are striving rather to bring it to confusion than to defend and glorify it in loyal devotion. In their thirst for gain and their desire for transient fame they set themselves against all that pertains to religion and the righteousness of God. This is the greater cause of grief to us because, having taken upon ourself the government of the Church in such a difficult crisis, we can neither carry it on properly nor abandon it with safety. But, knowing what strength of faith and persistence God has granted to you, and having in you the confidence which belongs to a most faithful son of St. Peter, we desire you to have no doubts whatever of our constant affection for you and our ready support of your powers.

As regards the king, you may fully understand our purpose and our wishes. So far as God gives us to know, we believe there is no one more anxious or more desirous for his present and future glory than ourself. It is our wish at the first available opportunity to come to an understanding with him through our legates upon the matters which we think important for the welfare of the Church and the honor of his kingly office — with fatherly affection and admonition. If he will then listen to us we shall rejoice for his sake as well as for our own. Of a certainty he will find his profit in maintaining justice in accordance with our advice and warnings.

But if — which God forbid! — he shall repay our love with hate and show contempt toward Almighty God for the high office conferred upon him, then may the judgment which declares, "Cursed be he that keepeth back his sword from blood!" not fall upon us in the providence of God. For we are not free to set aside the law of God for the sake of any person, neither to draw back from the path of rectitude for any favor of men, according to the word of the Apostle, "If I were still pleasing men I should not be a servant of Christ."

To Beatrice and Matilda of Tuscany, Urging Them to Refuse Support to the Bishops of Lombardy and Advising Them of His Relations with Henry IV

Book I, 11, p. 17.   June 24, 1073.

Gregory, Roman pontiff-elect, to Beatrice and her daughter Matilda, greeting in the Lord Jesus Christ.

As St. Gregory [I] says in a certain book of Commentaries upon Job concerning human conduct: "It is fixed by the divine judge how much everyone is to suffer by adversity and how far he is to enjoy prosperity. Whoever, therefore, in times of temptation is led by fear of the one or hope of the other to stray from the right path shows that he neither hopes in God nor respects the appeal of Holy Writ." We speak of this because neither you nor we, nor anyone who desires to share in the adoption of the children of God, should consider our own advantage, that is, what may profit or injure us, but rather should diligently study and strive to hold fast the righteousness of God, which never fails to bring us happiness. For it is written: "Blessed are they that suffer for righteousness' sake."

You know, beloved daughters of St. Peter, how openly the bishops

of Lombardy have dared to uphold the heresy of Simony by bringing a curse in the form of a blessing upon the simoniac Godfrey, a
man excommunicated and condemned for that crime, and, under
the guise of ordination, have set up an execrable heretic. Those
people who have long been hurling stones and arrows against the
Lord have now come out into the open field, overturning religion
and beating against the immovable rock of the Holy Roman Church
and are beyond a doubt precursors of Antichrist and satellites of
our ancient foe. How dangerous it is to favor or support them,
may Your Prudence learn from the words of the blessed Gregory:
"Failure to resist such men with all your might is nothing less
than to deny your faith."

Wherefore we exhort Your Excellencies and beg you most earnestly to avoid all communion with them and to give no aid or
counsel to their party. In this matter let no worldly considerations,
vain, transitory and deceptive as these are, influence you; for by
the mercy of God and of St. Peter, no wiles of your enemies can
harm you if a clear conscience supports your minds.

As to the bishop-elect of Lucca, we can give you no answer except that we know him to be a man of such learning in the sacred
writings and with such good judgment that he must know his
right hand from his left. If he shall turn to the right we shall rejoice greatly; but if — which God forbid! — he shall turn to the
left, it will certainly be a grief to us; but we will not give our
approval to impiety through the grace or favor of anyone.

And as to the king: As you have learned from our former letters,
it is our intention to send pious men to him, by whose admonitions
and the help of God we may be able to bring him back to loyalty to
his mother, the Holy Church of Rome, and give him detailed instructions as to the proper form of assuming the empire. But if,
contrary to our hopes, he shall refuse to listen to us, we cannot and
we ought not to turn aside from our mother, the Roman Church,
which has cherished us and has often brought forth other children
from the blood of her sons; so God protect us! And surely it is
safer for us to resist him even unto death in defense of the truth
and for our own welfare than to give way to his will by consenting
to iniquity and so rush on to our own ruin.

Farewell in Christ, and be assured that we hold you in the most
heartfelt affection.

To Archbishop Manasses of Reims, in Defense of the Monastery of S. Remi

Book I, 13, p. 21.   June 30, 1073.

Gregory, bishop and servant of those who serve God, to Manasses, archbishop of Reims, greeting and apostolic benediction.*

If you would consider carefully, beloved brother, the importance of your position, the obligations of your office, the statutes of the divine law and the reverence and affection which you owe to the Holy Roman Church, you would surely not allow the requests and admonitions of the Apostolic See to be so frequently set at naught in your diocese. It is a serious fault in a case of this sort for you to call forth or to wait for the word of reproof. We cannot without peril to our soul neglect whatever duty is imposed upon us by our commission, and still less do we think it safe for us to bring it to confusion through our own willful action.

Your Prudence ought surely to remember how often our lord and predecessor, Pope Alexander of reverend memory, and we ourselves have admonished you as well by letter as by legates in the case of the monastery of S. Remi, begging and urging you not to let the apostolic patience be wearied by the complaints of the brethren made under urgent necessity. They demanded that you should not appoint to the position of abbot a person whom the sacred canons would exclude and that you would not bring the place to poverty by diverting the property of the monastery from the use of the congregation, but would cause such an one to be set over the abbey according to the rule, whose piety and learning would be equal to providing carefully for outward requirements and also for spiritual discipline.

This you promised us repeatedly by your own legates to do; but, so far, you have taken no pains whatever to fulfill your promises. On the contrary, as we have learned from various reports, you are treating that venerable House more harshly with every day. Not to mention the destruction of temporal goods, you are oppressing the sacred persons of the brethren with contemptuous cruelty.

This being so, your own cleverness can understand how seriously your fault in this affair affects you, and how our chagrin preys

---

* This is the first letter in the *Registrum* after Gregory's consecration as pope, and consequently the first to show the complete formula of salutation. See I, 52 and IV, 20.

upon us that the authority of the Apostolic See has not been able
to prevail with you for peace and quietness toward the House and
the brethren for whom you ought long since to have shown the
affection of a father. Up to the present, however, we have thought
best to try to influence you as our beloved brother by gentle exhortation, begging and warning you in the name of the blessed Apostles Peter and Paul, that if you desire to have in future any hope
in our brotherly affection you will without delay cause some one
to be appointed abbot according to the rule, who is well suited for
the office, and also that you will make such further corrections and
improvements as the needs and the claims of the monastery demand, so that we shall have to listen to no further complaints of
the brethren. But if finally you shall refuse to reverence St. Peter
in this matter and shall scorn our love and charity, then beyond a
doubt — we regret to say it — you will call down upon yourself
our apostolic severity and wrath.

To the Adherents of the Papacy in Lombardy, Warning Them against Godfrey, Simoniacal Bishop of Milan

Book I, 15, p. 23. July 1, 1073.

Gregory, bishop, servant of those who serve God, to all faithful
followers of St. Peter, prince of the Apostles, especially to those
dwelling in Lombardy, greeting and the apostolic benediction.

I desire you to know, beloved brethren, as many of you do know
already, that we are so placed that, whether we will or no, we are
bound to proclaim truth and righteousness to all peoples, especially
to Christians, according to the word of the Lord: "Cry aloud;
spare not, lift up thy voice like a trumpet and declare unto my
people their transgressions!" And elsewhere: "If thou shalt not
declare his wickedness unto the wicked, I will require his soul at
thy hand." Also saith the prophet: "Cursed be he that keepeth
back his sword from blood!" that is, he that keepeth back the
word of preaching from reproving the carnally minded. We make
this prelude because, among the many ills which afflict the whole
world, certain ministers of Satan and heralds of Antichrist in
Lombardy are striving to overturn even the Christian faith and
thus are bringing down the wrath of God upon themselves.

As you well know, during the life of Guido, called archbishop of
Milan, Godfrey had the audacity to purchase, like any vile wench,

that church which once through the merits of Mary, most glorious
Virgin and Mother of God, and through the fame of that most
noted doctor, St. Ambrose, shone forth among the churches of
Lombardy by its piety, its freedom and its own peculiar glory —
that is to say, he prostituted the bride of Christ to the Devil and
befouled her with the criminal heresy of Simony by trying to separate her from the catholic faith.

Hearing of this the Roman Church, mother of you and, as you
know, mistress [*magistra*] of all Christendom, called together a
council from several countries and, supported by the approval
of many priests and members of divers orders, through the authority
of St. Peter, prince of the Apostles, pierced him with the lance of
anathema as an enemy of the catholic faith and of the canon law,
together with all those who took his part. This right of excommunication, as even the enemies of the Church cannot deny, was
approved of old by holy fathers and has been confirmed and is still
confirmed by Catholics through all the holy churches.

Wherefore, beloved brethren, in the name of Almighty God,
Father, Son and Holy Spirit, and of the blessed Peter and Paul,
chiefs of the Apostles, we warn, exhort and command you to have
no dealings whatever with the aforesaid heretic Godfrey, seeing
that to side with him in this crime is to deny the faith of Christ.
Resist him by whatever means you can as sons of God and defend
the Christian faith whereby you are to be saved. And let no pride
of men deter you; for he who is with us is greater than all, is ever
unconquered, and it is his will that we labor for him, and he will
give the crown to those who fight fairly, as the Apostle promises.
For our captain [*dux*] is wont to crush the many and the proud by
means of the few and the humble, and to confound the things that
are strong by the things that are weak. Such is the will and pleasure of our invincible prince.

May Almighty God, who especially entrusted his sheep to St.
Peter and gave him rule over all the Church, strengthen you in
your devotion to him so that, delivered from your sins by his authority, you may have grace to withstand the enemies of God and
win their hearts to repentance.

To Gerald of Ostia, Legate to Spain, Chiding Him for Failure
to Report to the Holy See

Book I, 16, p. 25. July 1, 1073.

Gregory . . . to Gerald, bishop of Ostia, greeting and apostolic
benediction.

It has always been the custom, and a very necessary one, that
whenever a legate of the Apostolic See has held a council in a dis-
tant country he should return at once and report fully upon what
he has done. We are therefore surprised and greatly troubled, our
brother, that you, after the recent synod at which so many subjects
came up for discussion, have neither returned yourself nor sent
your colleague, disregarding both our need and our expectations.
It is indeed a satisfaction to us that you made the journey to Spain
upon business of the Holy Roman Church; but it was your duty as
a man of good judgment to dispatch either the companion whom
we appointed for you or some one else who was present at the
synod and who would be able to give in your place a complete explanation of everything he had seen and heard. In that way we
could review the whole matter, confirm what we approved and
modify with intelligent judgment what needed modification.

Although your letter gave us some idea of what you had done,
we were unable, in your absence and with no one here to explain
the proceedings in your stead from personal knowledge, to give
answer to many persons, some of whom were complaining that they
had been unjustly excommunicated, others that they had been
irregularly deposed and others that they had been undeservedly
disciplined — and all this because of the vagueness of the charges
and our desire to uphold your authority. To make no replies or to
delay them a long time implies disrespect or, considering the prolonged danger to those under censure, even cruelty.

In the case of William, so-called archbishop of Auch, whose restitution you have requested, you have yourself caused us some embarrassment. You have stated that he was deposed solely because
he had knowingly held communication with an excommunicated
person and yet that in his trial upon charges made against him he
did not clear himself canonically, though he was willing to do so —
excepting those charges which it is admitted were disregarded by
our lord and predecessor, Pope Alexander.

All this has troubled us not a little, and we find great difficulty in replying to you, as well as to others. However, after consulting with our brethren, our fellow-bishops and the cardinals, we have come to the following decision: that the aforesaid bishop of Auch ought not to be deposed upon the sole ground that he held communication with the excommunicated person, but that he should be acquitted under the condition that he shall be able to clear himself of other charges in such a way that no suspicion may attach to you and no dishonor may come to us. Otherwise you are to reserve the decision in this matter for a hearing before us.

You are aware that Pontius, called bishop of Bigorre, who, you say, was deposed upon similar charges, came personally to us; but out of regard for your dignity we gave no reply to his complaints. But now, since similar rules should be applied in similar cases, we are writing to say to you that if, after careful inquiry into the accusations against him, no other fault can legally be found which ought to be punished with canonical severity, he is to be restored to his office. Further, my brother, make no delay in sending me in writing at the earliest opportunity a true statement of your own efforts.

To Duke Wratislaw of Bohemia, Commending to Him the Papal Legates

Book I, 17, p. 27. July 8, 1073.

Gregory to Wratislaw, duke of Bohemia, and to his brothers, greeting and apostolic benediction.

We give thanks to Almighty God that you have received with all due respect our legates, Bernard and Gregory, sent from this Holy and Apostolic See to your country, and have given them honorable treatment as befitted your lofty station and on account of your reverence and devotion toward the blessed Peter and Paul, chief among the Apostles. In return we offer you our good will.

Through the negligence of our predecessors and the indifference of your forefathers, who ought to have made a request to this effect, messengers of the Apostolic See have but seldom been sent to your country, and therefore certain ones among you have thought of this as a novelty and, not reflecting on the word of the Lord, "He that receiveth you receiveth me; and he that rejecteth you rejecteth me," have shown contempt for our legates, thus despising, not them, but the very word of Truth itself by refusing them the

[handwritten: writes a letter to correct someone's manners]

respect which is their due. By this action they have made it clear as day that they have so heaped up the measure of their condemnation that, in accordance with the judgment of the Truth, a millstone shall be hanged about their necks and, unless they repent, they shall sink into the depths of perdition because they have caused the Lord's little ones to fall. *[handwritten: /// out of proportion a bit? Why?]*

Your brother Jaromir, bishop of Prague, once our friend, is reported to be so greatly opposed to our legates, Bernard and Gregory, that, if the facts are as stated, he seems to have been following in the footsteps of Simon Magus against the chief of the Apostles. Wherefore we beg you to take counsel with our legates and with your brother, and that you will urge him earnestly on your own account and in our name to listen to the instructions of our legates, and whatever sentence they may pronounce and however severe their judgment may be, this Church will never deny him a fair hearing.

But if he refuses to do either of these things, we shall confirm the sentence of deposition passed by our legates and shall unsheath the sword of apostolic wrath against him even to his destruction, so that he, and through him many others, may learn by experience how great is the authority of this See. We are forced unwillingly to this action, nor dare we hide the boldness of it. For we are driven on by the word of the prophet Ezekiel [33, 8] upon peril of our own ruin: "If thou dost not speak to warn the wicked from his way, that wicked man shall die in his iniquity but his blood will I require at thine hand." And elsewhere [Jer. 48, 10]: "Woe to him who keepeth back his sword from the incorrigible sinner." But do you so act in this and in other matters that honor may be increased to you in this world and that you may obtain abundant and eternal blessing through the mediation of the Apostles. *[handwritten: more threat]* *[handwritten: saving people by punishing them for wickedness]* *[handwritten: Pope is in a good...]*

[handwritten: place for manipulation]

To Duke Rudolf of Swabia, concerning Henry IV

Book I, 19, p. 31.   Sept. 1, 1073.

Gregory ... to Rudolf, duke of Swabia, greeting ....

Although your zeal in the past has made it clear that you are devoted to the honor of the Holy Roman Church, your recent letter shows your fervent affection for it and proves how greatly you surpass all the other princes of those parts in this respect. Among other welcome expressions therein, this seemed especially calculated *[handwritten: ?]*

to advance the glory of the imperial government and also to
strengthen the power of Holy Church, namely, that the empire and
the priesthood should be bound together in harmonious union. For,
as the human body is guided by two eyes for its physical illumina-
tion, so the body of the Church is guided and enlightened with
spiritual light when these two offices work together in the cause of
pure religion.

Wherefore we desire Your Excellency to know that we have no
ill will toward King Henry, to whom we are under obligation because he was our choice as king, and because his father of honored
memory, the emperor Henry, treated me with especial honor among
all the Italians at his court, and at his death commended his son
to the Roman Church in the person of Pope Victor [II] of reverend memory. Nor, so God help us, would we willingly hate any
Christian man, according to the word of the Apostle: "If I give
my body to be burned, and if I bestow all my goods to feed the
poor and have not love, I am nothing." But, since the harmony of
Empire and Priesthood ought to be pure and free from all deceit,
it seems to us highly important first to take counsel with you and
the empress Agnes, the countess Beatrice, and Rainald, bishop of
Como, and other God-fearing men. Then, after you have thoroughly understood our wishes, if our reasons seem sound to you, you
may come to an agreement with us; but, if you find that anything
should be added to our arguments or stricken from them, we shall
be ready, with God's approval, to accept your advice.

Wherefore we urge you to strive ever more earnestly to increase
your loyalty to St. Peter and to come without delay to his shrine,
both to offer your prayers and for the sake of the great advantage
it may bring. You will place St. Peter on both accounts so greatly
in debt to you that you will enjoy his intercession both in this life
and in the life to come.*

TO THE CLERGY AND PEOPLE OF CARTHAGE, REGARDING PERSECUTION OF THEIR BISHOP

Book I, 22, p. 36.   Sept. 15, 1073.

Gregory . . . to the clergy and Christian people of Carthage,
greeting . . .

[The letter begins with a long exhortation to patience under persecution and then continues as follows:]

* See ep. I, 27.

I groan as I think of these things, dearest children, I weep as I write them, and I send them to you with the deepest sorrow in my heart. The report has come to us that certain among you in defiance of the law of Christ have impiously brought such charges against Christus Cyriacus, our venerable brother and your archbishop and master, nay your truly anointed, before the Saracens, and have so assailed him with abusive arguments that he was accounted a robber and handed over as deserving of stripes. O, wicked example! O, shame upon you and the holy, universal Church! Christ is taken prisoner anew, is condemned by false accusers and false witnesses and delivered over to be scourged as a thief! And by whom? By those who are supposed to believe in his incarnation, to reverence his passion and to accept his other sacred mysteries. Are we to keep silence about these things or are we to cry aloud and to reprove them with tears? It is written: "Cry aloud, and spare not." And elsewhere: "If thou shalt not warn the wicked man from his wicked way, his blood will I require at thine hand." I am bound, therefore, to cry aloud; I am bound to reprove you, lest your blood be required at my hand and lest I be punished at the bar of a fearful, a just and unchanging God. And so I lay bare the secret places of my fatherly love and mercy toward you in this way, partly because a journey hither over the wide and perilous sea is no easy matter for you, and partly because I know not how so to discriminate between the reasons for anger, for sorrow and for ill will as to reach a definite decision.

I admonish and command you by my apostolic authority that, as the foul stench of your audacity and your unheard-of wickedness have brought deep sadness to our heart, so the sweet savor of your repentance and amendment may turn our heart to gladness. But if you fail to do this, I will smite you with the sword of anathema according to law and will proclaim the curse of St. Peter and of ourself upon you.

TO ERLEMBALD OF MILAN, URGING LENIENCY TO THE PENITENT FOLLOWERS OF GODFREY AND ADVISING OF PAPAL RELATIONS WITH HENRY IV

Book I, 26, p. 43.   Oct. 9, 1073.

Gregory . . . to Sir Erlembald of Milan, greeting . . .
We are rejoiced to hear your message telling of your zeal in

defense of the faith and the restoration of our holy religion, and we were not lacking in good will to aid you; but, being busied with other cares, we can only briefly reply to your many inquiries.

As to those associates of that excommunicated person who desire to return to you for pay, and as to sons of fathers and fathers of sons who hold to the anathematized Godfrey, and as to those whose restoration without money you do not approve — toward whom, however, we warn you to be lenient — if any of these wish to join your party, we commit the decision to your good judgment according to your best knowledge and ability. Or, if any, in penitence for their errors, desire to come to us for absolution, let them know that they shall be graciously received and considerately treated.

You need have no great fear of the bishops who are trying to support your opponent, for Beatrice and her daughter Matilda, who are deeply attached to the Roman Church, together with some of the greatest princes of the kingdom, are striving to bring about harmony between the king and ourself. Against him we have no hatred, nor ought we to have, unless — which God forbid! — he should choose to act contrary to our holy religion. It is confidently believed that the king will meet our wishes in other affairs of the Church and especially will assent to our disposition of your case. Try by every honorable means to win over Bishop Gregory of Vercelli. He promises to submit himself entirely to our orders. "Finally be strong in the Lord and in the strength of his might," seeking his favor by prayers and almsgiving and in purity of heart, that he may deign to bring your wishes and ours to perfection.

HENRY IV TO GREGORY VII, PROMISING SUBMISSION AND EXPRESSING SELF-REPROACH

Book I, 29(a), p. 47. Aug.-Sept., 1073.

To the most watchful and best beloved lord, Pope Gregory, by divine will invested with the apostolic dignity, Henry, by the grace of God King of the Romans, presents his due and faithful service.

Kingdom and priesthood, if they are to be duly administered in Christ, need his continual support, and therefore, my beloved lord and father, they must never be in dissension but must inseparably cleave to each other in the bonds of Christ. For in this way and no other can the harmony of Christian unity and the institution of the Church be held in the bond of perfect love and peace.

But we, who by God's will have now for some time held the kingly office, have not in all respects shown toward the priesthood such reverence and honor as was due to it. Not without reason have we borne the sword of justice entrusted to us by God; but we have not always unsheathed it as we should have done against the guilty. Now, however, somewhat repentant and remorseful, we turn to your fatherly indulgence, accusing ourselves and trusting to you in the Lord that we may be found worthy of absolution by your apostolic authority.

Alas for me, guilty and unhappy that I am! Partly through the impulses of my deceitful youth, partly through the seductive counsels of my advisers, I have sinned against heaven and before you with fraudulent disloyalty and am no more worthy to be called your son. Not only have I encroached upon the property of the Church, but I have sold churches themselves to unworthy persons, men poisoned with the gall of Simony, men who entered not by the gate but by other ways, and I have not defended the churches as I ought to have done.

But now, since I cannot regulate the churches alone, without authority from you, I most earnestly beg your advice and help in this and in all my affairs. Your directions shall be scrupulously followed in all respects. And first, in regard to the church of Milan, which has fallen into error through my fault, I beg that it may be restored according to law by your apostolic sentence and that then you will proceed to the regulation of other churches by your authority. I shall not fail you, so God will, and I humbly beseech your fatherly support in all my interests.

You will soon receive letters from me by the hands of most trustworthy messengers and from these you will, please God, learn more fully what remains to be said.

To Lanfranc of Canterbury, concerning St. Edmund's Abbey

Book I, 31, p. 51. Nov. 30, 1073.

Gregory . . . to Lanfranc, archbishop of Canterbury in England, greeting . . .

It is a matter of no little wonder to us under what pretext or with what intention you are allowing the so-called bishop Arfastus to deceive the Holy Roman Church and to disobey the orders of our predecessor, Alexander of blessed memory. We are well aware

that Your Wisdom fully understands that the Holy Roman Church,
through its God-given right, claims for itself the consecration of
churches, priests and bishops. No license obtained from any other
source can validate their services. Rome has given, and with God's
help will continue to give, its aid to its own in this matter, since
they have come to Rome and have sought help and counsel from
the Apostolic See.

Now with what presumption the so-called bishop Arfastus resists these rules, I know not — unless it be perchance, "I will set
my seat in the North and be like unto God." Why you keep silence
about this I wonder greatly. And yet, having no more doubt of
you than of ourself we urgently beg Your Fraternity to act in
our place, to crush out absolutely this absurd claim of Arfastus and
no longer allow the Abbey of St. Edmund's to be disquieted in any
way contrary to the decree of our predecessor. He, by causing that
abbot to be ordained as priest at Rome, received him and the abbey
over which he presides under the protection of the Apostolic See.
We cannot, therefore, be blind to the fact that injuries done to him
affect us as well, involving as they do contempt for our authority.

For this reason also we beg you to advise King William, specially
beloved son of Holy Roman Church, not to listen to the empty arguments of Arfastus by which his own singular wisdom is greatly
lowered in the general esteem. But if Arfastus shall continue his
resistance, command him and Abbot Baldwin by apostolic authority to come to Rome for a settlement of the affair.

To the Bishop of Lincoln, in the Case of a Deposed Priest

Book I, 34, p. 55.   Dec. 2, 1073.

Gregory . . . to Remedius, bishop of Lincoln in England, greeting . . .

The bearer of these presents, whom your letter charged before
us with the crime of homicide, cannot, by any sanction of the holy
fathers, be permitted to serve the sacred altar in future. Nor is it
fitting that we should give assent to his restitution and thereby go
against the canonical rules — God forbid! Nevertheless, if Your
Compassion shall find that he is showing before God fruits meet for
repentance for the crime he has committed, then do you in charity
see to it that he is supplied with some support from the Church
so that he may not be crushed by poverty and disregard the things

same vigor
for

of God. While he can never, upon any condition, be worthy to receive priestly orders, still he may properly have some provision
from the Apostolic See.

Further, we have seen fit to comply with your request and to
send you absolution for your sins by authority of the chief Apostles,
Peter and Paul, in whose stead we unworthily serve, provided however that you abide in good works, lament your past excesses and,
so far as in you lies, show the dwelling-place of your body to be a
temple pure before God. As to your request that we command
your services as far as you can know how to please us, this is our
special demand: that you aid us by your prayers, that we may together be worthy of eternal joy.

To the Bishop of Chalon-sur-Saône, against Philip I

Book I, 35, p. 56. Dec. 4, 1073.

Gregory ... to Roclin, bishop of Chalon, greeting ...

We have learned from trustworthy sources that among the
princes of our time who have laid waste the Church of God by
putting it up for sale with wicked greed and have trampled under
foot the mother to whom, in accordance with the Lord's command,
they owe honor and reverence, holding her in subjection as their
handmaid, King Philip of France has so greatly oppressed the
Gallican churches that he seems to have reached the very summit
of this hateful iniquity. This has the more offended us in the case
of that kingdom on account of its well-known reputation for good
judgment, piety and power, and for its great devotion to the Roman church. We were so greatly disturbed, not only on account of
our general responsibility, but by the actual destruction of churches
themselves, that we ought to have reproved more severely such
audacious attacks upon our holy religion. He, however, gave us
every assurance through his chamberlain Alberic that he would
respect our judgment and would reform his own life and set the
churches in order.

We desire, therefore, to test the value of this promise in the case
of the church of Mâcon, long deprived of its pastor and reduced
almost to nothing. It is our wish that he shall permit the archdeacon of Autun, elected by the unanimous choice of clergy and
people and, as we have heard, with the approval of the king himself, to be set over the church of Mâcon as its bishop, the appoint-

ment to be made, as it should be, without payment. If he shall refuse to do this, let him understand beyond all doubt that we will
no longer suffer this ruination of the Church but will meet such
obstinate persistence in disobedience with canonical severity by authority of the blessed Apostles Peter and Paul. For either the king
himself, abandoning the evil merchandise of simoniacal heresy,
shall allow suitable persons to be promoted to the government of
the Church, or the French people, unless they desire to reject the
Christian faith, shall be smitten by the sword of a general anathema and will refuse to obey him in future.

[margin note: threatens to excommunicate France???]

This we have taken pains to entrust to your watchfulness, beloved brother, that you may convey it to the king and may make
every effort, by petition and exhortation and by every other means,
to persuade him to allow the church of Mâcon and every other
church to be provided with pastors according to the canon law.

[margin note: what is canon law?]

We have laid this duty upon you because we knew the excellence
of your judgment and your personal intimacy with the king. But
if we have overlooked anything which ought to be mentioned, let
your own keen intelligence supply it. May you so labor in this commission that you may win both the favor of God and our good will.

To Count William of Burgundy, Urging Him to Send Troops to Italy

Book I, 46, p. 69. Feb. 2, 1074.

Gregory . . . to Count William of Burgundy, greeting . . .
Your Prudence may remember how affectionately the Roman
Church received Your Mightiness not long since and how greatly
it enjoyed your visit. Nor can you in decency forget the promise
which you made to God before the tomb of Peter, chief of the
Apostles, in the presence of our venerable predecessor, Pope Alexander, and of an innumerable company of bishops, abbots and
people of many nations, that whenever necessary your force would
not be lacking if it were called for in defense of the property of St.
Peter.

Wherefore, remembering the noble repute of your honor, we beg
and require of your prudence and your zeal that you bring together
a military force to protect the freedom of the Roman Church and
if need be that you come hither with your army in the service of
St. Peter. We beg you also to send this same summons to the

count of St. Giles, father-in-law of Richard, prince of Capua, and
to Amadeus, son of Adelaide of Turin, and others whom you know
to be loyal to St. Peter and who made the same promise with hands
upraised to Heaven. If we decide to send a definite reply to Your
Prudence, send back word to us by the same messenger, who will relieve us of all doubts. And let that same messenger of yours come
by the way of the countess Beatrice; who, with her daughter
and her son-in-law, Duke Godfrey of Lorraine, is promoting this
enterprise.

We are not, however, trying to bring together this force of fighting men for the sacrifice of Christian blood, but in order that our
enemies, learning of the expedition, may fear to join battle and be
the more easily won over to the right side. We are hoping also that
another advantage may come from this, namely, that when the
Normans are pacified we may cross over to Constantinople in aid
of the Christians who, oppressed by frequent attacks of the Saracens, are urging us eagerly to reach out our hands to them in succor.
The troops we have with us are sufficient against those Normans
who are in rebellion against us. And be assured that you and all
who shall join you in this undertaking will receive a double — nay,
as we believe a manifold — reward from Peter and Paul, chiefs of
the Apostles.

To Matilda of Tuscany, Conveying Pious Exhortations

Book I, 47, p. 71. Feb. 16, 1074.

Gregory . . . to Matilda, his beloved daughter in Christ, greeting
and the apostolic blessing.

How great are my care and my unceasing devotion to your welfare and that of your kindred, he alone knows who searches the
mysteries of the heart and who understands better than I myself.
But if you weigh the matter carefully you will, I think, perceive
that I ought to take care, by the love I bear you, that you should
not abandon those [who belong to you] in order that you may devote yourself solely to the salvation of your own soul. For love, as
I have often said and shall continue to say, "seeketh not its own."
Among the weapons against the prince of this world which, by
God's grace, I have supplied to you, the most potent is, as I have
suggested, a frequent partaking of the Lord's body, and I am therefore directing you to entrust yourself wholly to the unfailing

protection of the Mother of God, reminding you of the teaching of St. Ambrose in regard to the taking of the Lord's body. [Quotations from Ambrose, Gregory I and Chrysostom.]

This, then, I have written you, best beloved daughter of St. Peter, that your faith and confidence in receiving the body of the Lord may constantly increase. This treasure and these gifts, and not gold or precious stones, your soul requires of me, in love of your father, the prince of Heaven — though you might receive from other priests gifts more worthy of your deserts. But now concerning the Mother of God, to whom above all I have committed you, do now commit and shall never cease to commit you until, as we hope, we shall meet her face to face, what can I say of her whom earth and heaven cease not to praise, though never as her merits deserve! May you believe beyond all doubt that, as she is higher and better and more holy than all human mothers, so she is more gracious and tender toward every sinner who turns to her. Cease, therefore, every sinful desire and, prostrate before her, pour out your tears from an humble and a contrite heart. You will find her, I surely promise you, more ready than any earthly mother and more lenient in her love for you.

To the Bishop and People of Genoa, in the Case of a Woman Falsely Accused of Adultery

Book I, 48, p. 74. Feb. 26, 1074.

Gregory . . . to Hubert, bishop of Genoa, and all the clergy and people of that place, greeting . . .

Hearing of the mistake you have made, we are greatly alarmed at your danger, since we learn that the sacrament of marriage, consecrated by divine commandments and laws, is being viciously profaned among you. It is written: "What God hath joined together let no man put asunder." And the Truth absolutely forbids a man to put away his wife, save only for adultery.

Now it is reported to us that one Ansaldus, a fellow citizen of yours, has been compelled by his father to separate from his wife, who is falsely accused of adultery, and to refuse to admit her trial by purgation to discover the truth, though she strenuously demands it. This is contrary to all laws, human and divine, and we therefore by our apostolic authority command you as bishop and all the rest of you, that if the woman voluntarily offers herself for a legal investigation, she shall quietly be accepted in expectation of a just verdict, and if by God's mercy she shall be proved innocent, then you are by no means to allow her to be separated from her husband.

But if the father of the aforesaid Ansaldus or any other person shall presume to prevent or interfere in these directions which we give by divine authority, then we admonish Your Fraternity as bishop, by our apostolic authority, to set aside all personal considerations and at once to smite the guilty with the sword of anathema, to cut them off from the body of the Church, and fail not to inform us by letter of your action, that we may put the final sanction upon it. We desire also that you make your plans to present yourself here at the earliest possible moment.

GREGORY SUMMONS THE FAITHFUL TO DEFEND CONSTANTINOPLE
Book I, 49, p. 75.   March 1, 1074.

Gregory . . . to all who are willing to defend the Christian faith, greeting . . .

We desire to make known to you that the bearer of these presents upon his recent return from beyond the seas visited us at the threshold of the Apostles. From him, as also from many others, we have learned that a people of the pagans have been pressing hard upon the Christian empire, have cruelly laid waste the country almost to the walls of Constantinople and slaughtered like sheep many thousand Christians. Wherefore, if we love God and acknowledge ourselves to be Christians, we ought to be deeply grieved by the wretched fate of that great empire and the murder of so many followers of Christ. But it is not enough to grieve over this event; the example of our Redeemer and the duty of brotherly love demand of us that we should set our hearts upon the deliverance of our brethren. For as he offered his life for us, so ought we to offer our lives for our brothers. Be it known, therefore, that we, trusting in the mercy of God and in the might of his power, are preparing in every possible way to carry aid to the Christian empire as soon as may be, by God's help. We adjure you, by the faith in which you are united [to them] in the adoption of the sons of God, and by authority of St. Peter, prince of the Apostles, to be stirred with compassion by the wounds and the blood of your brethren and the peril of the empire and willingly to offer your powerful aid to your brethren in the name of Christ.

Whatever decision you may make in this matter by God's mercy, pray report it to us without delay by trustworthy messengers.

To Archbishop Manasses of Reims, regarding the Monastery of S. Remi

Book I, 52, p. 78.   March 14, 1074.

Gregory . . . to Manasses, archbishop of Reims, greeting . . .

[margin note: When he wants to ask a favor]

The Roman Church has long since received you into the embrace of her motherly love and cherished you with peculiar affection and distinguished favor. Especially did we so highly approve of your advancement that we cannot escape grave responsibility if you do anything which would bring dishonor upon your rank or would be unbecoming to your dignity.

When, therefore, we hear reports of you which are unsuited to your dignity we are very deeply grieved and can no longer hide our feelings. Among other complaints that have come to our ears, that of the monastery of St. Remi greatly disturbed us and roused our anger against you. But now, since we have learned that you have brought that house into better order than we had known or hoped for by placing there an honorable and learned man, you have refreshed our heart with exceeding happiness. The abbot is indeed

[margin note: In what cases would an abbot not be good?]

wholly satisfactory to us, and if he is equal to the burden of governing the two abbacies of Metz and Reims, we should give him our approval, because he is a man of piety and learning. Otherwise, if the load is too much for him, as he himself thinks, and lest he should break down under its weight, we beg Your Prudence and enjoin upon you by our apostolic authority that with his advice and consent and with God's help you will appoint there a suitable ruler through election by the congregation according to the Rule of St. Benedict. You will understand that the honorable and orderly regulation of the government of that House will be as precious to us as if it were the Abbey of St. Paul in Rome.*

To Siegfried of Mainz, concerning the Case of Prague vs. Olmütz

Book I, 60, p. 87.   March 18, 1074.

Gregory . . . to Siegfried, archbishop of Mainz, greeting . . .

A certain report quite unworthy of you has reached our ears,

---

* Reference to I, 13 and IV, 20 shows Gregory's persistent care in protecting religious houses from the aggressions of their episcopal superiors.

but we should have paid no attention whatever to it were it not for the fact that, from the letter which you sent us about the case of the bishops Jaromir of Prague and John of Moravia [Olmütz], we learn that you have got the same idea into your head, namely, that the affair about which they are in controversy and which has already been brought so many times to the attention of the Apostolic See should be transferred from our judgment to the tribunal of your personal opinion. As it is therefore evident that your advisers neither know nor care very much about the rights of apostolic authority, we invite you to go over with us the canonical traditions and the decrees of the holy fathers, so that, recognizing the enormity of your presumption, you may perceive at once your faults of negligence and of audacity.

When at first Bishop John of Moravia, in his desire to defend the rights of the church over which he presides, was suffering many insults and reproaches and even, as we have heard, bodily injuries and still could not obtain justice, you showed no concern and took no pains to inquire into the case. But, after the Apostolic See had heard the complaint of the aforesaid bishop and had labored by letter and by its legates to reach a just decision and to settle the controversy, then at length Your Cleverness waked up and took notice of the affair. You thought it should be referred to you for discussion and wished to drag back into the depths of renewed contention and struggle a brother who through an apostolic decision was floating into a haven of justice and peace.

Therefore, although, on the one hand your neglect of duty, and on the other your arrogance toward the Apostolic See may well have roused our indignation, nevertheless we make use of apostolic leniency toward you and warn you with affectionate calmness not to venture into such irregular and ill-advised proceedings. You will understand that apostolic decisions cannot be reversed — I do not say by you, but by any patriarch or primate. You are not to attribute to yourself any rights as against the Holy Roman Church nor make any attempt against her, seeing that without her abundant favor you cannot maintain yourself in the place you hold, as you well know.

With the help of God and by authority of the blessed Peter and according to long standing precedent in the Apostolic See, we shall proceed to a just decision and shall determine and confirm to the church of Olmütz whatever rightly belongs to it.

THE FIRST BOOK

To Hugo of Cluny, Urging Him to Come to Rome

Book I, 62, p. 90. March 19, 1074.

Gregory . . . to Hugo, abbot of Cluny, greeting . . .

Welcome and sweet to us are your words; but they would give us far greater satisfaction if your affection toward the Roman Church were more ardent. That the warmth of your devotion is cooled we perceive by this sign: that we are still deprived of the solace of your presence though we have so often asked for it.

We cannot believe that this is owing to your other engagements, unless it were that Your Holiness is avoiding trouble and through a certain indolence putting off the more important matter to a more convenient season. Know then, that while we have borne your continued refusal up to now with surprise, we can no longer endure it without great anxiety and trouble of mind. You should remember how many and great responsibilities we placed in the hands of you and our colleague Gerald of Ostia. Now through your absence these have either come to nothing by neglect or cannot be brought to a fitting conclusion, because when we sent the afore-said bishop [Gerald] across the mountains to the king [Henry IV] we calculated that you would come here. Therefore, greatly disturbed, we urgently enjoin upon Your Devotion to visit us as soon as possible in the many and great tribulations that oppress us. We are carrying, weak as we are and though it is beyond our strength of body and of mind — we are carrying alone at this critical time a ponderous load not only of spiritual but also of secular affairs. We live in daily dread of breaking down under the burden and cannot find anywhere aid or support in this world.

And so we beg you and your brethren by Almighty God, as we have begged you ever since we were ordained, to pray earnestly to God in our behalf, for unless we can obtain divine aid through the prayers of them and of other loyal hearts we cannot escape peril to ourself and, what we still more dread, to the Church.

May Almighty God, from whom all good things do proceed, make you and those committed to your care so to live in this mortal life that you may attain to the true and immortal life under divine guidance.*

---

* The halting style of this letter seems to betray the writer's embarrassment in dealing with the shortcomings of one of his most important supporters.

To the Kings of Leon and Castile, Urging Support for the Roman Church

Book I, 64, p. 93.   March 19, 1074.

Gregory . . . to Alfonso and Sancho, kings of Spain, likewise to the bishops under their rule, greeting . . .

Your Diligence is aware that the blessed Apostle Paul signified his intention to visit Spain and that afterward seven bishops were sent from Rome by Peter and Paul to give instruction to the Spanish peoples, and that after the abolition of idol-worship they founded Christianity, established religion, taught the order of divine service and dedicated churches with their blood. How great the harmony between Rome and Spain was in faith and in the practice of the sacred functions, is matter of common knowledge. But, after the kingdom of Spain had been long polluted by the madness of the Priscillianists, degraded by the treason of the Arians and separated from the Roman ritual, through the invasion first of the Goths and then of the Saracens, not only was religion brought low, but also her secular power was ruined.

Wherefore I exhort you as dearly beloved sons, that like good children, even after long separation, you at last recognize the Roman Church as your true mother, and in this you shall find us to be your brother. May you, like the other kingdoms of the west and the north, accept the order and ritual of the Roman Church — not those of Toledo nor any other but of that Church which was founded by Peter and Paul upon a solid rock through Christ and consecrated in blood, and against which the gates of Hell, that is, the tongues of heretics, have never been able to prevail. You have no doubts from what source you received the beginnings of your religion; receive then from the same source the holy ritual of the church service which is shown in the letter of Pope Innocent to the bishop of Gubbio, which is in the decrees of Hormisdas sent to the church of Spain, which the councils of Toledo and Braga prove and which your bishops who came recently to us after the meeting of a council promised in writing to adopt and confirmed it in our hand. . . .

To Bishop Gerald of Sisteron, in Defense of the Monastery of St. Martin de Cruis

Book I, 67, p. 96. March 21, 1074.

Gregory . . . to Gerald, bishop of Sisteron, greeting and apostolic benediction — if he shall be obedient.

Michael, a priest of the church of Cruis, has complained to us that you have invaded that church, knowing that it is the peculiar property of St. Peter, that you have seized its estates, made prisoners of its priests and clergy and compelled them by violence to swear fidelity to you contrary to law and right.

Now, since you are well aware that Ananias and Sapphira were punished with death because they did not give to St. Peter what they had promised, by whose instigation if not that of the Devil did you venture upon such an invasion, inflict such an outrage and commit such a sacrilege against the chief of the Apostles?

Wherefore, by our apostolic authority we command you, the moment you have read this letter, without excuse or delay immediately to set free our church of Cruis, to liberate its priests and clerks, to restore all the property you have carried away from there and allow them to serve God there in peace and quiet under the rule of St. Peter and in our protection.

But if you feel that you have any rights of jurisdiction over the aforesaid church, then do you, together with those canons of ours already mentioned, come before us that you may receive full justice at our hands. If you fail to do this, understand that you will be excommunicated by apostolic authority.

To William of England, in Reply to Congratulations

Book I, 70, p. 101. April 4, 1074.

Gregory . . . to William, king of the English, greeting . . .

Through your grief, my beloved son, at the decease of our predecessor, Alexander of blessed memory, as well as your joy at our promotion, we are assured beyond a doubt of your sincere loyalty to your mother, the Holy Roman Church, and of your will to defend her with all your might. For, when you heard of her widowhood, as it were, you were deeply grieved, but were consoled and rejoiced by our advancement and begged us urgently and humbly by letter to inform you as to our situation, showing the devotion of a good son, a son who loves his mother with his whole heart. Fulfill, then, by your actions, beloved son, the confession of your lips; make your words effective in the spirit of Christ himself who said: "If a man love me he will keep my words"; and elsewhere: "The proof of love is the display of works." Cease not to labor for righteousness and have such zeal in defense of the churches committed to your care that you may prepare healing for your soul, may wipe out the stain of sin and make yourself of such sweet odor that you may say with the Apostle: "For we are a sweet savor of Christ." We counsel you, warn and exhort you, to set the things of God above all earthly interests. For this is the one thing the neglect of which may bring ruin to your power and drag you down into the depths.

We have spoken thus urgently, best beloved, because we believe you to be among all kings the one above all the rest who cherishes what we have written.

As to our situation, about which you inquire so eagerly, it is this: Against our will we took command of the ship when she was tossed upon a troubled sea by the violence of storms, the shock of the whirlwind and of waves as high as heaven. Yet she steers her dangerous course with good courage around rocks hidden or towering into the air. The Holy Roman Church, over which we unworthily preside, is daily and continuously shaken by diverse temptations, by many persecutions of hypocrites, by the snares of heretics and treacherous opposition, and is driven hither and thither by the secret or open hostility of temporal powers. To meet all these and many other dangers and provide against them is under God our special care and duty; by these cares we are consumed day and night, by these and their like we are torn in pieces. Though for the moment our situation may seem a fortunate one to the children of this world, nevertheless — and we thank God it is so — the things of this world are of necessity displeasing to us. Thus we live, and by God's help we will continue so to live.

The Privilege of St. Stephen [at Caen] as to which you have written is the salvation of your soul. In regard to it we advise you to act as our legates, Peter and Johannes Minutus, shall judge to be in accordance with canon law. But if it shall seem to you that the Privilege goes too far, remember that the more you grant to St. Stephen in the name of God and St. Peter, the greater shall surely be the reward which you will receive from them.

As to the property of St. Peter in England, we enjoin upon you to guard it as your own. We entrust it to your generosity as if it were yours, that you may have Peter as your faithful and loyal debtor and may fairly call upon him for aid as one who knows how much you have done for him.

To KING PHILIP I OF FRANCE, ASKING PROTECTION FOR THE CHURCH OF BEAUVAIS

Book I, 75, p. 106.   April 13, 1074.

Gregory . . . to King Philip of France, greeting . . .

You have borne witness to us by letter and by messengers that you desire to obey St. Peter, chief of the Apostles, devotedly and as befits your station and to give attention to our admonitions in whatever pertains to affairs of the Church. This being well established in your heart by divine inspiration, we ought greatly to rejoice that Your Highness, thus inclined to reverence toward God, gives careful attention to what belongs to the function of a king.

Wherefore we exhort Your Highness in the name of St. Peter and in all charity beg of you to strive to please God and, among other things, to repair so far as in you lies the injury done by you to the church of Beauvais as befits the greatness of your name and dignity. We beg you to consider with us the fame and glory in which your predecessors, those most famous and most illustrious kings, were held throughout almost the entire world. Their royal majesty was ever piously devoted to the enlarging and defending of churches and continued liberal and scrupulous in maintaining justice.

Later, however, as this energy began to be dulled by the perversion of human and divine law, the splendor, the honor and the power of the whole realm were changed along with the corruption of morals, and the lofty fame and dignity of the kingdom declined. To remind you of these and other similar matters frequently and, if need be, with stern reproof is a duty imposed upon us by the office we have assumed.

While, then, it is neither safe nor optional for us to hide the word of preaching or to repress it in any place, nevertheless the greater the dignity and the higher the person, so much greater diligence and eloquence ought we to show in pointing out the right way to him, as we are commanded by the Lord through his proph-

et: "Cry aloud and spare not! Lift up thy voice like a trumpet!"
Especially is this true at a time when the power of Christian
princes ought to be gathering with us in the camp of that same
king for the protection of the Christian host.

Since therefore you stand forth as the sole heir to the nobility
and glory before God and men of those who were before you in the
kingship, we exhort you to imitate their virtues and, fulfilling
the divine justice with all your strength, to restore and maintain the
churches as far as you are able, that Almighty God may protect
and exalt the government of your kingdom by the right hand of
his power and may grant you the crown of everlasting glory as
your reward in the life to come.

To the Countesses Beatrice and Matilda, Asking Safe-Conduct for Werner of Strasbourg

Book I, 77, p. 109.   April 15, 1074.

Gregory . . . to the Duchess [*duci*] Beatrice and her daughter,
Matilda, greeting . . .

The prophet bears witness that Almighty God, whom we are
commanded to imitate, despises not the humble and contrite heart,
and so we, sinner though we be, and though we cannot clearly
enough perceive contrition in the hearts of others, ought not to conceal or treat as of no importance what has come to our knowledge.
Werner, bishop of Strasbourg, after he had shamefully disgraced
the dignity of his order by his sins and was summoned for reproof
by our lord Pope Alexander of reverend memory, alone of all the
bishops in Germany, of whom many, befouled not only by carnal
offenses but also by the plague of Simony, had been summoned
likewise, presented himself at the threshold of the Apostles, begged
for a judgment in humble attitude and, fearing the apostolic
scourge, declared and confessed his sins and prostrated himself
upon his face. Smitten by the apostolic judgment he is now on his
way hither to ask the apostolic mercy, having shown his repentance
and his obedience by such self-discipline, fasting and pilgrimages
that my colleagues felt and declared him worthy of our compassion
as far as the circumstances of the time would allow.

Now, although we have not granted him restoration to his episcopal dignity as he desired, still what good would it do to enforce
the full rigor of the canon law upon him at this crisis when perhaps

if he were removed no successor could be found except one who was able to pay heavily for the place?

But I beg you to consider what you did against him, how dishonorable it was to you, what a cause of shame to me and of offense against St. Peter and the Apostolic See that hidden peril should lurk in these parts for pilgrims for whom there ought to be especial protection, and that we who have forbidden this to other rulers should be charged with complicity on account of our intimate relations with you, especially since we commended our brother to your protection with the greatest confidence.

Wherefore we earnestly beg and warn Your Excellencies to mitigate his wrongs as far as you can, with all kindness and open display of regard, allowing him to go on his way and, as we requested in our above-mentioned letter, to give him safe-conduct to Sir Erlembald of Milan, understanding that we have given him warning by letter to refrain from any hostile action toward you or yours in this affair.

To Dionysius of Piacenza and to the other Lombard bishops who came to us we have allowed no part of their episcopal functions except the confirmation of children in case of necessity, but we have held the reins of the whole situation in our hands so that there may be room for repentance to those who are set right by our indulgence or [even] to those who are obstinate. But since we suspect that you, out of your affection and reverence for the Holy Roman Church, are criticizing us for this action, we have remembered that St. Peter, our father and prince of the Apostles, did not disdain to give satisfaction to the disciples who were murmuring against him, and therefore we have been willing to give you an account of our actions, seeing that we have not up to the present time given you more positive assurances of the affection in which we are bound to you. Nor has it escaped our notice how various the opinions and judgments of men about us are; for in the same cases and regarding the same actions some accuse us of cruelty while others think we are too lenient. To these critics we know no better answer than that of the Apostle: "With me it is a very small thing that I should be judged of you or of man's judgment."

And now may Almighty God, the true searcher of hearts, teach both us and you to do his will and bind his law upon our hearts.

To Whom It May Concern, regarding the Property of the Abbey of Reichenau

Book I, 82, p. 116.   May 6, 1074.

Gregory [to all to whom this letter may come].*

Although it belongs to the office of universal supervision which — unworthy as we are — we have assumed through the blessed Peter, chief of the Apostles, to watch carefully and labor to avert all attacks upon churches and sacred places, we are doubly bound, as it were, to protect by the aid and shield of apostolic authority those places which are included on an equality with others within the general membership of the Holy Roman Church and at the same time are superior to others in the privilege of special protection.

Among these the monastery of Reichenau is attached to this Holy and Apostolic See by a certain peculiar and personal line of descent. We are therefore greatly disturbed by the scattering of its properties and have decided to declare to all to whom notice of this our letter may come the decree of our lord and predecessor, Alexander [II] of reverend memory, in this case together with our own confirmation of the same.

Our aforesaid lord pope was unable to induce Robert, a simoniac usurper of that monastery, by persuasion or by threats either to resign his abbacy or to present himself before the apostolic tribunal to render an account of his occupancy. When, therefore, he learned the facts: that Robert had given up another abbacy and canvassed for this one by bribery, he smote him with the dart of anathema by a synodal decree — unless he should repent — and under the same condemnation forbade all persons to hold the benefices belonging to that monastery which they had received from him, canceled all his acts by apostolic decree and ordered the bishop of Constance to publish all these enactments by letter throughout his bishopric. By the grace of God this was carried out so far as his mad usurpation of the abbacy was concerned, but it did not bring about the abandonment by his supporters of the property of the monastery which they had received from him contrary to divine justice.

Therefore, since that chief abomination of heresy has been removed, we have appointed Ekkehard, well-beloved son of St. Peter,

* Apparently added by the compiler to replace the usual formula.

a member of that House, chosen by his colleagues and carefully examined by ourselves, as his successor, and it is our desire that the monastery after its prolonged afflictions may return in peace to the cultivation of monastic piety. Likewise we lay under the ban of anathema all those who have received feudal holdings of the abbey from the aforesaid Robert in return for their allegiance and support in his evil deeds. For if he, as the author and promoter of such practices, could not hold the place which he aspired to win by heretical methods, by what laws or by what right can they hold what they acquired by a sacrilegious compact?

We, therefore, by our apostolic authority, command all faithful servants of Christ to whom these presents may come, not to admit them to any share in the Christian communion, seeing that they already have the reward of sin and death for their devilish greed and insolence.

To the Empress Agnes, Acknowledging Her Services in the Cause of Peace between Empire and Papacy

Book I, 85, p. 121. June 15, 1074.

Gregory . . . to Agnes, most Christian empress, greeting . . .

We rejoice and exult in the Lord that the light of your activities has spread even to us, and that the results of your labors, if not quite as great as you could wish, have yet brought praise and glory to God, happiness to us, and to yourself the crown of a perfect reward. Nor should your hope be limited or checked because the desire of Your Holiness could not be perfectly fulfilled; for he who with an unwavering will ceases not to do all in his power, brings all to perfection in the sight of God.

We know for a truth that you labor mightily for peace and harmony in the Church Universal and that you desire beyond words and strive with untiring diligence for everything that can cement Empire and Papacy together in mutual charity. The most important thing for this unity of affection you have already accomplished, namely, that your son King Henry is restored to the communion of the Church and his kingdom delivered from the general peril. While he was placed outside this communion we were prevented from dealing with him by the fear of divine vengeance, but his subjects were bound up with his offense through the necessity of daily intercourse.

With regard to other and less important matters, although we have no doubt whatever that Your Poverty [*sic*] will be ready to act, still we are constrained to urge upon Your Highness by our faith in Christ for the revealing of your joy that you persist in such holy endeavor. We are also notifying your son that your advice and your merits have been of the greatest value and that Your Holiness will see with satisfaction how mercifully divine grace has looked upon him.

Be it further known to Your Highness that we are just now hard pressed in the cause of St. Peter, chief of the Apostles, and that your devoted Beatrice and Matilda, daughters to us both, are laboring day and night in our behalf, following your example and imitating you as faithful pupils of their lady and mistress. Through you a new example of ancient joy comes to my memory — through you, I say, I am reminded of those women who once sought their Lord in the sepulcher. For as they first of all the disciples came to the Lord's tomb in the wondrous ardor of their affection, so you have visited the Church of Christ laid in the sepulcher of affliction before many others — nay, before almost all the princes of the world in pious service. You strive with all your strength that she may rise again to her state of freedom and, taught as it were by angelic answers, you call others to the support of the struggling Church.

Wherefore await without anxiety the revelation of supreme glory and eternal life which is in Christ Jesus, and in the company of those women you shall enter the presence of our Savior with the angelic host and enjoy peace forever with him as your leader. Your inquiries about your daughter Matilda we have received with joy, and we congratulate Your Holiness that you are so deeply concerned for her welfare. She, in fact, is devoted to you with heart and soul and desires your glory as the joy of her own salvation. We too pray earnestly for her, and, though our own merits can little commend our prayers to God, yet we trust that, aided by the virtues of Peter, whose servant we are, they may not be wholly worthless in the sight of God.

And so, receiving your approval with all due respect, we beg you to remember both her [Matilda] and ourself in your prayers. And may we so aid each other with mutual intercession before God that the Christian love which binds us here on earth may prepare for us seats and joy together in the kingdom and presence of our Father.

william
of Aquitaine

THE SECOND BOOK

To Count William of Poitou, regarding the Annulment of His Marriage

Book II, 3, p. 126. Sept. 10, 1074.

Gregory . . . to William, count of Poitou, greeting . . .

Thanks and praise to God Almighty that he has entered the innermost places of your heart and has turned you to his love and fear and given you strength to obey his commandments and to overcome the desires of the flesh. We have learned that you have given up what was dearest to you in this world and have agreed to separate yourself from your wife because of her close relationship to you.* Of a truth, the more severe the struggle by which you have conquered the desire of your heart and humbled yourself more completely before the law of God, so much greater the glory and infinite the reward which you may beyond all doubt expect to have prepared for you.

Wherefore to us also comes a more abundant joy because in this discipline of yours we perceive the certain hope of your salvation and the preservation of that nobility which by the grace of God has always distinguished your House. For the nobility of a race is greatly corrupted when offspring are produced from an unlawful marriage. And Your Highness should be the less surprised at our insistence because the Roman Church, which has always had such great and peculiar affection for you, for your family and your whole kinship, could not allow you to remain in such great peril. We dare not, however, grant your request that that lady may remain under your control until a future synod, in spite of the petition of your sister [the empress Agnes] whom we regard with filial affection, knowing as we do how the snares of the Devil prompt men with especial eagerness toward forbidden indulgence. Therefore remove her so absolutely from your neighborhood that

* Count William of Poitou and duke of Aquitaine, brother of the empress Agnes, married as his third wife Hildegard, daughter of King Robert of Burgundy. His maternal grandfather was the adopted son of a brother of King Robert.

your self-control and your reverence to God may be an example to all men and the Devil may be unable by any cunning to imperil your salvation. [Here follows a brief passage referring to the threatened excommunication of Isambert, bishop of Poitiers.]

Your assurance of readiness to act in the service of St. Peter was very welcome to us, but it has not seemed best to write you anything definite at present concerning an expedition, because the report is that the Christians beyond seas have, by God's help, driven back the fierce assault of the pagans, and we are waiting for the counsel of divine Providence as to our future course. But for your good will a full reward is in store at the hand of God, and if the necessity shall arise we shall have firm confidence in your promises as of a beloved brother and son.

To the Clergy of France, against Philip I

Book II, 5, p. 130.   Sept. 10, 1074.

Gregory . . . to Archbishops Manasses of Reims, Richer of Sens and Richard of Bourges and to Bishop Adraldus of Chartres and the other bishops of France, greeting . . .

For a long time now the kingdom of France, once renowned and mighty, has been declining from its glorious position and with increasing evil behavior has been stripped of a great part of its power. Within this period the pinnacle of its honor and the whole aspect of its outward appearance seem to have fallen in ruin. Through neglect of law and contempt for justice, every kind of cruel, wretched and intolerable compact is there made with impunity and, begun as license, is now accepted as custom. Some years since, when through weakness of the royal power wrongs were neither prohibited by law nor punished by authority, enemies fought among themselves as if by some law of nature, each for himself, and laid in stores of arms and supplies to avenge their own wrongs. In these confusions slaughter, burnings and all that war brings in its train occurred throughout the land, a thing to be deplored indeed but not to be wondered at.

But now everyone, as if smitten with some horrible pestilence, is committing every kind of abominable crimes without any impelling cause. They regard neither divine nor human law; they make nothing of perjury, sacrilege, incest or mutual betrayal. Fellow citizens, relatives, even brothers, capture one another for the sake of plunder, extort all the property of their victims and leave them to end their lives in misery, a thing unknown anywhere else on, earth. Pilgrims going to or returning from the shrines of the Apostles are captured, thrust into prison, tortured worse than by any pagan and often held for a ransom greater than all they have.

Of all these things your king — who is to be called a tyrant rather than a king — is the cause and fountainhead under the inspiration of the Devil. Every stage of his life was stained with vice and crime, and since he began his wretched and unhappy reign he has not only led his people into crime by the laxity of his rule but has encouraged them to every unmentionable and forbidden deed by the example of his own aims and actions. Nor has it seemed to him enough to incur the wrath of God by the wasting of churches, by adultery, plunder, perjury and fraud of many kinds, for which we have often reproved him. From merchants returning recently from many parts of the world to a certain fair in France he seized vast quantities of money like a robber, a thing not hitherto told of any king, even in legend. He, who ought to be the guardian of law and justice, stands forth as the worst of plunderers and does this in such wise that his wrongdoings are not confined to the kingdom he rules but are spread throughout the world to the confusion of many peoples and, as I believe, to his own destruction.

Since, then, the sentence of the supreme judge is in no wise to be avoided, we beg you and in all charity counsel you to have a care for yourselves lest the curse of the prophet fall upon you: "Cursed be the man who holds back his sword from blood," that is to say, as you well know, he who holds back the word of admonition from rebuking sinful men. For you, my brethren, are at fault, seeing that you beyond a doubt encourage his evil doing by not rebuking his infamous deeds with sacerdotal strictness. Further — we grieve to say it — we greatly fear that you will receive judgment, not as shepherds but as hirelings, who, seeing the wolf tearing the flock of the Lord, take to flight and hide yourselves in silence like dogs too weak to bark. Indeed we are the more disturbed as to your peril because we can imagine no excuse for you in the judgment of the future, since we can see no reason for your silence unless we are to accuse you either of connivance, if — as we cannot believe — he commits these wrongs by your suggestion, or else of negligence, if you are too indifferent to his ruin. How both these accusations are to be avoided, especially in the function of dispensation entrusted to you, do you who know the obligations of the pastoral office consider for yourselves. For if you suppose that it is contrary to law and to respect for the fealty you have vowed to him for you to restrain him from crime, you are greatly mistaken. We can prove by every reason that he is far more loyal who rescues another from the shipwreck of his soul, even against his will, than he who allows him to perish in the deadly whirlpool of his sins. And as to fear, it is idle to speak of that, since if you work together and are constantly armed in defense of justice your strength will be so great that by faithful discipline you may turn him from his wonted evil courses without any danger to yourselves and may deliver your own souls. Even though fear and the peril of death should threaten you, still you ought not to surrender the independence of your priestly office.

Wherefore we beg you and warn you by our apostolic authority to come together and take counsel for the welfare of your country, and your own reputation. Address the king jointly upon the peril of the kingdom and of himself. Show him to his face how criminal are his deeds and his policies. Strive earnestly to persuade him to make good the plunder of the above-mentioned merchants, knowing as you do that unless this is done he will rouse no end of discord and hostility among many peoples. Further, let him amend his evil ways, abandon the practices of his youth and begin to restore the dignity and glory of the kingdom by adhering to righteousness, and let him be the first to give up what is wrong that he may compel others to do what is right. But if he shall refuse to hear you and, casting aside the fear of God, shall continue to harden his heart, contrary to his royal dignity and the welfare of the kingdom and of himself, then declare to him as from our own lips that he shall no longer escape the sword of apostolic discipline. And so do you, as commanded and bound by apostolic authority, following the example of your mother, the Holy Roman and Apostolic Church, in due faith and obedience, separate yourselves from all service and communion with him and forbid throughout all France the celebration of public divine worship. But if even this discipline does not bring him to his senses we desire to leave no doubt in the mind of anyone that we shall, with God's help, make every possible effort to deprive him of his kingly rule in France. And if we find you lacking in zeal in this great and necessary work, we shall no longer be in doubt that he remains incorrigible through his reliance upon your support and shall smite you as allies and accomplices of his crimes with the spear of the same punishment and shall deprive you of your episcopal offices.

God and our own conscience bear us witness that it has never entered our mind to make these proclamations at the request of anyone or for any reward but that, moved solely by our profound grief that so noble a kingdom and so vast a people should go to ruin through the fault of one abandoned wretch, we neither could nor ought to dissemble or keep silence.

Mindful, therefore, of that saying of divine wisdom, "The fear of man bringeth a snare, but whoso putteth his trust in the Lord shall be safe," so act and so carry yourselves as to show your liberty of mind and tongue, having no fear of man and bearing the downfall of your own weakness, but comforted in the Lord and in the power of his strength, like good soldiers of Christ, rise to the height of present and future glory.

Further, we urgently request and command you to summon Sir Lancelin of Beauvais and order him in the name of St. Peter and by our apostolic authority to set free and unharmed our liegeman Fulcher of Chartres, whom he captured on his return from the shrine of the Apostles, and to restore all his goods. If he refuses to do this do you proceed against him with both secular and spiritual weapons until you have compelled him to set free this pilgrim of St. Peter and to restore or refuse to accept whatever ransom he may have received or contracted for.

To Bishop Jaromir of Prague, regarding Controversies with Bishop John of Olmütz and Duke Wratislaw of Bohemia

Book II, 6. p. 133. Sept. 22, 1074.

Gregory . . . to Bishop Jaromir of Prague, greeting and apostolic benediction — though he does not deserve it.

When you came to the Apostolic See during the present year we received you in our apostolic clemency far more kindly and leniently than your deeds deserved. But you, rendering evil for good as your custom is, in contempt of our good will and our apostolic authority, had the presumption to set yourself against our decree concerning the property in dispute between you and Bishop John of Moravia [Olmütz] and, what is especially offensive to us, you declared falsely that you had done this with our approval.

Our recollection is that we gave judgment that the Moravian bishop should hold the land and other property in dispute in peace and quiet until a future synod. Of this we expressly notified your brother, the duke, in writing, and you confirmed it, promising us in our hand that you would in no way interfere.

Further, quite recently you brought certain new charges against your brother, Duke Wratislaw — which we now see were made falsely — namely, that he was disputing your right to a certain castle of St. Wenceslaus and to a provostship. In this you accomplished nothing except that we warned him by letter that if he felt he had done you wrong, he should do what was right in the matter for our sake — or rather for the love of God. Therefore, on this occasion also, you both made up a lie about us and acted contrary to our decree. I should like to know if you have no shame nor fear that for reasons such as these not only your office is imperiled, but that out of this fraternal hatred not even the grace of Christian faith is left to you?

We therefore order you in the name of St. Peter and by our apostolic authority to restore to the Moravian bishop the castle which you so fraudulently captured and all the other property in dispute. We decree also that you come in person or send suitable agents to Rome for a settlement of this case, and further that you forward this notice at once to the Moravian bishop so that he too may prepare himself or his agents for the journey.

It is further reported to us that you still continue to disturb the peace which ought to exist between you and your brother, the duke, in many ways, especially that you are excommunicating subjects of his without canonical grounds or legal process — a perilous thing for you, since, as the blessed Gregory [I] says, "He who lays bonds upon the innocent destroys his own power of binding and loosing." Wherefore we admonish you never to venture to brandish the sword of anathema hastily or rashly over anyone, but to determine the guilt of each person by careful previous investigation. And if any question arises between you and the subjects of your brother, first confer with him in a friendly and brotherly way that he may compel his own people to do right. But if he shall refuse justice to you or shall allow the rashness of his men to break out against you without punishment, then inform us at once, and with God's help we will see to it that the cause of complaint shall be settled by fitting admonition and without delay.

To DUKE WRATISLAW OF BOHEMIA, REFERRING TO THE MATTERS TREATED IN NUMBER 6

Book II, 7, p. 135.   Sept. 22, 1074.

Gregory . . . to Wratislaw, duke of Bohemia, greeting . . .

Your messenger has arrived here bringing proofs of your great devotion and loyalty and has duly presented the hundred marks of silver of your standard weight which you sent to St. Peter under the form of a tribute. We received this with gratitude, but we welcome your affection still more eagerly, extending, as it were, the arms of our spirit towards you as we perceive your mind and will to be more and more kindled with reverence for the Apostolic See. The blessed Peter, whom you love and before whom you humble the loftiness of your power, will beyond a doubt abundantly reward you and cause you to rejoice in his protection both now and in the life to come.

We are further gratified that, in obedience to our admonitions, you have made peace with your brother, Jaromir, bishop of Prague. When he presented himself this year before the Apostolic See, we treated him far more leniently than his faults deserved. But he, making an unworthy requital, had no sooner returned home, as we learned from undoubted evidence, than he presumed to interfere in the case of a castle and other property about which he had a controversy with the Moravian bishop John, contrary to our injunction and contrary also to the promise which he had given in our hand, and even falsely declaring that we had authorized him to do this. In what words and how briefly we reproved him for this falsehood and deception you may clearly see from the copy forwarded to you of the letter that we sent him.

Wherefore we beg Your Highness and in the name of St. Peter admonish you no longer to permit him to enjoy the fruits of his deceit. Unless he at once restores to the Moravian bishop the castle and other property in dispute according to our commands, do you oust him by force, make full restitution and defend the person of the bishop and the property of the church over which he presides from injury and oppression by evil men, for the love of God and the redemption of your own soul.

TO BEATRICE AND MATILDA, REGARDING ITALIAN AFFAIRS

Book II, 9, p. 138. Oct. 16, 1074.

Gregory . . . to the Duchess Beatrice and her daughter Matilda, greeting . . .

It will not have escaped your notice that various reports have reached me about you, as is usually the case where the affection and unity of friends are the object of envy. Indeed if we chose to listen to such tales there are but few in whose sincere devotion we could trust. But, without any suspicion whatsoever, we say to you in all truth that we have no more confidence in any prince of this world than in you, and this we have learned from your words, your deeds, your pious zeal and the splendid steadfastness of your faith. Nor have we any doubt that your regard for us shines with a pure light; for the servant is beloved through Peter and Peter in his servant.

This will inform you that, contrary to the expectation of all my attendants, I have overcome the weakness of my body and am now in good health again — a cause for mourning rather than for rejoicing. For my soul longed with great desire for that fatherland where he who has a care for labor and sorrow grants rest and refreshment to the weary.

But, preserved thus far for our accustomed labors and our endless anxieties, we suffer hour by hour, as it were, the pangs of a woman in labor, so that we scarce hold the rudder of the ship that is sinking before our eyes. The law and the religion of Christ have almost everywhere so completely gone to ruin that Saracens or whatever pagans you please are holding more firmly to their usages than those who have received the Christian name and for whom is prepared an inheritance of eternal glory in their Father's kingdom are guarding the precepts of the law of God. So it is no wonder that we long to desert the fortress of this life in the hope of divine consolation, seeing that, placed as we are, we pay the penalty by the mere contemplation of the perils that crowd in upon us.

Be it further known to you that Robert Guiscard has often sent word to us that he desires to place himself in our hands with prom-

ises of loyalty as binding as any that could or ought to be given by
anyone to any lord. But, considering certain good reasons why
this should be postponed until now, we are awaiting the decision of
divine judgment and of our apostolic representatives. Besides, we
are informed that one of you [Beatrice] is proposing to cross the
Alps at about this time, but we are extremely anxious to have an
interview with you both before then, desiring to have your advice
in our affairs as our sisters and daughters of St. Peter. As for
ourself, you may have every confidence that whatsoever we know
or can do by God's grace is frankly laid before you, and be assured
that you are remembered daily in our prayers and earnestly commended to God by us, sinful though we be.

Further, you are aware that Marquis Azzo [of Este] has given
us his solemn promise to present himself before us whenever he
shall be summoned to render an account of his marriage. We have
therefore sent a summons in this case to him, to William, bishop of
Pavia, and to Herbert, bishop of Modena, who are acquainted with
the relationships of the woman, in order that we may get at the
truth of the matter and, with God's help, render a just decree.
Wherefore may it be your good pleasure to notify the aforesaid
marquis by trusty messengers that he is free to pass through your
territory, both going and returning, so that no fear of violence
from you may interfere with the working of Christian law in this
case.

To Archbishop Udo of Trier, Ordering an Investigation of the Bishop of Toul

Book II, 10, p. 140.   Oct. 16, 1074.

Gregory . . . to Udo, archbishop of Trier, greeting . . .

We urge you, our brother, to give as prompt and careful attention to the matters we are entrusting to you as the nature of the
case and the circumstances will permit. We hope that you will so
consider both in the affair described below, that we may find you,
as we believe you to be, our faithful and devoted fellow worker.

This monk of Toul, said to be a clerk, came to us and complained
that his lord, said to be bishop of Toul, was enraged against him
and that he had been driven into exile and deprived of all his
goods, and he prayed to be relieved from his distress by apostolic
charity. We inquired carefully how this had happened to him, and

he replied that he had demanded of the bishop a certain benefice which he claimed as lawfully belonging to the office of custos which he held. The bishop, angered by this demand, not only refused him the benefice but forbade him upon his obedience to perform any duties of his office. To this he replied that he owed the bishop no duty of obedience because he [the bishop] had sold archdeaconates, consecrations of churches, and even churches themselves, and had thus made himself guilty of the heresy of Simony. Further, he charged that the bishop had lived in open relations with a certain woman, by whom he had had a child, and report had it that he had joined himself to her by a solemn promise and by a marriage after the manner of laymen. Some said also that he had bought his way into the episcopal office.

When the bishop heard all this he spoke with this monk and also with others of the brethren about making amends as if he repented of the sins that had been brought to light, but finally broke out into a public display of anger against this man.

Shortly afterward in the absence of the bishop some of his men-at-arms, knowing his wishes, endangered the peace of this man and threatened him to his face within the cloister. When he learned that his life and honor were being plotted against he went away secretly, hoping that his absence would moderate the violence of this excitement. But the bishop straightway ordered that all his goods should be seized and sold, and he made his complaint that he had long been living in poverty and exile.

This seems to me against due order and very unjust. If the charges are true the bishop — nay the ex-bishop — hated, not this man, but his own conscience and ought to be brought to trial. But if they are false — as I hope they are — still it was not right that the man should be seized and flogged by soldiers but rather that he should be disciplined according to the law of the Church. Wherefore it is our will that you, my brother, being advised and supported by apostolic authority, invite our beloved colleague, Hermann, the venerable bishop of Metz, to join with you in summoning the bishop of Toul to your presence. You are to order him to receive this clerk back into his cloister free from all danger to his life and safe from every form of insult. He shall restore to him the office of custos together with the benefice which he demanded, if he has a lawful claim to it, also all the other rights which lawfully belong to him, together with his provostship and his mastership of the scholars, and all the goods which were taken from him, and shall make good all the damage so unjustly inflicted upon him.

Then call the clergy of Toul together and give them strict orders upon their obedience and under penalty of anathema to disclose to you whatever they may know as to the life of the bishop and his accession to office, and after you have probed the truth from every side, fail not to inform us in writing at or before the synod which we are to hold during the first week of Lent what we ought to think of the matter. But if the bishop shall be proved innocent — as we hope he may be — of these many and grave charges we shall see to it with God's help that the rash offense of the clerk in seeking a hearing from us shall be duly corrected. If, however, the bishop shall not be able to clear himself of the charges brought against him, then in no wise is it to be endured that the wolf shall hold the shepherd's place.

We have ordered this letter to be plainly [or openly] sealed in order that we might give you the more complete authority.

To King Solomon of Hungary, Claiming Suzerainty over That Kingdom

Book II, 13, p. 144. Oct. 28, 1074.

Gregory . . . to Solomon, king of Hungary, greeting . . .

Your letter to us arrived late owing to delay on the part of your messenger. It would have been more graciously received at our hands had not your ill-considered condition been so grievously offensive to St. Peter. For, as you may learn from the chief men of your country, the kingdom of Hungary was long since offered and devotedly surrendered to St. Peter by King Stephen as the full property of the Holy Roman Church under its complete jurisdiction and control. Furthermore, the emperor Henry [III] of pious memory, after his conquest of that kingdom, in honor of St. Peter sent to his shrine a spear and a crown, and in celebration of his triumph delivered the insignia of sovereignty to the place where he knew the headship of that power belonged.

This being so you, nevertheless, who in other respects also have widely departed from the character and quality of a king have, as we hear, degraded the right and the honor of St. Peter as far as you could by accepting a kingdom which is his as a fief from the king of the Germans. If this is true, you yourself know how much favor

from St. Peter or good will from ourself you can expect. You cannot
receive these, or hope to reign long without apostolic reproof unless
you correct your fault and acknowledge that the scepter of the kingdom which you hold is a fief of the apostolic and not of the royal
majesty. For neither fear nor favor nor any respect of persons shall,
so far as in us lies, prevent us from claiming with God's help every
possible honor due to him whose servant we are.

[margin note: two centers of power vying for dominance]

If you are prepared to correct these wrongs and to order your
life as becomes a king, then beyond a doubt you shall enjoy in full
measure the affection of the Holy Roman Church as a beloved son
of a mother, and also our own friendship in Christ.

To the Bishops of Strasbourg and Basel, Ordering Them to Settle the Rival Claims to Wardenship over a Convent

Book II, 14, p. 146.   Oct. 29, 1074.

Gregory . . . to Bishops Werner of Strasbourg and Burchard of
Basel, greeting . . .

We assume that you are aware of the fact that our lord Pope Leo
[IX] of blessed memory granted in full sovereignty to the Holy
Roman Church, over which he presided with holy fidelity, the convent of the Holy Cross situated in his ancestral territory and built
at his own expense, in order that that venerable place might do
more efficient service to God under the protection and freedom
of St. Peter. But, as we learn by trustworthy information, his
nephews Hugo and Gerard, seeking their own profit rather than
the things that are of God, and having no fear of excommunication
by that most holy man, are in conflict as to the wardenship [*advo-
catia*], are plundering the convent property and handing over to
their fighting men through sacrilegious invasion funds established
for the support of the maids of God.

[margin note: are these his legates?]

Wherefore we urgently request and command you, our brethren,
by the love and obedience due to St. Peter, to summon them both
to meet you in some suitable place, to inquire carefully into both
sides of the case and use your best endeavors to put an end to their
rivalry. You are not, however, to deviate in any way from the
terms laid down in the privilege of our father, Pope Leo. It is
there ordered, among other things, that the oldest member of his
family in the estate [*castrum*] of Egisheim should be the sole

tenant of the wardenship and that this right should continue forever in the hands of his family. — ?

In accordance with this provision it is our opinion that Gerard
has a better claim than Hugo to administer the wardenship, because
we understand that he is the elder. If you also agree in this opinion then, in the name of St. Peter and by our apostolic authority
and your own right as bishops, do you prohibit Hugo from interfering in any way in this matter of the wardenship and from in-
flicting upon the convent or upon its property of whatsoever kind
any injury or inconvenience. Otherwise let him understand that he
can in no way escape the stroke of the apostolic sword but shall be
cut off, not only from the favor of St. Peter, but from the communion of the whole Church and shall be condemned and excommunicated by the judgment of the Holy Spirit and by apostolic
decree.

Let us hear by letter at the earliest possible moment what action
has been taken in this case.

To Count William of Poitou, against King Philip I of France

Book II, 18, p. 150.   Nov. 13, 1074.

Gregory . . . to William, count of Poitou, greeting . . .

Although the evil deeds of Philip, king of France, have undoubtedly come to your knowledge, still we have thought it worth
while to inform you how greatly we are aggrieved thereby.

Among other crimes in which he has gone beyond not only
Christian but even pagan princes, and after the various spoliations
of churches which he has been pleased to destroy, he has so far
forgotten all respect for his royal dignity as to plunder certain
Italian merchants traveling in your country, driven thereto by
avarice rather than by any reasonable motive. We have called
upon the bishops of France to summon him in this case and we now
exhort you, as one having a true regard for St. Peter and for ourself, and, as we believe, saddened by his and our peril, to join with
some of the higher nobility of France and call his attention to his
evil deeds. You are to enjoin upon him to reject the counsels of
the wicked and follow those of the wise and good, to cease from his
destruction of churches and change his conduct to conform to the
example of the good kings of France and immediately to cease

from the robberies above referred to whereby pilgrims of St. Peter are held up, taken prisoner and molested in divers ways.

If he shall accept your advice we will treat him with all due respect. But if he shall persist in his perverse attitude and shall lay up the wrath of God and of St. Peter against him for the hardness of his heart, then with God's help and according to the measure of his iniquity, we will without hesitation separate him in a Roman synod from the body and communion of Holy Church, and with him whoever shall pay him the honors and obedience due to a king, and his excommunication shall daily be confirmed upon St. Peter's altar. For we have long borne with his iniquities; long have we overlooked his insults to Holy Church on account of his youth. But now his misconduct has become so scandalous, that even if he were as brave and powerful as the pagan emperors who inflicted such torments upon the holy martyrs we could not be moved by any fears to leave such iniquities unpunished.

To Archbishop Liemar of Bremen, Calling Him to Obedience

Book II, 28, p. 160.   Dec. 12, 1074.

Gregory . . . to Liemar, archbishop of Bremen. [No greeting.] *Oh*.

Since we have learned that you are unmindful of the favor with which the Holy Roman Church has been willing to honor you, and that you have forgotten the promise and the canonical obligation by which you bound yourself to be the loyal and obedient servant of the Holy Roman Church, we are justly aggrieved and angered against you, whom we believed to be our faithful son. Alas for the perversion of morals and the altered times! The man whom we believed to be an impregnable wall of defense for the Holy Roman Church, over which we unworthily preside, and for ourself, whom we held to be a guardian of the faith, ready if need were to take the sword of Christ in virtue of his office as well as of the above-mentioned obligations, for the Holy Roman Church and for ourself and our successors — this man we now find to be an enemy both to her and to us and we must endure his insults and suffer a disgraceful, unprecedented and undeserved repulse.   *drama queen*

You placed every possible hindrance in the way of our legates, Bishops Albert of Palestrina and Gerald of Ostia, whom we sent into your country to summon a convention of archbishops, bishops, abbots and pious clergy, and in our place, supported by our au-

thority, to correct whatever needed correction and to make necessary additions to your religious order. You forbade the synod to
be held and when you were summoned by them to Rome at a fixed
date, namely the feast of St. Andrew, you failed to appear.

Wherefore we summon and order you, by our apostolic authority,
to present yourself at the synod which with God's help will be held
in the first week of the coming Lent for the correction of these and
whatever other matters need correcting. In consequence of the
above-mentioned offenses we suspend you from all episcopal functions until you shall appear before us.

To Bishop Otto of Constance, Summoning Him to the Lenten Synod at Rome

Epistolae collectae, 8, p. 528.   Dec., 1074.

Gregory . . . to Otto, bishop of Constance, greeting . . .

A report has come to us with regard to Your Fraternity, which I
have heard with grief and regret — a report which, if it had been
made to us of the lowest member of the Christian community, would
undoubtedly have called for a severe disciplinary sentence. While
we were zealously striving to wipe out the heresy of Simony and to
enforce the chastity of the clergy, inspired by apostolic authority
and the authentic opinions of holy fathers, we enjoined upon our
colleague, the venerable archbishop of Mainz, whose suffragans are
numerous and widely scattered, that he should diligently impress
this decree upon his whole clergy, in person and through his assist-
ants, and should see that it was carried out without exception.

To you also, who preside over the numerous clergy and the widespread population of the church of Constance, it has, for the same
reason, seemed good to us to send a special letter under our own
seal. With this as your authority you can more safely and more
boldly carry out our orders and expel from the Lord's holy place
the heresy of Simony and the foul plague of carnal contagion. The
apostolic authority of St. Paul is here of especial force, where,
counting in fornicators and adulterers with other vicious persons,
he gives this plain decision: "With such a one, no, not to eat."

Furthermore the whole body of the Catholic Church consists of
virgins or married persons or those holding themselves in restraint.
Whoever, therefore, is outside those three classes is not to be
counted among the sons of the Church or within the bounds of the

Christian religion. Wherefore we also, if we should know for certain that even the lowest layman was involved in concubinage, would cut him off completely from the body and blood of the Lord until he should perform due penance. How then shall one be the distributor or server of the holy sacraments who cannot in any wise be partaker of them? Further, we are urged to this by the authority of the blessed Pope Leo [I] who deprived subdeacons of the right to marry, a decree to which his successors in the Holy Roman Church, especially that famous doctor Gregory [I], gave such force of law that henceforth the marriage bond has been absolutely forbidden to the three orders of priests, levites and subdeacons.

But when we, in our pastoral forethought, sent word to you that these orders were to be carried out you, not setting your mind on the things that are above, but on the things that are upon the earth, loosed the reins of lust within the aforesaid orders so that, as we have heard, those who had taken concubines [*mulierculis*] persisted in their crime, while those who had not yet done so had no fear of your prohibitions. Oh, what insolence! Oh, what audacity, that a bishop should despise the decrees of the Apostolic See, should uproot the precepts of holy fathers — nay more, by orders from his high place and his priestly office should impose upon his subjects things contrary and repugnant to the Christian faith.

Wherefore we command you to present yourself before us at the approaching synod in the first week of Lent to give answer according to canon law as well for this disobedience and contempt of the Apostolic See as for all the other offenses charged against you.

TO THE PEOPLE OF CONSTANCE, DEFENDING HIS ACTION AGAINST THEIR BISHOP

Epistolae collectae, 9, p. 529. Dec., 1074.

Gregory . . . to the clergy and laity of high and low degree dwelling within the bishopric of Constance who are faithful to the Christian law, greeting . . .

We have sent to our brother, your bishop Otto, letters of exhortation, in which we enjoined upon him by our apostolic authority and the obligation of our office that he should banish entirely the heresy of Simony from his church, should see to it that the chastity of the clergy was preached with energy and should insist upon its maintenance with episcopal watchfulness. For this duty is

so well laid down for us by evangelical and apostolic writings, by
decrees of recognized councils and by the teachings of famous
scholars that we cannot cloak or neglect it without grave peril to
our soul and injury to Christian people.

But, as we are informed, your bishop has not been led by reverence for St. Peter or respect for his own office to carry out our
fatherly counsel. He has, so we understand, committed not only
the sin of disobedience but also of rebellion in that he has openly
permitted to his clergy actions contrary to our commands — nay,
to the commands of St. Peter — allowing those who had concubines
[*mulierculas*] to keep them, and those who had not to take them
unlawfully and rashly. When we learned this we were greatly
disturbed and wrote him a second letter expressing our anger and
laying down still more sharply the same orders. We have summoned him also to a Roman synod, which is to be held in the first
week of the coming Lent, to give an account of himself and to explain the grounds of his disobedience, if he has any rational ones,
before the whole assembly.

We are sending you word of this, my beloved sons, out of regard
for your welfare. It is perfectly evident, if he chooses to set himself in open opposition to St. Peter and the Holy Apostolic See,
that a man who dishonors his father and mother cannot exact
obedience from those who are loyal sons of their fathers and
mothers. It is a shame that he who refuses to submit to a master
should claim to be a master over pupils. Now therefore, as we have
said, we proclaim by our apostolic authority to all adherents of
God and St. Peter that if he shall persist in his obstinacy, you are
to show him neither reverence nor obedience. Nor are you to have
any fear that this may be a peril to your souls. For if, as we have
so often said, he chooses to set himself against the apostolic commands, we, by authority of St. Peter, do absolve all persons from
their duty of obedience to him. And even though one be bound to
him by an oath, so long as he remains in rebellion against Almighty
God and the Apostolic See, one is not under any obligation of
fidelity. For no one is bound to obey any person in opposition to
his Creator, who is above all; but we are bound to resist one who
sets himself against God, so that, compelled by this pressure, he
may learn to seek the way of righteousness. What a peril it is and
what a departure from the law of Christ to refuse obedience, especially to the Apostolic See, you may learn from the sayings of

the blessed prophet Samuel as expounded by the most holy Pope Gregory in the last book of his *Moralia*. That you may have these in mind we send them to you in writing so that you may know beyond a doubt that we are telling you no new things but are simply setting forth the teaching of holy fathers.

[Here follows a long quotation from Gregory's *Moralia* commenting upon I Samuel 15, 22-23.]

To KING HENRY IV, OFFERING FRIENDLY ADMONITIONS
Book II, 30, p. 163. Dec. 7, 1074. *when rebellion were still happening*

Gregory . . . to King Henry, greeting . . .

Beloved son: Although you have not settled the case of the church of Milan in accordance with your repeated letters and promises, still we have heard with great satisfaction that you treated our legates kindly and graciously, have duly corrected certain church matters and have sent to us by the said legates becoming greetings and assurance of devoted service. Further we rejoice greatly that, as your mother, the august empress Agnes of pious memory, constantly assured us, and as the bishops, your legates, now confirm, you are determined to root out completely the heresy of Simony from your kingdom and to use every effort to cure the inveterate disease of clerical unchastity.

The countess Beatrice and her daughter Matilda, our daughters and your most loyal subjects, have given us no little pleasure by their letters telling of your friendship and sincere attachment, which we were most glad to receive. By their advice and the persuasion of your august and best beloved mother we have been induced to send you this letter. And so, sinner that I am, I have kept and shall keep you in mind in the solemn service of the Mass above the bodies of the Apostles, humbly beseeching that Almighty God may confirm you in your present good intentions and may grant you still better things to the advantage of his Church. I further warn you and exhort you with sincere affection to take to yourself in these matters such advisers as will consider yourself, not your property, and will promote your welfare, not their own profit. If you follow their advice the Lord God whose cause they represent to you will be your gracious defender.

As to the Milan affair: If you will send to us wise and pious men and if it shall appear by their weighty arguments that the decree

MILAN

of the Roman Church, twice confirmed by synodal authority, can or ought to be modified we shall not hesitate to follow their well-considered judgment and turn to a wiser course. But if this shall prove to be impossible, then I beg and conjure Your Highness, for the love of God and by your reverence for St. Peter, freely to restore its rights to the church of Milan. Then finally you may know you have won the true power of a king, if you shall bow before Christ, the king of kings, for the restoration and defense of his churches, remembering the words of him who said: "Them that honor me I will honor, and they that despise me shall be lightly esteemed."

Further, be it known to Your Highness that we have written to Siegfried, archbishop of Mainz, summoning him to a synod which, by God's favor, we propose to hold in the first week of the coming Lent. If he shall not be able to come, let him send legates to represent him at that council. We have also directed the bishops of Bamberg, Strasbourg and Speyer to present themselves and give an account of their accession and their manner of life. But if — such is the insolence of the men — they shall delay in coming, we beg you to compel them by your royal power. And with them we wish you to send confidential messengers who may give us a trustworthy report of their accession and way of life, so that after we have learned the truth from their recital we may the more surely render an unquestioned judgment.

spies?

To Henry IV, Setting Forth Gregory's Plan for a Crusade

same   Book II, 31, p. 165.   Dec. 7, 1074.   *same day*

Gregory . . . to the glorious King Henry, greeting . . .

If God would grant by some act of his grace that my thoughts might lie open before you, I know beyond a doubt that no person could separate you from my sincere affection. But even as it is, I have entire confidence in his mercy, that it shall one day become clear that I am truly devoted to you. For to this I am directed by the common law of all Christian men; to this the majesty of empire and the mild sway of the Apostolic See impel me; so that if I do not love you as I ought, I am trusting in vain in the mercy of God through the merits of St. Peter.

But, since I desire to labor day and night in the Lord's vineyard, through many dangers even unto death, I will always strive with

CRUSADE

God's help to preserve a sacred and merited affection not only towards you whom God has placed at the summit of earthly affairs and through whom many may be led either to wander from the path of rectitude or to observe the faith of Christ, but also toward the least among Christians. For he who should try to approach the marriage feast of the king without this wedding garment will suffer a monstrous disgrace. Alas! Those who are daily plotting to sow discord between us pay no attention to these truths, that with these nets prepared at the Devil's prompting they may catch their own advantage and conceal their own vices by which they are madly calling down upon themselves the wrath of God and of St. Peter. I therefore warn and exhort you, my best beloved son, to turn your ear away from them and listen without reserve to those who seek not their own but the things that are of Jesus Christ and who do not set their own honor or profit above righteousness, so that through their counsel you may not forfeit the glory of this life, but may gain with confidence the life that is in Christ Jesus.

Further, I call to your attention that the Christians beyond the sea, a great part of whom are being destroyed by the heathen with unheard-of slaughter and are daily being slain like so many sheep, have humbly sent to beg me to succor these our brethren in whatever ways I can, that the religion of Christ may not utterly perish in our time — which God forbid! I, therefore, smitten with exceeding grief and led even to long for death — for I would rather stake my life for these than reign over the whole earth and neglect them — have succeeded in arousing certain Christian men so that they are eager to risk their lives for their brethren in defense of the law of Christ and to show forth more clearly than the day the nobility of the sons of God. This summons has been readily accepted by Italians and northerners, by divine inspiration as I believe — nay, as I can absolutely assure you — and already fifty thousand men are preparing, if they can have me for their leader and prelate, to take up arms against the enemies of God and push forward even to the sepulcher of the Lord under his supreme leadership.

I am especially moved toward this undertaking because the Church of Constantinople, differing from us on the doctrine of the Holy Spirit, is seeking the fellowship of the Apostolic See, the Armenians are almost entirely estranged from the Catholic faith and almost all the Easterners are waiting to see how the faith of the Apostle Peter will decide among their divergent views. For it is the call of our time that the word of command shall be fulfilled which our blessed Savior deigned to speak to the prince of the Apostles: "I have prayed for thee that thy faith fail not: and when thou art converted, strengthen thy brethren." And because our fathers, in whose footsteps we, though unworthy, desire to walk, often went to those regions for the strengthening of the Catholic faith, we also, aided by the prayers of all Christian men, are under compulsion to go over there for the same faith and for the defense of Christians — provided that the way shall be opened with Christ as our guide — for the way of man is not in his own hand, and the steps of a man are ordered by the Lord.

But, since a great undertaking calls for the aid and counsel of the great, if God shall grant me to begin this, I beg you for your advice and for your help according to your good pleasure. For if it shall please God that I go, I shall leave the Roman Church, under God, in your hands to guard her as a holy mother and to defend her for his honor.

Advise me at the earliest possible moment of your pleasure in this matter and what your divinely inspired judgment may determine. If I did not have better hopes of you than many suppose, these exhortations would be in vain. But since there is perchance no man whom you can completely trust in regard to the sincerity of my affection for you, I leave to the Holy Spirit, which can do all things, to show you in its own way what I ask of you and how great is my devotion to you, and may it in the same way so dispose your heart toward me that the desires of the wicked may come to naught and those of the righteous may increase. These two desires are keeping incessant watch upon us two — though in different ways — and are fighting according to the wishes of those from whom they proceed.

May Almighty God, from whom cometh every good thing, cleanse you from all your sins by the merits and the authority of the blessed Apostles Peter and Paul, and make you to walk in the way of his commandments and lead you into life eternal.

To Bishop William of Pavia, concerning the Marriage of His Sister Matilda with Marquis Azzo of Este

Book II, 35, p. 171.   Dec. 16, 1074.

Gregory . . . to William, bishop of Pavia, greeting . . .

Although you appear to have set yourself so greatly in opposition to us that we ought not even to send you our apostolic benediction — seeing that you neither came to us at the time appointed nor sent a valid excuse, nevertheless we would rather be charged with too great leniency than punish your disobedience with canonical severity. Wherefore, by our apostolic authority, we summon you to come to the synod which, please God, we are to hold during the first week of Lent and there make answer in the case of your sister.

Though it is perfectly clear that she had married the marquis Guido, a relative of the marquis Azzo, and though it was established by oath and by witness in our presence that your sister and Azzo were within the fourth degree of relationship, we will nevertheless grant you a hearing at that synod, so that, if you are confident that you have a good defense and can disprove the evidence and the oaths presented before us, their marriage may stand. Otherwise, if you cannot do this at that time or if you fail to come to the synod, we forbid by our apostolic authority that any further question be raised. In the oath by which we held the aforesaid Azzo we took the precaution to add that if you should present good reasons he might, with our permission, take back your sister and keep her as his wife.*

To Matilda, Wife of Marquis Azzo of Este, in the Matter of Her Marriage within the Prohibited Degrees

Book II, 36, p. 172.   Dec. 16, 1074.

Gregory . . . to Matilda, greeting . . .

That it was proved by witnesses and by oaths in our presence that you had formerly been married to a relative of Azzo and in addition that you and Marquis Azzo were related in the fourth

---

* The relationship referred to in this and the following letter was a double one: first between Guido, a former husband of Matilda, and Azzo; second, between Azzo and Matilda herself. Neither of these connections is quite positively established. Breslau, *Jahrbücher Konrads II*, I, 421-422.

degree, those who were present at the inquiry could have informed you. Therefore, since we bound Marquis Azzo by oath to have no relations with you as his wife, we now order you, in the name of St. Peter, to refrain absolutely from all marital intercourse with him and to do such penance for the wrong you have committed that you may recover the favor of God and avert the disgrace of such foul incest.

But if perchance you feel that you are suffering from a prejudiced judgment and believe you can disprove the oaths and witnesses of your consanguinity, we will give you a hearing at the approaching synod at Rome, where with God's help we will turn neither to the right nor to the left in executing justice but will deliver a just sentence.

To THE COUNTESS MATILDA, URGING HER TO JOIN A CRUSADE

Epistolae collectae, 11, p. 532. Dec. 16, 1074.

[No salutation.]

How serious my intention and how great my desire to go overseas and with Christ's help carry succor to the Christians who are being slaughtered like sheep by pagans, I hesitate to say to some persons lest I seem to be moved by too great fickleness of purpose. But to you, my most dearly beloved daughter, I have no hesitation in declaring any of these matters; for I have more confidence in your good judgment than you yourself could possibly express.

Therefore, when you have read the letter which I have written to the faithful beyond the Alps, pray use your utmost efforts to furnish whatever aid and counsel you can in the service of your Creator. If, as some say, it is beautiful to die for one's country, it is most beautiful and glorious indeed to give our mortal bodies for Christ, who is life eternal. I am convinced that many men-at-arms will support us in this work, that even our empress will be willing to go with us to those parts and to take you with her, leaving your mother here to protect our common interests, so that with Christ's help we may be safe in going.

If the empress will come, her prayers joined with yours may rouse many to this work. And I, provided with such sisters, would most gladly cross the sea and place my life, if need be, at the service of Christ with you whom I hope to have forever at my side in our eternal home.

Pray send me word as soon as possible of your decision in this matter and also of your coming to Rome, and may Almighty God deign to grant you his blessing, leading you from strength to strength, that our universal mother may long rejoice in you.

To the Doge and People of Venice, Urging Them to Support the Patriarchate of Grado

doge?

Book II, 39, p. 175. Dec. 31, 1074.

Gregory . . . to the doge Domenico and the people of Venice, greeting . . .

We suppose it is well known, not only to those who have been associated with us but also to many of yourselves, that from an early age we have been friendly to your country and to the independence of your people, and that on this account we have incurred the hostility of certain princes and nobles. And after we took upon ourself, unworthy though we are, the duties and burdens of the apostolic government, our affection for you became the more ardent because care for your welfare was more strictly enforced upon us by the obligation of universal supervision.

We therefore have sent a letter to you to rouse Your Excellency to consider the high repute of your ancient dignity, lest by long neglect — which God forbid! — you might have cause to mourn the loss of an honor which you are not striving to defend while it is still intact. For you are aware that by divine dispensation your land has been honored above many others with the dignity of a patriarchate, a title the loftiness of which is so majestic and so unusual that not more than four of them exist in the whole world.

This being so, nevertheless this great honor and glory of the priestly office has sunk so low in your hands through lack of worldly goods and loss of its power and has fallen so far below the honor becoming to its rank that its meager resources would seem insufficient for the dignity or even for the necessities of an ordinary bishopric. We therefore charge you with being ungrateful and unmindful of such a bounteous gift of divine beneficence, and we fear that, like degenerate offspring, you are wasting the heritage of a noble mother, namely, the church of Grado, and are thereby becoming of small significance, whereas, next to the Apostolic See you are the most distinguished people of the western world.

patriarchate?

We call to mind that the patriarch Dominicus [III] of blessed memory, predecessor of this present one [IV], wished to abandon his place on account of his poverty. And now this one declares that he is crushed by the same distress. Wherefore we admonish you as our beloved sons to be mindful of your former nobility and glory and no longer to disregard the dignity conferred upon you and the good will of the Apostolic See toward you, but to come together and take counsel how to maintain the honor of the patriarchate in due respect and with an increase of temporal resources and how, with God's help, you may restore it to its former eminence.

Our colleague, the present patriarch, has indicated to us that you, the doge, and many of your people have the best of good will in this matter. For this reason we begin by appealing to your loyalty to carry out your good intentions. Whatever may be the result of your deliberations, pray report to us at once by letter or trusty messengers. If you shall come to a decision worthy of the fame and honor both of yourselves and of that sacred office, we shall be grateful, as you will deserve. But if any unworthy pretext shall cause you to draw back, be assured that we will not suffer the name of so great a ministry to be debased among you or to be deprived of its due honor.

To Rudolf of Swabia and Berthold of Carinthia, against Simony and Concubinage

Book II, 45, p. 182. Jan. 11, 1075.

Gregory . . . to Rudolf, duke of Swabia, and Berthold, duke of Carinthia, greeting . . .

We are aware that you are giving intelligent consideration to the wretched desolation of the religion of Christ, which in these days has, for our sins, been brought so low that no man living has ever seen a more unhappy time, nor can such be found recorded since the days of our blessed father Silvester. But the chief and primary cause of these calamities is in us, who have been raised to govern the people or have been called and established as bishops for the welfare of their souls. From the leadership of those who have taken upon themselves either civil office or spiritual rule come, as from certain first principles, the weal and woe of their subjects. If, then, they seek only their own glory and the lusts of this world, they cannot live without confusion to themselves and to their people.

Pursuing their own evil desires they both bind the laws of their own authority by their own fault and loose the reins of sin to others by their example. Nor do they go wrong through ignorance or without thought, but resisting the Holy Spirit with presumptuous obstinacy they reject laws which they understand and set at naught the apostolic decrees.

The archbishops and bishops of your land are well aware — and it should be known also to all the faithful — that the sacred canons forbid that those who have been appointed to any degree or function of holy orders through the heresy of Simony, that is by the use of money, shall have the right to administer any office in Holy Church; also that those who are guilty of fornication shall celebrate Mass or serve at the altar in the lower orders. These rules, although formerly neglected, our holy and apostolic Mother Church from the time of the blessed Pope Leo [IX] has repeatedly ordered to be received and enforced in councils and by means of messengers and letters under the authority of St. Peter. But until the present time bishops with very few exceptions have refused to obey them, have made no effort to prohibit or to punish these execrable practices, not reflecting that according to Scripture "rebellion is as the sin of witchcraft, and stubbornness [or disobedience] is as idolatry."

Since, therefore, we are sure that the sacred offices are unworthily performed and the people led astray by those who despise the apostolic commands — nay, those of the Holy Spirit — and who encourage the sins of their subjects by criminal indulgence, it is very fitting that we, upon whom above all others rests the care of the Lord's flock, should keep watch against these evils by some other method. For it seems to us far better to reënforce the divine justice by new policies rather than allow the souls of men to perish by neglect of law.

Wherefore we now turn to you and to all in whose loyalty and devotion we have confidence, begging you and directing you by apostolic authority, no matter what bishops may say or not say, not to recognize those whom you shall prove to have been promoted or ordained simoniacally or to be under the charge of fornication. These orders you are to publish and urge at the king's court and elsewhere in assemblies of the kingdom, and you are to prevent such persons, to the best of your ability, even by force if that be necessary, from serving at the sacred mysteries. But if any persons begin to babble against you, saying that this is none of your affair, make them this answer: that they shall not interfere in the matter of your welfare and that of your people, but shall come to us and discuss the question of obedience which I have enjoined upon you.

As to you, Rudolf, duke and best beloved son of St. Peter, we have every confidence that you earnestly desire that spirit of religion about which you have asked our advice, and we will suggest what seems to us the most appropriate form of satisfaction: whatever money you can remember receiving for the appointment of clergymen in a church, apply this either to the needs of that same church if possible, or to the support of the poor, to the end that you may be freed from every stain of guilt and may deserve to be numbered among the chosen citizens of the kingdom of Heaven.

TO HUGO OF CLUNY, ASKING SYMPATHY FOR THE BURDENS OF THE PAPAL OFFICE

Book II, 49, p. 188.   Jan. 22, 1075.

Gregory . . . to Hugo, abbot of Cluny, greeting . . .

If it were possible, I should greatly desire you to understand fully what anxiety oppresses me, what toil renewed day by day wearies and disturbs me by its increasing burden, so that your brotherly sympathy might incline you toward me and cause you to pour out your heart in floods of tears before God, that Jesus, the man of poverty, through whom all things were made and who is ruler over all, might stretch forth his hand and deliver me from my misery with his wonted mercy. Often have I besought him, according to his word, that he would either take me out of this life or would show favor to our common mother through my service. Yet up to the present time he has not delivered me from my great suffering nor has my life been of value, as I had hoped, to that mother in whose chains he has bound me. A vast and universal grief and sadness walls me about because the Church of the East is falling away from the Catholic faith by the instigation of the Devil, and through all its members that ancient enemy himself is slaughtering Christians in all directions, so that the members are destroyed in their bodies while their head is slaying them in spirit.

And again, when I review in my mind the regions of the West, whether north or south, I find scarce any bishops who live or who *was there not a concept of pride in your religion?*

were ordained according to law and who govern Christian people in the love of Christ and not for worldly ambition. And among secular princes I find none who prefer the honor of God to their own or righteousness to gain. As to those among whom I live, Romans, Lombards and Normans, as I often say to them, I find them worse than Jews and pagans.

And now to return to myself: I find myself so weighed down by the burden of my own actions, that I have no hope of salvation save only in the mercy of Christ. For if I did not hope for a better life and one more useful to Holy Church, I would under no conditions remain at Rome where, as God knows, I have lived under compulsion for the last twenty years. So it is that between the suffering daily renewed and the hope none too plain before me, I am crushed by a thousand woes, and suffer a living death waiting for him who bound me in his chains, led me back to Rome against my will and has beset me there with a thousand anxieties. I cry out to him repeatedly: "Hasten and delay not! Hasten and die not, and deliver me for the love of the blessed Mary and of St. Peter." But, since praise is of no value, and holy prayers avail not in the mouth of a sinner whose life is not praiseworthy and whose deeds are of this world, I pray and beseech you to urge with watchful care those who deserve to be heard for the virtue of their lives, that they pray God for me in that love and devotion which they owe to our universal mother.

And, because we ought to use either hand as a right hand in crushing the savagery of the wicked, it becomes our duty, when there is no prince to care for such matters, to keep watch over the lives of religious men. We enjoin upon you in brotherly love that, so far as are able, you lend your aid with watchful zeal, warning, urging and exhorting those who love St. Peter, that if they really wish to be his sons and his soldiers they do not prefer the princes of this world to him. For these can yield them only what is wretched and transient, while he promises eternal blessings, absolving them from all their sins and leading them into their heavenly home by the power committed to him.

I desire to know more clearly than the day who are really faithful to St. Peter and who are no less devoted to that heavenly prince for the sake of their heavenly glory than to those to whom they are subject for temporal and miserable rewards.

To King Sancho I of Aragon, concerning an Invalid Bishop

Book II, 50, p. 190.   Jan. 24, 1075.

Gregory . . . to Sancho, king of Spain [Aragon], greeting . . .

Since we have learned that Your Royal Highness is inclined toward the Holy and Apostolic See with pious affection and devotion, we desire that you and your kingdom should be raised to all due honor and we wish to offer our apostolic good will, not only in this present, but at all times, to you and to your interests in sincere affection.

But in the case of the Aragonese bishopric as to which you consulted us and expressed a certain wish, after long and careful consideration and consultation with members of the Roman Church, we perceive that your plan is not advisable, since there are canonical decrees against it. As you know, our colleague Sanctius, a bishop of Aragon, came to us complaining of great bodily infirmity and asking our permission to resign his bishopric on the ground that he was so nearly broken down by sickness that he could no longer properly perform his duties. In order to do this more easily he suggested to us two clerks, either of whom, he said, would have your approval as well as his own for the place. When we asked him about their life and conversation, we found them in every respect good and honorable men, except for the fact that they were the sons of concubines, and since the holy canons forbid the promotion of such persons to the priesthood, we did not think it wise to approve them, so that no act of ours contrary to the canons might be used as a precedent for the future. The Holy and Apostolic See is accustomed to tolerate many things for well-considered reasons, but never to deviate from the canonical tradition in its official decrees.

Therefore be it known to Your Affection that we advised the bishop to continue, as far as he was able, to perform the spiritual functions of the bishopric, to ask the help of his provincial colleagues and to appoint some clerk to carry on the less important and outside business, who should be competent for such representation and, in case of need, could perform the episcopal functions. After a year or more of this arrangement, if meanwhile by God's grace the bishop should recover his health he should continue to watch over the flock of the Lord; but if his infirmity should increase and he should no longer be able to carry on the trust committed to him, then, if the conduct of the substitute should be approved, let a report be sent to the Apostolic See together with letters from you and the bishop and the witness of the clergy of that church, and so after careful deliberation a final and appropriate reply shall be sent to you under divine approval. We should not have sent you such a positive statement, except that our feelings of brotherly compassion for a bishop seeking release and alleging the hindrance of his own infirmity would not permit us to refuse him a hearing.

Give this matter, then, beloved son, careful consideration and aid the bishop so far as you can to carry out our directions, that you may be worthy of the assistance of Peter, chief of the Apostles, in governing the people committed to your care, that you may through his merits be delivered from your sins and may enjoy eternal blessedness in the kingdom of Christ and of God.

To Swen, King of Denmark, Urging Friendly Relations and Assistance to the Holy See
Book II, 51, p. 192.   Jan. 25, 1075.

Gregory . . . to Swen, king of Denmark, greeting . . .

While we were still in the diaconate we often received letters and messengers with tokens of your affection, and from these we gathered that you were well disposed toward us. Later, however, when we had been raised to a more lofty station of duty and service, we found that your loyalty had grown cool in the absence of personal intercourse and was lacking in your letters, for no fault of ours so far as we are aware. Yet now we are so much the more strictly bound to care not only for kings and princes, but for all Christians as the universal government entrusted to us brings the interests of all men closer and more specifically to us. But since we have learned that you are distinguished above other kings as well by your skill in letters as by your zeal for the advancement of the Church, we have addressed you with more confidence, believing that we should benefit thereby the more readily, the more you are known to excel in learning and judgment.

We beg and exhort you, therefore, to administer the kingdom committed to you according to God's law, to bear the name of Royal Highness with that special quality of virtue which belongs thereto, so that you may always show that in your own heart reigns

that spirit of justice under whose governance you rule your subjects. For you know that glory and the vain joys of this world are
transient and deceptive. You know that all flesh is daily hastening
to its end and that death surely awaits us whether we will or no.
You know that kings and paupers alike shall become dust and
ashes, that we shall all meet the stern sentence of the judgment to
come, and that this judgment is so much the more to be dreaded by
us priests and kings and other princes as we shall give account for
ourselves and for those who are subject to us. Strive, then, my best
beloved, so to live and reign that you may in that day behold the
face of the eternal king and judge without fear and, as a reward
for rightly carrying the glory of this world, may receive from God
the incomparably lofty crown of the heavenly kingdom.

This will also inform you that we dispatched messengers to you
who were to give answer and make arrangements in regard to the
matters about which you made requests to the Apostolic See in the
time of our lord Pope Alexander touching the question of a metropolitan see and other topics. On account of the troubles in Germany, however, they saw that the journey would be a perilous one
and came back to us. Now, if any of these questions are of importance to you and you are willing, as we have several times heard
from your own messengers, to commit yourself and your kingdom
with loyal devotion to the prince of the Apostles and to have the
support of his authority, pray dispatch trustworthy legates to us
without delay, so that, having learned your wishes in all details we
may take deliberate counsel and may be able to see and to determine
what reply to make to you and what measures to take in the whole
affair.

Further, if our Holy Roman Mother Church shall have need of
your help in fighting men, we desire to know by sure advices what
we may expect of you. There is, not far from here, a very rich
maritime province now in the hands of base and miserable heretics,
where we should be glad to place one of your sons as duke and
prince and defender of the Christian faith, provided that you are
willing, as a certain bishop of your country has reported you propose, to give him as a soldier to the apostolic court, together with a
considerable following of loyal troops.

DECREE OF THE LENTEN SYNOD OF 1075 IN THE CASE OF
PRAGUE VS. OLMÜTZ

Book II, 53, p. 197.   March 2, 1075.

Believing that there is no more suitable and lasting method of
keeping in mind and forever recording the truth of legal and business transactions than by committing them to writing, we desire by
these presents to inform not only those now living but also those to
come that the long-drawn-out controversy between our colleagues,
Bishops John of Moravia [Olmütz] and Jaromir of Prague, concerning certain titles and estates has at length been settled by an
agreement made at the Apostolic See.

The case was brought before us and the whole council there
assembled in the second year of our pontificate, many of our
brethren sitting with us in the Church of Our Saviour, and the two
above-named bishops being present. The investigation was long
and thorough, but the case proved to be involved in such uncer-
tainty and such complications that it could not be carried through
to a complete discovery of the truth upon the evidence there produced. But, in order that their dispute should no longer rouse fraternal hatred or excite other dangerous feelings on one side or the
other, we determined, with the approval of our brethren, that it
should be equitably disposed of as follows: that all the property in
dispute should be equally divided, each to hold one part free from
all interference and both in the meantime to investigate carefully
whether they could produce clearer evidence either in writing or by
trustworthy witnesses.

To this end, and lest an endless opportunity for keeping up the
strife back and forth should be given, we prescribed a term of ten
years, so that the one who should be confident of obtaining justice
by well-founded proofs should be free to make a declaration and
follow up the rights of his church within the above term. If meanwhile either one or both should die — which God forbid! — the
successors should be bound by the same agreement. But if either
party should allow this term to elapse in silence or without furnish-
ing proof of the truth and justice of his claim, then he should have
no further opportunity for making a declaration or for bringing up
the matter again.

The aforenamed bishops, being reconciled in our presence and, as
it appeared, accepting our decision gratefully, were dismissed to

their homes with the apostolic benediction and in brotherly affection.

We ordain by our apostolic authority that this decree be observed by all inviolate and unbroken forever.*

To Manasses of Reims, in the Case of Bishop Roger of Châlons-sur-Marne

Book II, 56, p. 209.   March 4, 1075.

Gregory . . . to Manasses, archbishop of Reims, greeting . . .

If you were as conscientious as you ought to be in the administration of your pastoral office, the case of the clergy of the church at Châlons so often brought before us would have been settled long ago. But since it has been drawn out until now through your negligence and the disobedience of the bishop of the place, we have been forced to come to the relief of the oppressed clergy and to curb the rebellious spirit of the disobedient bishop with apostolic severity.

In various ways this bishop of Châlons has shown contempt for our orders. First, when summoned to a synod he failed to appear. Receiving in person from our own lips directions for restoring the property of his clergy, he paid no attention to them. Then again, warned by a letter from us, he refused to carry out our orders. We have therefore concluded that for this monstrous insolence of disobedience he ought to be deprived of his episcopal office and have commissioned you to carry out this judgment strictly and without delay. And finally, we give you strict orders to enjoin upon him in our name to restore to the clergy without any reservation the property and benefices taken from them, wherever they may be situated, adding also the value of the use which they have lost from the time of our first order. With this alternative: that if he shall refuse to obey this our command he shall be wholly excluded from the body and blood of the Lord until he shall learn through obedience to bow his neck before that Holy Roman Church against which he has not been ashamed to rebel. If our legates shall arrive in France before October first, let him prepare to present himself before them for his expurgation; if not let him appear before ourself without fail at the feast of All Saints.

* Read in connection with II, 6 and 7, this document gives a fairly complete picture of Gregory's policy in cases of conflict between rival bishops.

To the Monks of Romans-sur-Isère, Confirming Them in Their Privileges and Lands

Book II, 59, p. 212. March 9, 1075.

Gregory ... to the brethren dwelling in the monastery of Romans-sur-Isère, greeting ...

We have received the assurances of your loyal affection which you have sent us by your messengers.

You ask us to endow you with the Roman Freedom, which your church has hitherto held from our predecessors. You write also, to our great joy, that certain ones among you have entered upon the life of canons regular and that you have granted to them certain properties of your church, and you ask us to confirm these grants by our authority. We congratulate you upon your good resolution and, praying that you may go on to still better things, we grant your petition at the intercession of our son Hugo, bishop of Die, and out of our affection for you, endowing you with the Roman Freedom as you request.

The properties which your provost Hermann and yourselves have granted and confirmed to your regular brothers as mentioned in your letter to us — namely, whatever portion of church property they were known to hold previously — we also grant and we permit whoever among you may wish to join them under the rule to do so, and whatever property of his own any one may have given them, we also allow. We further ordain by our authority that the property and privileges of the church — when those who now hold them shall go over to the regular life or shall depart from this world — and lands which shall henceforth be given to the church, shall belong to the table of the regular brothers there residing and no one shall henceforth be created or ordained there as canon unless he shall declare his intention to live under the rule. We ordain by our apostolic authority that no one shall be set over you as provost or abbot or as administrator of any church stewardship unless he shall have been elected by the brothers who are living under the rule according to God's order. We forbid any one to violate these wholesome ordinances of ours, by the might of the Holy Spirit and the power conferred upon us by God.*

* This very involved passage seems to be a general guarantee of the property and privileges of those of the brethren who were prepared to bind themselves to a strict enforcement of the Rule. It gives a not too clear picture of the process of monastic "reform" under Gregory VII.

We have entrusted the consecration of your church, which you asked to have reinstated by a legate of the Apostolic See, to our son, the bishop of Die, who is at once a child of Romans and of Vienne.

To Anno of Cologne, concerning the Chastity of Priests
Book II, 67, p. 223. March 29, 1075.

Gregory . . . to Anno, archbishop of Cologne, greeting . . .

It is well known that the church of Cologne, of all churches in the kingdom of Germany, has been from its earliest years so closely bound to the Holy and Apostolic See, which we by God's will serve, by ties of loyalty, affection and obedience, that it stands toward her in peculiar intimacy and gracious devotion as a most precious daughter toward her mother. This habit of mutual good feeling coming down to us from our predecessors I am prepared not only to continue but to enlarge and increase in every way as circumstances shall permit.

On this account, beloved brother, I beg and counsel you upon your obedience with the more confidence and trust, and by authority of our common lord, St. Peter, I command you to apply yourself with more energy to preaching and enforcing the celibacy of the clergy according to the edicts of the fathers and the authority of the canons, together with all your subordinates, so that the service of a pure and unspotted family may be offered to the bride of Christ who knows no spot or wrinkle. You, my brother, know that these orders are not of our own invention but that we proclaim them as decrees of the ancient fathers, taught to them by the inspiration of the Holy Spirit, and in pursuance of the duty of our office, lest we incur the penalty of the slothful servant by hiding in silence the Lord's treasure which is demanded again with interest. It has ever been and ever shall be the province of this Holy Roman Church to provide new edicts and new remedies against newly increasing excesses, and these, sent forth under the sanction of reason and authority, no human being may lawfully declare to be invalid. We are moved also by dread of that curse proclaimed by Solomon [Samuel?]: "Obedience is that without which one who seems to be loyal is convicted of disloyalty."

Now, for the more complete and efficient execution of the orders we have given, we urge you to call a council of your fellow bishops.

Gather there as large an assembly as possible, make a clear statement of the canon law and the authority of the Apostolic See as well as your own and that of the assembled brethren. Expound at length, as God shall give you knowledge, how great is the virtue of chastity, how necessary it is for all grades of the clergy and how fitting for the chamberlains of the virgin bridegroom and the virgin bride. Then declare firmly that it shall no longer be permitted them to carry on the functions which up to the present time they have usurped to their own destruction, but that it will be more bearable for them completely to resign their offices than to impose upon their Savior a criminal and grievous servitude and thus heap up wrath for themselves from the very source which ought to bring them a reward.

But if trouble and persecution shall come to you for the strict execution of these commands, look back to him who said: "Be of good cheer; I have overcome the world." You shall learn beyond a doubt that we shall be found prepared at every moment and armed with the shield of St. Peter to hold back your enemies if we can and to keep you under our protection.

We desire you also to know that action was taken at the [Roman] synod against the heresy of Simony, for decrees against this were put forth by the holy fathers of ancient times, and it was forbidden in the strongest terms that church offices should be sold in any manner whatsoever, or that any price should be taken for the laying-on of hands. If any person has been ordained in this way we remove him utterly from the celebration of the Mass and the reading of the Gospel, and we lay upon you the strictest orders to observe these directions.

To Bishop Cunibert of Turin, on the Rights of Bishops over Monasteries

Book II, 69, p. 226. April 9, 1075.

Gregory . . . to Cunibert, bishop of Turin. [No greeting.]

It was your duty, beloved brother, in view of the reverence which you owe to St. Peter, prince of the Apostles and master of the Church Universal, loyally to maintain unity and concord with us in the bonds of charity and peace and to aid our efforts to further the cause of Christ and help them to bear fruit, at least in matters pertaining to yourself and in business transactions with you. But, on the contrary, to our infinite surprise and grief, the complaints of the brethren of the monastery of St. Michael and the manifold injuries which, as we learn from various reports, you have inflicted upon them, give us the clearest proof that you have forgotten our affection for you, have set yourself against us and have done your best to bring to nought what we are striving to accomplish. You ought to remember how many and how great efforts both our lord and predecessor, Pope Alexander of blessed memory, and we ourselves made during your recent visit to the Apostolic See in behalf of the peace and quietness of that monastery, so that the Devil, always envious of the welfare and peace of the servants of God, should not be able to pour out the poison of his iniquity upon them and turn their devoted souls away from their earnest meditation, prayer and service to God. Upon this matter you made us the fairest promises: namely, that you would make a suitable agreement with the abbot covering all details or, if this could not be done, that without any injury to the monastery you would refer the matter for final settlement to the verdict of an apostolic inquiry. Nevertheless, as we are informed, since your visit here you have been far more severe and cruel toward that venerable place than before and have not ceased to say and do whatever could injure it, not only by violence from without but through episcopal interference as well.

vague

On this account we are greatly stirred against you, having seen our apostolic authority despised, our efforts wasted and our advice, our prayers and our warnings disregarded, so that you neither can nor will keep the peace with the servants of God, which we desire to preserve with such regard for justice as God may give us to know.

Do you imagine that bishops were given the power and the right in their government as pastors to oppress at pleasure the monasteries which lie within their jurisdiction, or to repress the enthusiasm for the religious life to the advantage of their own precedence by forcibly exacting one thing after another and by making use of their power? Are you not aware that the holy fathers generally exempted monasteries from the control of bishops, and bishoprics from the supervision of a metropolitan see, because of oppression by the higher prelates, and by grants of perpetual privilege sanctioned their adhesion to the Apostolic See as chief members to their head? Read through the privileges of the holy fathers and you will find that in most monasteries the intervention even of archbishops is prohibited unless requested by the abbot, so that the monastic quiet might not be disturbed by the visits and conversation of secular persons.

Therefore, in order that we may not be compelled to act upon their authority and example in the case of the monastery of St. Michael, and that you, while you are making exorbitant demands, may receive what justly belongs to you, we admonish and command you either to make your peace with the abbot by a mutual consideration of the whole affair or, if this be impossible on account of wrongdoing, to accept these presents as a summons to the Apostolic See at the coming feast of St. Martin, so that with God's help we may be able to end your controversy and bring it to a just conclusion. And meanwhile we give order by the same authority that you shall not venture to injure or disturb the abbot, or the monastery, or its servants, or the lands or goods thereto belonging, whether in your own person or through any one of your people, either by a summons to a synod or by any kind of interdict or by any sort of annoyance. Those of that party whom you have placed under the ban of anathema, although you did this unlawfully, still out of our brotherly affection we grant you the privilege of absolving them. And if in this matter you delay or upon any pretext refuse to obey us, understand that we by our apostolic authority declare those persons to be freed from all the bonds of your interdict or excommunication.

So act then, my beloved brother, that we may not seem to have addressed you in vain. Trust our counsel, accept our warnings and no longer involve us, who are already burdened with many cares, in the labor of this case. Do not refuse us your brotherly and hearty coöperation in establishing peace with the monastery, lest if you continue to set yourself in opposition to us — or rather to St. Peter — you plunge into still more serious fault and incur irreparable harm by your own action. For if in future you shall undertake to drag this case into litigation upon error and beyond the evidence of documents, or to do any kind of violence to the monastery, we shall cause that House with all that belongs to it to be given perpetual independence, subject to no superior under God excepting the Holy Roman Church, so that it may be able to serve God in the holy profession of religion free from all annoyance.

PASTORAL LETTER TO THE PEOPLE OF BOHEMIA

Book II, 72, p. 232.   April 17, 1075.

Gregory . . . to all the people of Bohemia, of high or low estate, greeting . . .

In virtue of the See which we, unworthy though we be, have to administer, we are under obligation alike to believers and unbelievers; to believers, that they may hold the course upon which they have entered; to unbelievers, that they may come to acknowledge their Creator and, repenting of their evil doing, may be converted. Therefore, learning from bishops of your country who came to the shrine of the Apostles that some of you are walking in the way of the ordinances of God while others are running into danger through their evil ways, we have tried to admonish you with fatherly love, that the good may become better and that those who are living blameworthy lives may show themselves freed from blame.

We exhort you with your whole heart and soul and strength to love God and your neighbor as yourself; to keep the peace among you, without which no man shall see God; to live in chastity, both clergy and laity; to pay faithfully tithes to God, from whom comes life and all that, sustains life; to show proper respect for your churches; to devote yourselves to charity and hospitality.

All these and whatever else touches the safety of your souls, although we know that your own clergy are competent to teach them to you, still it is evident that our words are accepted more willingly and more eagerly on account of your reverence for St. Peter, and this very eagerness of yours compels us to confirm what others may give you, and thus to pay the debt of exhortation the more completely, as you give more faithful attention to our admonitions.

Do you then, best beloved, setting aside all carnal desires, turn your thoughts to the joys of your eternal fatherland in Heaven and so by faithful service make St. Peter your debtor, to whom is given above others the power to bind and loose here on earth, that after the dissolution of this earthly dwelling, toward which we move nearer day by day whether we will or not, to be soon thereafter turned to worms and ashes, you may enjoy his most efficient advocacy before the final judge.

call to
christianity
aimed at lower classes

To Boleslav of Poland, concerning the Organization of the
Polish Church

Book II, 73, p. 233. April 20, 1075.

Gregory ... to Boleslav, duke of Poland, greeting ...

Since honor paid to agents and stewards is a part of the respect
due to their masters, the work and service of agents is doubtless
welcomed with great joy — by those, I mean, who are known to
respect the persons and authority of their superiors. By this token
we perceive that Your Excellency is sincerely devoted to St. Peter,
prince of the Apostles, and that you are showing your reverence with
eager enthusiasm, namely, the fact that you have desired to make
him your debtor by honoring him with liberal offerings and, as we
trust in God, have earned this reward.

Wherefore we also, who are called and desire to be his servant,
have responded to your love in Christ and are anxious to extend to
you in such ways as seem needful and honorable to you the minis-
tration of the office to which we, unworthy as we are, were ordained
and established by the mysterious will of God and in obedience
to the apostolic leadership — and this the more earnestly, the more
clearly we perceive your faith and love to be prompt in obedience
and zealous in well-doing.

But, since the due order and wise administration of the Christian
religion depend primarily, under God, upon the pastors and rulers
of God's flock, our first attention must be given to the fact that the
bishops of your country, having no fixed metropolitan see and
placed under no superior control, are free to wander at their own
will hither and yon contrary to the regulations of the holy fathers.
Then again, the bishops are so few and their parishes so large that
they are unable properly to perform the duties of their office toward their people. For these and other reasons, therefore, which we
will not mention here, we have sent these messengers to confer with
you in regard to the care of the Church and the upbuilding of
the body of Christ, which is the congregation of the faithful, and
as to needed reforms, either to settle matters according to the decrees of the holy fathers or to refer them to us for our decision.
Give ear to them, therefore, as to ourself, remembering that in
sending forth his disciples to preach the Gospel, Christ said: "He
that heareth you heareth me; and he that despiseth you despiseth
me." Assist them with your own counsel and your kind favor that

their efforts among you may bear fruit, for the sake of the apostolic message which they bring you.

We further pray and warn you in the Lord that, having ever before your eyes the end of your life, the day of whose coming you know not, and the fear of the last judgment, you strive to exercise the power entrusted to you by an administration prudent and pleasing to God, thus preparing for yourself riches in good works and laying a fixed and stable foundation for the life eternal. For you must know that the supreme arbiter will require of you that which he has committed to your care and that you must render him the more strict account the greater are the powers and the rights of judgment you possess.

Now may Almighty God, whose majesty is above all principalities and kingdoms, direct your heart and your actions to every good work in all prudence and virtue, so that when the course of this uncertain and swiftly passing life is finished you may be worthy to attain to true and eternal glory through the merits and intercession of St. Peter and St. Paul, chiefs of the Apostles. And when the pride of your enemies has been subdued by Jesus Christ our Lord, may he grant you the joys of peace and quietness so that you may judge from the gifts of the present how greatly those of the future are to be desired.

If these joys are a true delight to you, in the midst of them all preserve the law of charity which you seem to have violated in the matter of the money you have taken from the king of Russia. Therefore, while sympathizing greatly with you, we beg you, for the love of God and St. Peter, to make restitution of whatever was taken by yourself or by your people, knowing, as you do, that no one who unjustly takes the goods of others can in any wise enter the kingdom of Christ and have his part in God. May this be received by you in the same spirit of charity in which we send it, for the salvation of your soul.

To Demetrius, King of the Russians, and His Queen, Granting the Kingdom to Their Son Jaropolk

Book II, 74, p. 236.   April 17, 1075.

Gregory . . . to Demetrius, king of the Russians, and the queen, his spouse, greeting . . .

Your son, visiting the shrine of the Apostles, came to us and, desiring to obtain that kingdom by a grant from St. Peter through our hands, and having given proof of his devoted loyalty to that same Peter, chief of the Apostles, made his demand with prayerful submission. He declared without reserve that his petition would be ratified and confirmed by your consent if it should be granted under the favoring protection of the apostolic authority.

To his promises and his petition, because they seemed to be authenticated by your consent and by the devotion of the petitioner, we finally gave our assent and in the name of St. Peter transferred the government of your kingdom to him. We did this, however, with the intention and desire that the blessed Peter, by his intercession before God, may guard you and your kingdom and all your possessions and may permit you to hold your kingship in all peace, honor and glory to the end of your lives, and when this earthly warfare shall be accomplished, may obtain for you eternal glory in the presence of the supreme King. Your Serene Highnesses are aware that in whatever lawful matters you may seek the approval of this See in time of need, your requests will be granted. *alliances*

Furthermore, that these and other subjects not included in this letter may be more firmly fixed in your minds, we have dispatched these messengers, of whom one is well known as a faithful friend of yours, who will explain in detail what is here written and will supply by word of mouth what is missing. May you show yourselves friendly and accessible to them out of respect for St. Peter, whose ambassadors they are. Give them a patient hearing and unquestioning credit; and whatever arrangements they may see fit to establish by authority of the Apostolic See, allow no evil influence to interfere, but aid them with the favor of your sincere affection.

And may Almighty God enlighten your minds and lead you through earthly prosperity into eternal glory.

THE THIRD BOOK

To KING HENRY IV, PRAISING HIS EFFORTS AT REFORM

Book III, 3, p. 246. July 20, 1075.

Gregory . . . to King Henry, greeting . . .

Among other praiseworthy actions, my beloved son, to which you are reported to have risen in your efforts at self-improvement, there are two that have specially commended you to your holy mother, the Roman Church: first, that you have valiantly withstood those guilty of Simony; and second, that you freely approve, and strenuously desire to enforce, the chastity of the clergy as servants of God. For these reasons you have given us cause to expect of you still higher and better things with God's help. Wherefore we earnestly pray that you may hold fast by these, and we beseech our Lord God that he may deign to increase your zeal more and more.

But now, as regards the church of Bamberg, which according to the ordinance of its founder [King Henry II] belongs to the Holy and Apostolic See as the shoulder to the head, that is, as a most intimate member, by a certain special bond of duty, we are greatly disturbed and we are forced by the obligation of our office to come to the rescue of its distress with all our powers. That simoniac so-called bishop Hermann, summoned to a Roman synod this present year, failed to appear. He came within a short distance of Rome, but there halted and sent forward messengers with ample gifts, trying, with his well-known trickery, to impose upon our innocence and, if possible, to corrupt the integrity of our colleagues by a pecuniary bargain. But when this turned out contrary to his hopes, convinced of his own damnation he hastily retreated and, soothing the minds of the clergy who were with him by smooth and deceitful promises, declared that if he were able to regain his own country he would resign his bishopric and enter the monastic life.

How he kept these promises Your Highness, beloved son, well knows. With increasing audacity he plundered the clergy who were upholding the welfare and the honor of their church, and had not your royal power restrained him, as we are informed, he would have completely ruined them. After careful consideration of these outrages we removed him from his episcopal and priestly office. Further, as he dared to oppress the church of Bamberg, under the apostolic patronage of St. Peter, more cruelly and more harshly than before, we placed him in the bonds of anathema until he should lay down his usurped dignity and, nevertheless, present himself for trial before the Apostolic See.

Now, therefore, most excellent son, we ask Your Highness and urge you by our dutiful obligation to take counsel with men of piety and so to regulate the affairs of that church according to God's order, that you may be worthy of divine protection through the intercession of St. Peter, in whose name and under whose patronage the church was founded.

What I have written regarding this case to our colleague Siegfried, bishop of Mainz, and the clergy and people of Bamberg, you may learn with certainty from the letters dispatched to them.[*]

To SIEGFRIED OF MAINZ, URGING HIM TO CALL A GERMAN COUNCIL AND ENJOINING ACTION AGAINST SIMONY AND FORNICATION

Book III, 4, p. 248. Sept. 3, 1075.

Gregory . . . to Siegfried, archbishop of Mainz, greeting . . .

In your letter, my brother, you have brought forward many excuses [for not calling a German Council], plausible and from a human point of view valid, nor would they seem to me without force if such reasoning could excuse us before the judgment seat of God. It does indeed seem a reasonable explanation that the kingdom is in confusion, with wars, rebellions, hostile invasion, ruin of your property and the fear of death which seems to threaten our brethren from the hatred of the king, and also the dread lest men from different and mutually hostile sections coming together in one place might break out into violent conflict. All these seem to be amply sufficient excuses.

But, if we consider the wide difference between divine and human judgments, we find scarcely any pretext that we could safely offer in that last day for drawing back from the rescue of souls — not the loss of property, nor the assaults of the wicked, nor the wrath of the mighty, nor the sacrifice of our safety or of life itself.

* Book III, 1 and 2, of the same date and practically the same content as 3.

This is the difference between hirelings and shepherds: that when the wolf comes the hireling fears for himself, not for the sheep, abandons his flock and flees, leaving them to destruction; but the shepherd who truly loves his sheep does not desert them when danger approaches, and does not hesitate to sacrifice even his life for them.

Wherefore it belongs to us zealously to fulfill the duties of the shepherd, for the glory of God to guard the safety of his sheep, to urge our fellows to keep watch over his flock, and bid them walk straight forward as leaders of the sheep. For if we keep silent when we see them wandering and do not try to call them back to the right path, are we not ourselves in fault, shall we not be convicted of wandering? For he who fails to correct a fault commits it himself. And why did Eli the priest perish at Shiloh? And what did the Lord say by the prophet: "Cursed be he who holds back his sword from blood!" — that is, holds back the word of preaching from destroying the carnal things of life?

And now let us come to a matter which is at present weighing upon our mind and which is, as it were, the reason of this our discourse, namely, how we can bear with patience the reports we have received as to the conduct of our brother, the bishop of Strasbourg, not a few of which we know by trustworthy information to be true. We desire and command you, therefore, to investigate carefully one of them about which we are still in doubt, that is, the infection with the heresy of Simony. Whatever you discover with certainty upon this point, fail not to inform us at once, so that if the report be true the Church of Christ may be cleansed of this foulness and his soul may be rescued from destruction. But if, as we rather pray, it be false, then may this great calumny be turned away from him with the help of divine grace.

And now let those who say that the council which we have proclaimed ought to be postponed answer this question: What would the soldiers of a king do when they had been summoned to prepare for war and the enemy was already in the king's court with fire and sword? Let them say whether they ought to rush to arms and crush the enemy or idly watch what he is about? For what are those evil spirits doing but striving unceasingly to lay waste the Church of Christ with the flames of their vicious lives? And what ought those royal soldiers, the holy priests, to do, but to rise up against their fury, armed with the shield of priestly charity and girded with the sword of the divine word? As for what you say, that certain brethren cannot come to the council on account of the enmity of their prince, we say that it is enough for them if they send some of their clerks to answer for them.

But, since we are aware that you are being dissuaded by many carnally minded persons from working diligently and faithfully in the Lord's vineyard for the welfare of souls lest you suffer loss of fortune and incur the enmity of the powerful, we exhort and command you, in the name of Almighty God and by authority of St. Peter, that you venture not to turn aside from the straight way through fear or favor of anyone or through any loss of earthly goods, but that, so far as the Holy Spirit may grant, you shall diligently inquire into everything and report to us immediately whatever you ascertain. We ought to regard it as a shameful thing that the soldiers of this world daily stand up to fight for their earthly prince and shrink not from deadly conflict, while we, who are called priests of God, will not fight for our king who created all things out of nothing, and who did not hesitate to suffer death for us and has promised us an eternal reward.

This also we enjoin upon you, my brother, that you make diligent inquiry into the simoniac heresy and fornication of your clergy, as you have been instructed by the Apostolic See, and that whatever you find has been committed in the past you punish according to law and thoroughly root it out, and give strictest orders that it shall not occur in future.

To Henry IV, Congratulating Him on His Victory over the Saxons

Book III, 7, p. 256. Sept., 1075.

Gregory . . . to King Henry, greeting . . .

When I received Your Majesty's letter the persons with whom I needed to consult with regard to my reply were absent from the city on account of the plague, and your messenger, who is also the bearer of this, was afraid to stay with me for the same reason. But, desiring to have the peace which is in Christ, not only with you whom God has placed at the summit of human affairs, but also with all men, and to give every one his right, we wish to cleave [to you] with heart and soul.

For I know, and I believe you too know, that those who truly love God and who have no dread of the Roman Church and the Roman Empire as avengers of their faults, eagerly desire to bring about peace and concord between us by their actions and by their prayers. Wherefore I have good reason to believe that you have begun to entrust our affairs — nay, the affairs of the whole Church — to pious men devoted to me and sincerely anxious that the status of the Christian faith may be restored. To put it briefly, I am prepared by their advice and with the blessing of Christ to receive you into the bosom of the Holy Roman Church as lord, as brother and as son and to give you my support as far as may be, asking of you only that you do not scorn to hear my warnings as to your salvation and that you do not refuse to pay due honor and glory to your creator. For it is a most shameful thing to refuse to our creator and redeemer the honor which we demand from our brethren and fellow servants. May we, then, be mindful of the divine promise which declares: "Them that honor me will I honor, and they that despise me shall be lightly esteemed." And let us sacrifice to him what is pleasing to us in this world that we may be partakers of spiritual gifts in the world to come.

As to the rebellion of the Saxons which has been broken by you through the judgment of God, this is a cause for both rejoicing and regret because of the great sacrifice of Christian blood. See to it that under these circumstances you maintain the honor and justice of God rather than promote your own advantage. It is safer for any prince to punish a thousand evil-minded persons in a just cause than to put a single Christian to the sword for the sake of his own glory. For he who said, "I seek not mine own glory," is the creator and ruler of all things. We provide truly for our own salvation when we prefer the glory of God in all our actions.

In the case of Hermann, formerly called bishop of Bamberg, Your Highness will have learned from our letter sent by a certain clerk of that church to you and to our colleague Siegfried, archbishop of Mainz, and to the clergy of the aforesaid church, that he has been deposed by apostolic authority from all his episcopal and priestly dignities and placed under the bond of anathema, because he dared to add the crime of sacrilege to that of simoniacal heresy and to plunder the church committed to his care like a tyrant. Wherefore we call upon you and command you in the name of St. Peter to see to it that a pastor be appointed to that church in accordance with the divine law, who with God's help may restore what the thief and robber has spoiled and replace what he has squandered.

May Almighty God, from whom all good things proceed, protect you with his love in this life and lead you with double triumph into the life eternal through the merits and intercession of the blessed Apostles Peter and Paul.

To Tedaldus of Milan, on His Candidacy for the Bishopric
Book III, 8, p. 259.   Dec. 8, 1075.

Gregory . . . to Tedaldus, a clerk of Milan, greeting . . . if he shall be obedient.

It is reported to us by persons who are loyal to us and friendly to you that you desire and request our friendship. We offer this to you freely without request and are most ready to grant it when you ask for it, provided we are convinced that you are willing to conform to our directions — or rather, to God's will — in the things that are of God. For in the cause which you appear to have taken up you have increased our anxiety by the need of very serious reform and have involved yourself in unbecoming conduct. In this case we feel that it would be alike dangerous for us to exceed the bounds of fairness and to relax the rule of justice or pass it over in silence.

We believe that Your Prudence has not failed to know that to the episcopal see into which you have been thrust, another person, still surviving, was assigned and that, unless some special exception was made for good reasons, there was no vacancy for you or for anyone else according to canonical or apostolic law. What shall we say of the man [Godfrey] who strove with wicked desire for the place denied him by justice, who spared not sacrilegious violence and plunder, and whose criminal ambition, which he refused to give up, led him on to his own damnation and ruin? As to him who is with us [Atto] and whom we have recognized as bishop-elect in that church, we have not been able to see any reason why we should repudiate him.

Wherefore, with the approval of our conscience and with sincere affection for you, we summon you, if you really love the church and desire to free both it and yourself from dangerous confusion, to present yourself at the next synod, which we have set, God willing, for the first week of the coming Lent; or, if you prefer, at the threshold of the Apostles before the synod. Thus, after a fair examination, with God's help, you may follow whatever course you find safe for yourself, free from every obstacle or peril to your soul. And have no doubt that if justice shall require us to withdraw support from him who is with us, we shall give our consent and our aid to your promotion, to the honor of Almighty God and of St. Ambrose.

To relieve you of all suspicion of danger we promise and grant a safe-conduct by the hands of our daughters, Beatrice and Matilda, so that no interference may be caused by us or our allies to you or your companions, but that you may remain safe and without offense under God's protection, in your persons and your property, both coming and going.

Meanwhile we forbid you, in the name of Almighty God and by the apostolic authority of St. Peter, to accept any grade of holy orders, remembering that if you do not now consider yourself to be within our obedience you will repent it when you shall find yourself so deeply involved through your own rashness that you cannot extricate yourself when you wish to do so. If then some persons who do not regard the things that are of God should begin to advise and persuade you to the contrary, telling you how great a protector you have in the king, what strength in your noble birth and what support among your fellow citizens, do not imagine that you are safe in trusting to them, bearing in mind what is written, "Cursed is the man who puts his trust in men," and that the might of kings and emperors and every effort of men against the apostolic law and the omnipotence of God on high are counted as dust and ashes. Never can it profit you to become an obstinate and persistent rebel against divine and apostolic authority by the instigation of any person or through your reliance upon him.

To KING HENRY IV, ADMONISHING HIM TO SHOW MORE DEFERENCE
TO THE HOLY SEE AND ITS DECREES

Book III, 10, p. 263. Dec. 8, 1075 [or Jan. 8, 1076].

Gregory, bishop, servant of God's servants, to King Henry, greeting and the apostolic benediction — but with the understanding that he obeys the Apostolic See as becomes a Christian king.

Considering and weighing carefully to how strict a judge we must render an account of the stewardship committed to us by St.

start writing to King Henry
a lot by end of Book 2

Peter, prince of the Apostles, we have hesitated to send you the
apostolic benediction, since you are reported to be in voluntary
communication with men who are under the censure of the Apostolic See and of a synod. If this is true, you yourself know that'
you cannot receive the favor of God nor the apostolic blessing unless you shall first put away those excommunicated persons and
force them to do penance and shall yourself obtain absolution and
forgiveness for your sin by due repentance and satisfaction.
Wherefore we counsel Your Excellency, if you feel yourself guilty
in this matter, to make your confession at once to some pious bishop
who, with our sanction, may impose upon you a penance suited to
the offense, may absolve you and with your consent in writing may
be free to send us a true report of the manner of your penance.

We marvel exceedingly that you have sent us so many devoted
letters and displayed such humility by the spoken words of your
legates, calling yourself a son of our Holy Mother Church and
subject to us in the faith, singular in affection, a leader in devotion,
commending yourself with every expression of gentleness and reverence, and yet in action showing yourself most bitterly hostile to
the canons and apostolic decrees in those duties especially required by loyalty to the Church. Not to mention other cases, the
way you have observed your promises in the Milan affair, made
through your mother and through bishops, our colleagues, whom
we sent to you, and what your intentions were in making them is
evident to all. And now, heaping wounds upon wounds, you have
handed over the sees of Fermo and Spoleto — if indeed a church
may be given over by any human power — to persons entirely unknown to us, whereas it is not lawful to consecrate anyone except
after probation and with due knowledge.

It would have been becoming to you, since you confess yourself
to be a son of the Church, to give more respectful attention to the
master of the Church, that is, to Peter, prince of the Apostles. To
him, if you are of the Lord's flock, you have been committed for
your pasture, since Christ said to him: "Peter, feed my sheep,"
and again: "To thee are given the keys of Heaven, and whatsoever
thou shalt bind on earth shall be bound in Heaven and whatsoever thou shalt loose on earth shall be loosed in Heaven." Now, while
we, unworthy sinner that we are, stand in his place of power, still
whatever you send to us, whether in writing or by word of mouth,
he himself receives, and while we read what is written or hear the

why was it so serious

voice of those who speak, he discerns with subtle insight from what
spirit the message comes. Wherefore Your Highness should beware lest any defect of will toward the Apostolic See be found in
your words or in your messages and should pay due reverence, not
to us but to Almighty God, in all matters touching the welfare of
the Christian faith and the status of the Church. And this we say
although our Lord deigned to declare: "He who heareth you
heareth me; and he who despiseth you despiseth me."

We know that one who does not refuse to obey God in those matters in which we have spoken according to the statutes of the holy
fathers does not scorn to observe our admonitions even as if he had
received them from the lips of the Apostle himself. For if our
Lord, out of reverence for the chair of Moses, commanded the
Apostles to observe the teaching of the scribes and pharisees who
sat thereon, there can be no doubt that the apostolic and gospel
teaching, whose seat and foundation is Christ, should be accepted
and maintained by those who are chosen to the service of teaching.

At a synod held at Rome during the current year, and over which
Divine Providence willed us to preside, several of your subjects being present, we saw that the order of the Christian religion had
long been greatly disturbed and its chief and proper function,
the redemption of souls, had fallen low and through the wiles of the
Devil had been trodden under foot. Startled by this danger and by
the manifest ruin of the Lord's flock we returned to the teaching
of the holy fathers, declaring no novelties nor any inventions of our
own, but holding that the primary and only rule of discipline and
the well-trodden way of the saints should again be sought and followed, all wandering paths to be abandoned. For we know that
there is no other way of salvation and eternal life for the flock of
Christ and their shepherds except that shown by him who said:
"I am the door and he who enters by me shall be saved and shall
find pasture." This was taught by the Apostles and observed by
the holy fathers and we have learned it from the Gospels and from
every page of Holy Writ.

This edict [against lay investiture], which some who place the
honor of men above that of God call an intolerable burden, we,
using the right word, call rather a truth and a light necessary for
salvation, and we have given judgment that it is to be heartily
accepted and obeyed, not only by you and your subjects but by all
princes and peoples who confess and worship Christ — though it

is our especial wish and would be especially fitting for you, that you should excel others in devotion to Christ as you are their superior in fame, in station and in valor.

Nevertheless, in order that these demands may not seem to you too burdensome or unfair we have sent you word by your own liegemen not to be troubled by this reform of an evil practice but to send us prudent and pious legates from your own people. If these can show in any reasonable way how we can moderate the decision of the holy fathers [at the Council] saving the honor of the eternal king and without peril to our own soul, we will condescend to hear their counsel. It would in fact have been the fair thing for you, even if you had not been so graciously admonished, to make reasonable inquiry of us in what respect we had offended you or assailed your honor, before you proceeded to violate the apostolic decrees. But how little you cared for our warnings or for doing right was shown by your later actions.

However, since the long-enduring patience of God summons you to improvement, we hope that with increase of understanding your heart and mind may be turned to obey the commands of God. We warn you with a father's love that you accept the rule of Christ, that you consider the peril of preferring your own honor to his, that you do not hamper by your actions the freedom of that Church which he deigned to bind to himself as a bride by a divine union, but, that she may increase as greatly as possible, you will begin to lend to Almighty God and to St. Peter, by whom also your own glory may merit increase, the aid of your valor by faithful devotion.

Now you ought to recognize your special obligation to them for the triumph over your enemies which they have granted you, and while they are making you happy and singularly prosperous, they ought to find your devotion increased by their favor to you. That the fear of God, in whose hand is all the might of kings and emperors, may impress this upon you more than any admonitions of mine, bear in mind what happened to Saul after he had won a victory by command of the prophet, how he boasted of his triumph, scorning the prophet's admonitions, and how he was rebuked by the Lord, and also what favor followed David the king as a reward for his humility in the midst of the tokens of his bravery.

Finally, as to what we have read in your letters and do not mention here we will give you no decided answer until your legates,

Radbod, Adalbert and Odescalcus, to whom we entrust this, have
returned to us and have more fully reported your decision upon
the matters which we commissioned them to discuss with you.

THE ROMAN LENTEN SYNOD OF 1076
Book III, 10(a), p. 268. Feb. 14-20, 1076.

In the year of the Incarnation 1075, our lord Pope Gregory held
a synod at Rome in the church of Our Savior which is called the
Constantiniana. A great number of bishops and abbots and clergy
and laymen of various orders were present.

At this synod, among the decrees promulgated was the excommunication of Siegfried, archbishop of Mainz, in the following form:

In accordance with the judgment of the Holy Spirit and by authority
of the blessed Apostles Peter and Paul, we suspend from every episcopal
function, and exclude from the communion of the body and blood of the
Lord, Siegfried, archbishop of Mainz, who has attempted to cut off the
bishops and abbots of Germany from the Holy Roman Church, their
spiritual mother — unless perchance in the hour of death, and then only
if he shall come to himself and truly repent. Those who voluntarily joined
his schism and still persist in their evil deeds, we also suspend from all
episcopal functions. Those, however, who consented against their will
we allow time until the feast of St. Peter; but if within that term they
shall not have given due satisfaction in person or by messengers in our
presence, they shall thenceforth be deprived of their episcopal office.

Excommunication of the bishops of Lombardy

The bishops of Lombardy who, in contempt of canonical and apostolic
authority, have joined in a sworn conspiracy against St. Peter, prince of
the Apostles, we suspend from their episcopal functions and exclude them
from the communion of Holy Church.

[Here follows a list of excommunications of prelates and laymen
beyond the Alps, ending with the proclamation against King Henry
IV.]

Excommunication of Henry IV

O blessed Peter, prince of the Apostles, mercifully incline thine ear,
we [sic] pray, and hear me, thy servant, whom thou hast cherished from
infancy and hast delivered until now from the hand of the wicked who
have hated and still hate me for my loyalty to thee. Thou art my witness,
as are also my Lady, the Mother of God, and the blessed Paul, thy brother
among all the saints, that thy Holy Roman Church forced me against my

will to be its ruler. I had no thought of ascending thy throne as a robber, nay, rather would I have chosen to end my life as a pilgrim than to seize upon thy place for earthly glory and by devices of this world. Therefore, by thy favor, not by any works of mine, I believe that it is and has been thy will, that the Christian people especially committed to thee should render obedience to me, thy especially constituted representative. To me is given by thy grace the power of binding and loosing in Heaven and upon earth.

Wherefore, relying upon this commission, and for the honor and defense of thy Church, in the name of Almighty God, Father, Son and Holy Spirit, through thy power and authority, I deprive King Henry, son of the emperor Henry, who has rebelled against thy Church with unheard-of audacity, of the government over the whole kingdom of Germany and Italy, and I release all Christian men from the allegiance which they have sworn or may swear to him, and I forbid anyone to serve him as king. For it is fitting that he who seeks to diminish the glory of thy Church should lose the glory which he seems to have.

And, since he has refused to obey as a Christian should or to return to the God whom he has abandoned by taking part with excommunicated persons, has spurned my warnings which I gave him for his soul's welfare, as thou knowest, and has separated himself from thy Church and tried to rend it asunder, I bind him in the bonds of anathema in thy stead and I bind him thus as commissioned by thee, that the nations may know and be convinced that thou art Peter and that upon thy rock the son of the living God has built his Church and the gates of hell shall not prevail against it.

To Wi[l]fred of Milan, a Military Leader of the Pataria

Book III, 15, p. 276. April, 1076.

Gregory . . . to Wi[l]fred, a gentleman of Milan, greeting . . .

Now that you have shown by your letter that you are deeply concerned for the honor of the Christian faith, we have thought it right to reply to Your Prudence.

Be it known to you, then, that the Normans are negotiating for peace with us. They would gladly have done this earlier and would humbly have given satisfaction to St. Peter, whom they desire to have as their sole lord and sovereign under God, if we had been willing to meet their terms in certain particulars. And now we hope that this may soon be accomplished, not to the injury, but to the advantage of the Roman Church and that we may bring them back to their loyalty to St. Peter completely and permanently.

With the king of Germany also, some have urged us to make

peace. We have replied that we desire to be at peace with him if only he would strive to make his peace with God and according to our repeated warnings would set right what he has done wrong to the peril of Holy Church and the fulfillment of his own perdition.

But, since we have placed our faith and hope and all our thoughts in the strength of divine power, we desire that you also who, we understand, have again turned your courage and endurance to comforting the soldiers of Christ, should have a firm trust in God. Expect, therefore, his aid and comfort for yourself and for all who love righteousness and the law of God, and that those limbs of the Devil will do no further injury to our innocence than God shall permit. Behold, the Devil rules the whole world, rejoicing that his members are exalted, but he who said, "Be of good cheer; I have overcome the world," gives us a certain faith that he will straightway bring succor to his Church and will put the Devil and his members to utter confusion. For, as we consider the changes that have taken place of old and in our own time as well, we find that the rule of the Devil has ended the sooner the more it seemed to be exalted and to be getting the better of the Christian faith. Wherefore, take comfort in the Lord, beloved son, and in the power of his might comfort also those whom you know to be standing fast in the faith of Christ. But admonish those who have denied that faith by their actions that they may be ashamed to go on living in slavery to the Devil.

Whatever is lacking in this writing we will explain to you more fully when we have conferred with the liegemen of St. Peter and will do our best to bring aid to you with God's help.

And may Almighty God enlighten your mind through the merits of our sovereign Lord and of the blessed Apostles Peter and Paul and the prayers of St. Ambrose and so strengthen you in his law that you may be worthy to be numbered among those who shall judge the Devil and his members and shall reign with Christ forever.

To Rainerius, Bishop of Orleans, in Defense of the Cathedral Chapter

Book III, 17, p. 279. April, 1076.

Gregory . . . to Rainerius, bishop of Orleans, greeting — and the apostolic benediction if he shall be obedient.

We should be seriously offended against you, even to the point of punishing your rash audacity, were we not restrained by apostolic leniency.

You yourself can and ought to remember that our predecessor, Pope Alexander of reverend memory, having examined your deed of gift, confirmed the diaconate of Holy Cross *ex eadem praepositura* to your canons who claimed it, and under the ban of apostolic authority bound yourself and all [your] men to refrain from violence against the aforesaid priory through this privilege of his [the pope's] confirmation.* But you, entering into relations with the excommunicated Everard and, what is worse, taking bribes from him according to report, had the temerity to defy the anathema and, urged on by wicked pride, thought nothing of throwing the whole Church into confusion. We ought then to have checked your presumption by apostolic discipline, but until now we have borne with you in hopes of betterment in the future.

We command you, therefore, by our apostolic authority, to reconsider your former rashness, to allow your canons and Jocelyn, the holder of the priory, who is their choice, to possess it in all peace and safety and to do them no violence in future. It is our will that they shall have such complete and quiet possession of all the property of that priory that the privilege of our predecessor, Pope Alexander of blessed memory, may not seem to be infringed upon in the least particular.

We ordain further that between now and the feast of All Saints [November 1] you present yourself before us in person to render account of these and other charges made against you. Meanwhile all the aforesaid rights are to be held in peace by the canons and by Jocelyn, who holds his priory of them, and the same Jocelyn is also to hold his abbacy in peace, together with all other property real

* The text of this passage is obviously corrupt, but the sense appears to be that the bishop had entered into an agreement with the chapter securing their right to the appointment of the prior and that this agreement, confirmed by Pope Alexander II, had been violated by the bishop.

and personal thereto belonging, without any molestation whatsoever from you. Benedict also shall in the interim hold his canonry under the same guaranty of peace. We direct also that the canonry granted for the support of the poor, but said to have been diverted from that purpose and sold by you, shall be restored to its proper use.

If then you shall obediently follow our commands and admonitions, and shall patiently carry out all directions therein contained, we shall rejoice for the peace of the Church. Otherwise, understand that you are suspended from all episcopal functions and are cut off from the communion of the body and blood of our Lord Jesus Christ.

To Anazir, King of Mauretania, on the Maintenance of Friendly Relations

Book III, 21, p. 287. No date.

Gregory . . . to Anazir, king of the province of Mauretania Sitifensis in Africa. [No greeting.]

Your Highness sent to us within a year a request that we would ordain the priest Servandus as bishop according to the Christian order. This we have taken pains to do, as your request seemed proper and of good promise. You also sent gifts to us, released some Christian captives out of regard for St. Peter, chief of the Apostles, and affection for us, and promised to release others. This good action was inspired in your heart by God, the creator of all things, without whom we can neither do nor think any good thing. He who lighteth every man that cometh into the world enlightened your mind in this purpose. For Almighty God, who desires that all men shall be saved and that none shall perish, approves nothing more highly in us than this: that a man love his fellow man next to his God and do nothing to him which he would not that others should do to himself.

This affection we and you owe to each other in a more peculiar way than to people of other races because we worship and confess the same God though in diverse forms and daily praise and adore him as the creator and ruler of this world. For, in the words of the Apostle, "He is our peace who hath made both one."

This grace granted to you by God is admired and praised by many of the Roman nobility who have learned from us of your benevolence and high qualities. Two of these, Alberic and Cencius, intimate friends of ours brought up with us from early youth at the Roman court, earnestly desiring to enjoy your friendship and to serve your interests here, are sending their messengers to you to let you know how highly they regard your prudence and high character and how greatly they desire and are able to be of service to you.

In recommending these messengers to Your Highness, we beg you to show them, out of regard for us and in return for the loyalty of the men aforesaid, the same respect which we desire always to show toward you and all who belong to you. For God knows our true regard for you to his glory and how truly we desire your prosperity and honor, both in this life and in the life to come, and how earnestly we pray both with our lips and with our heart that God himself, after the long journey of this life, may lead you into the bosom of the most holy patriarch Abraham.

you done good Anazir

THE FOURTH BOOK

A General Apology to All the Faithful in Germany

Epistolae collectae, 14 (Jaffé, p. 535). 1076.

Gregory . . . to all bishops, dukes, counts and other loyal defenders of the faith in Germany, greeting . . .

We hear that certain among you are in doubt regarding our excommunication of the king and are asking whether he was lawfully condemned; also whether our sentence was pronounced with due deliberation and under authority of a legal right of inquiry. We have therefore taken pains to make clear to the understanding of all by what motives, as our conscience bears witness, we were led to this act of excommunication. And we do this, not so much in order to make public by our own complaint the several cases which, alas! are only too well known, as to silence the accusations of those who feel that we took up the sword of the spirit rashly and were moved rather by our own impulses than by a holy fear and a zeal for justice.

While we were still in the office of deacon, sinister and dishonorable rumors came to us regarding the conduct of the king, and we sent him frequent admonitions both by letter and by legates, for the sake of the imperial station and personal character of his father and mother as well as from our hope and wishes for his improvement, warning him to desist from his evil ways and, mindful of his noble birth and station, so to order his life as would be fitting for a king and, God willing, for an emperor. And later, when we had reached the dignity of Supreme Pontiff — unworthy as we were — and he had grown in years and in vice, we, knowing that God would require his soul at our hands the more strictly now that authority and freedom of action were given to us above all others, besought him the more earnestly in every way, by argument, by persuasion and by threats, to amend his life. He replied with frequent letters of devotion, pleading his frail and fickle youth and the evil counsels of those in power at his court and promising from day to day that he would comply with our instructions — he promised in words, but in fact he trampled them under foot with ever-increasing misbehavior.

In the meantime we summoned to repentance certain of his intimates by whose intrigues and advice he had profaned bishoprics and many monasteries, for money installing wolves instead of shepherds. We ordered them, while there was still time, to give back the church property, which they had received with sacrilegious hand through this accursed commerce, to its rightful owners and to give satisfaction to God for their sins by penitential service. But when we learned that they refused to do this after due time and continued in their accustomed evil ways, we cut them off from the communion and body of the whole Church as guilty of sacrilege and as servants and members of the Devil, and we warned the king to banish them from his household and from his counsels and to desist from all association with them as persons under excommunication.

But again, when the Saxon uprising against the king was gaining strength and he saw that the resources and defenses of the kingdom were failing him to a great extent, he wrote us a letter of supplication full of humility. In this letter he confessed his fault before Almighty God and St. Peter and ourself and besought us by our apostolic authority to correct his offenses in church affairs against the canon law and the decrees of holy fathers. He also promised to obey us in all respects and to give us his faithful aid and counsel. And afterward, being admitted to penance by our colleagues and legates, Humbert, bishop of Palestrina, and Gerald, bishop of Ostia, whom we had sent to him, he reaffirmed all these promises in their hands, taking his oath by the sacred scarfs which they wore around their necks.

Then some time later, after a battle with the Saxons, he performed his sacrifices of gratitude to God for his victory by promptly breaking his vows of amendment, fulfilling none of his promises, receiving the excommunicated persons into his intimate counsels and bringing ruin upon the churches as he had done before.

With the greatest grief, then, although we had lost almost all hope of his improvement after he had treated with scorn the gifts of the heavenly king, we decided to make a further attempt, desiring rather that he should listen to apostolic gentleness than that he should suffer from our severity. We therefore wrote warning him to remember his promises and consider to whom they had been made; not to imagine that he could deceive God, whose anger when he begins to give judgment is the more severe the longer his patience has endured; and not to dishonor God, who has honored him, or use his power in contempt of God and in despite of apostolic authority, knowing as he does that God resists the proud but shows favor to the humble.

Besides this, we sent to him three clergymen, his own subjects, through whom we gave him private warnings to do penance for his crimes, horrible to describe, but known to many and published through many lands and for which the authority of law, human and divine, commands that he should not only be excommunicated until he should give due satisfaction, but should be deposed from his royal office without hope of restitution.

Finally we warned him that, unless he should exclude the excommunicated persons from his intimacy, we could pass no other sentence upon him but that, being cut off from the Church, he should join the fellowship of the condemned, with whom, rather than with Christ, he has chosen to take his part. And yet, if he were willing to listen to our warnings and reform his conduct, we called upon God — and we call upon him still — to bear witness how greatly we should rejoice in his honor and his welfare, and with what affection we should welcome him into the bosom of Holy Church as one who, being the chief of a nation and ruling over a widespread kingdom, is bound to be the defender of Catholic peace and righteousness.

On the other hand, his actions prove how little he cares either for our written words or for the messages sent by our legates. He was angered that anyone should reprove or correct him, and could not be led back to any improvement, but, carried away by a still greater fury of self-confidence, he did not stop until he had caused almost all the bishops in Italy and as many as he could in Germany to suffer shipwreck of their faith and had compelled them to refuse the obedience and honor which they owed to St. Peter and the Apostolic See and which had been granted to these by our Lord Jesus Christ.

When, therefore, we saw that we had reached the limit: namely, first, that he refused to give up his relations with those who had been excommunicated for sacrilege and the heresy of Simony; second, because he was not willing, I will not say to perform, but even to promise repentance for his crimes, for the penance which he had sworn to in the hands of our legates was a fraudulent one; finally, because he had dared to divide the body of Christ, that is, the unity of the Church — for all these crimes, I say, we excommunicated him through the decision of a council. Since we could not bring him back to the way of salvation by gentle means, we tried, with God's help, to do so by severity, and if — which God forbid! — he should not be afraid even of the severest penalty, our soul should at least be free from the charge of negligence or timidity.

If, then, anyone thinks that this sentence was imposed illegally or without reason, if he is willing to apply common sense to the sacred law he will take our part, will listen patiently to what is taught, not by ourself but by divine authority, and is sanctioned by the unanimous opinion of the holy fathers, and he will agree with us. We do not believe that any true believer who knows the canon law can be caught by this error and can say in his heart, even though he dare not openly proclaim it, that this action was not well taken. Nevertheless, even if — which God forbid! — we had bound him with this chain without due cause or in irregular form, the judgment is not to be rejected on this ground, as the holy fathers declare, but absolution is to be sought in all humility.

Now do you, my beloved, who have not desired to forsake the righteousness of God on account of the wrath of the king or of any danger, take no thought of the folly of those who "shall be consumed for their cursing and lying," but stand fast like men and comfort yourselves in the Lord. Know that you are on the side of him who, as unconquered king and glorious victor, will judge the living and the dead, rendering to each one according to his works. Of his manifold rewards you may be assured if you remain faithful to the end and stand firm in his truth. For this we pray God without ceasing, that he may give you strength to be established by the Holy Spirit in his name. May he turn the heart of the king to repentance and cause him to understand that we and you love him far more truly than those who now favor and support his evil doing.

And if, under God's blessing, he shall return to his senses, no matter what he may be plotting against us, he shall find us always ready to receive him back into holy communion in accordance with your affectionate counsel.

To All in Authority in Germany, Urging Their Support in His Struggle with Henry IV

Book IV, 1, p. 289. July 25, 1076.

Gregory . . . to all his brethren in Christ, bishops, abbots and priests, dukes, princes and knights, all dwellers in the Roman Empire who truly love the Christian faith and the honor of St. Peter, greeting . . .

We render thanks to Almighty God, who for the exceeding love he bore to us did not spare his own son, but gave him for us all, to protect and govern his Church, beyond all our deserts, beyond the expectation even of good men. You know, beloved brethren, that in this time of peril when Antichrist is busy everywhere by means of his members, scarce one is to be found who truly loves God and his honor, or who prefers his commands rather than earthly profit and the favor of the princes of this world. But he who rejects not his own and daily changes sinners from his left side to his right has looked upon you with calm and favoring countenance and has set you up against his enemies to the healing of many nations, that it might please you rather to be steadfast in the perils of this present life than to set the favor of men above the glory and honor of the eternal king. So doing you will not pass over with deaf ears that saying of the prince of the Apostles, ''Ye are a chosen generation, a royal priesthood,'' and also, ''We ought to obey God rather than men.''

You well know, my brethren, for how long a time our Holy Church has had to bear the unheard-of wickedness and manifold wrongdoing of the king — would that I could call him Christian or [truly] your king — and what misfortunes it has suffered at his hands under the lead of our ancient enemy. Already during our diaconate we sent him words of warning out of our affection for him and our devotion to his parents, and after we came to the priestly office — unworthy as we are — frequently and earnestly have we striven, with the help of pious men, to bring him to his senses. But how he has acted against all this, how he has rendered evil for good, and how he has raised his heel against St. Peter and striven to rend in twain the Church which God entrusted to him you know, and it has been spread abroad throughout the world. But, since it belongs to our office to regard men and not their vices, to resist the wicked that they may repent, and to abhor evil but not men, we admonish you by authority of St Peter, prince of the Apostles, and call upon you as our beloved brethren to endeavor in every way to snatch him from the hand of the Devil and rouse him to a true repentance, that we may be able with God's help to bring him back in brotherly love into the bosom of that Church which he has sought to divide. This, however, in such ways that he may not be able by some fraud to disturb the Christian faith and trample our Holy Church under his feet.

But if he will not listen to you and shall choose to follow the Devil rather than Christ and shall prefer the counsel of those who have long been under excommunication for simoniacal heresy to yours, then we shall find ways under divine inspiration to rescue the already declining Church Universal by serving God rather than man.

Now do you, my brethren and fellow priests, by authority of St. Peter, receive and bring back into the bosom of our Holy Mother Church as many as shall repent of those who have not been ashamed to set the king above Almighty God and to deny the law of Christ, if not in words, at least by their deeds — as the Apostle says, "They profess that they know God; but in works they deny him" — these receive, that you may be worthy to rejoice in Heaven with the angels of God. In all things keep before your eyes the honor of your holy father, the prince of the Apostles. But all those, bishops or laymen, who, led astray by fear or the favor of man, have not withdrawn from association with the king, but by favoring him have not feared to hand over the king's soul and their own to the Devil — have no dealings or friendship with these unless they shall repent and perform the proper acts of penance. For these are they who hate and slay their own souls and the king's as well, and are not ashamed to throw the kingdom, their fatherland and the Christian faith into confusion. For, as we are subject to the word of the prophet: "If thou speakest not to warn the wicked from his wicked way . . . his soul will I require at thine hand," and again, "Cursed be he that shall hold back his sword from blood," that is, shall hold back the word of reproof from smiting those of evil life, so they, unless they obey, are subject to the wrath of the divine judgment and to the penalties of idolatry, as Samuel bears witness. And God is our witness that we are moved against evil princes and faithless priests by no question of worldly advantage, but by our sense of duty and by the power of the Apostolic See which continually

weighs upon us. It were better for us, if need were, to pay the
debt of mortality at the hands of tyrants rather than to consent in
silence to the ruin of the Christian law through fear or for any
advantage. We know what our fathers said: "He who does not oppose evil men out of regard for his station gives his consent; and
he who removes not that which ought to be cut out is guilty of the
offense."

May Almighty God, from whom all good things proceed, guard
and strengthen your hearts through the merits of Our Lady, the
Queen of Heaven, and the intercession of the blessed Apostles
Peter and Paul, and may he always pour upon you the grace of his
Holy Spirit that you may do what is pleasing to him. May you be
worthy to rescue his Bride, our Mother, from the jaws of the wolf,
and may you attain to his supreme glory, cleansed of all your sins.

To Bishop Hermann of Metz, in Defense of the Excommunication of Henry IV

Book IV, 2, p. 293. Aug. 25, 1076.

Gregory . . . to Hermann, bishop of Metz, greeting . . .

You have asked a great many questions of me, a very busy man,
and have sent me an extremely urgent messenger. Wherefore I
beg you to bear with me patiently if my reply is not sufficiently
ample.

The bearer will report to you as to my health and as to the conduct of the Romans and the Normans in regard to me. As to the
other matters about which you inquire — would that the blessed
Peter himself, who is many times honored or wronged in me his
servant, such as I am, might give the answers!

There is no need to ask me who are the excommunicated bishops,
priests or laymen; since beyond a doubt they are those who are
known to be in communication with the excommunicated king
Henry — if, indeed, he may properly be called king. They do not
hesitate to place the fear and favor of man before the commands of
the eternal King nor to expose their king to the wrath of Almighty
God by giving him their support.

He too feared not to incur the penalty of excommunication by
dealing with followers who had been excommunicated for the heresy
of Simony nor to draw others into excommunication through their
dealings with him. How can we think of such things but in the

words of the Psalmist: "The fool hath said in his heart there is no God," or again: "They are all gone astray in their wills."

Now to those who say: "A king may not be excommunicated," although we are not bound to reply to such a fatuous notion, yet, lest we seem to pass over their foolishness impatiently we will recall them to sound doctrine by directing their attention to the words and acts of the holy fathers. Let them read what instructions St. Peter gave to the Christian community in his ordination of St. Clement in regard to one who had not the approval of the pontiff. Let them learn why the Apostle said, "Being prompt to punish every disobedience"; and of whom he said, "Do not even take food with such people." Let them consider why Pope Zachary deposed a king of the Franks and released all his subjects from their oaths of allegiance. Let them read in the records [*registra*] of St. Gregory how in his grants to certain churches he not merely excommunicated kings and dukes who opposed him but declared them deprived of their royal dignity. And let them not forget that St. Ambrose not only excommunicated the emperor Theodosius but forbade him to stand in the room of the priests within the church.

But perhaps those people would imagine that when God commended his Church to Peter three times saying, "Feed my sheep," he made an exception of kings! Why do they not see, or rather confess with shame that, when God gave to Peter as leader the power of binding and loosing in heaven and on earth he excepted no one, withheld no one from his power? For if a man says that he cannot be bound by the ban of the Church, it is evident that he could not be loosed by its authority, and he who shamelessly denies this cuts himself off absolutely from Christ. If the Holy Apostolic See, through the princely power divinely bestowed upon it, has jurisdiction over spiritual things, why not also over temporal things? When kings and princes of this world set their own dignity and profit higher than God's righteousness and seek their own honor, neglecting the glory of God, you know whose members they are, to whom they give their allegiance. Just as those who place God above their own wills and obey his commands rather than those of men are members of Christ, so those of whom we spoke are members of Antichrist. If then spiritual men are to be judged, as is fitting, why should not men of the world be held to account still more strictly for their evil deeds?

Perchance they imagine that royal dignity is higher than that

of bishops; but how great the difference between them is, they may
learn from the difference in their origins. The former came from
human lust of power; the latter was instituted by divine grace.
The former constantly strives after empty glory; the latter aspires
ever toward the heavenly life. Let them learn what Anastasius the
pope said to Anastasius the emperor regarding these two dignities,
and how St. Ambrose in his pastoral letter distinguished between
them. He said: "If you compare the episcopal dignity with the
splendor of kings and the crowns of princes, these are far more in-
ferior to it than lead is to glistening gold." And, knowing this, the
emperor Constantine chose, not the highest, but the lowest seat
among the bishops; for he knew that God resists the haughty, but
confers his grace upon the humble.

Meantime, be it known to you, my brother, that, upon receipt of
letters from certain of our clerical brethren and political leaders
we have given apostolic authority to those bishops to absolve such
persons excommunicated by us as have dared to cut themselves
loose from the king. But as to the king himself, we have absolutely
forbidden anyone to dare to absolve him until we shall have been
made certain by competent witnesses of his sincere repentance and
reparation; so that at the same time we may determine, if divine
grace shall have visited him, in what form we may grant him absolution, to God's glory and his own salvation. For it has not escaped
our knowledge that there are some of you who, pretending to be
authorized by us, but really led astray by fear or the favor of men,
would presume to absolve him if I [sic] did not forbid them, thus
widening the wound instead of healing it. And if others, bishops in
very truth, should oppose them, they would say that these were
actuated, not by a sense of justice, but by personal hostility.

Moreover ordination and consecration by those bishops who
dare to communicate with an excommunicated king become in the
sight of God an execration, according to St. Gregory. For since
they in their pride refuse to obey the Apostolic See, they incur the
charge of idolatry, according to Samuel. If he is said to be of God
who is stirred by divine love to punish crime, certainly he is not of
God who refuses to rebuke the lives of carnal men so far as in him
lies. And if he is accursed who withholds his sword from blood —
that is to say, the word of preaching from destroying the life of the
flesh — how much more is he accursed who through fear or favor
drives his brother's soul into everlasting perdition! Furthermore

you cannot find in the teaching of any of the holy fathers that men accursed and excommunicated can convey to others that blessing and that divine grace which they do not fear to deny by their actions.

Meantime, we order you to ask our brother, the venerable archbishop of Trier, to forbid the bishop of Toul to interfere in the affairs of the abbess of Remiremont and, with your assistance, to annul whatever action he has taken against her.

But, concerning Matilda, daughter to us both and faithful servant of St. Peter, I will do as you wish. I am not yet quite clear as to her future status — *deo gubernante*. I wish you, however, clearly to understand that although I remember her late husband Godfrey as a frequent offender against God, I am not affected by his enmity toward me nor by any other personal feeling, but moved by my fraternal affection for you and by Matilda's prayers I pray God for his salvation.

May Almighty God, through the mediation of Mary, Queen of Heaven, ever virgin, and the authority of the blessed Apostles Peter and Paul granted by him to them, absolve you and all our brethren who uphold the Christian faith and the dignity of the Apostolic See from all your sins, increase your faith, hope and charity and strengthen you in your defense of his law that you may be worthy to attain to everlasting life.

To All the Faithful in Germany, Counseling Them to Choose a New King in the Event that Henry IV Can Not Be Brought to Repentance

Book IV, 3, p. 298. Sept. 3, 1076.

Gregory ... to all the beloved brethren in Christ, fellow bishops, dukes, counts and all defenders of the Christian faith dwelling in the kingdom of Germany, greeting and absolution from all their sins through the apostolic benediction.

If you weigh carefully the decree in which Henry, king so-called, was excommunicated in a holy synod by judgment of the Holy Spirit, you will see beyond a doubt what action ought to be taken in his case. It will there be seen why he was bound in the bondage of anathema and deposed from his royal dignity, and that every people formerly subject to him is released from its oath of allegiance.

But because, as God knows, we are not moved against him by any

pride or empty desire for the things of this world, but only by zeal
for the Holy See and our common mother, the Church, we admonish you in the Lord Jesus and beg you as beloved brethren to receive him kindly if with his whole heart he shall turn to God, and
to show toward him not merely justice which would prohibit him
from ruling, but mercy which wipes out many crimes. Be mindful,
I beg you, of the frailty of our common human nature and do not
forget the pious and noble memory of his father and his mother,
rulers the like of whom cannot be found in this our day.

Apply, however, the oil of kindness to his wounds in such a way
that the scars may not grow foul by neglect of the wine of discipline and thus the honor of Holy Church and of the Roman Empire
fall in widespread ruin through our indifference. Let those evil
counselors be far removed from him, who, excommunicated for the
heresy of Simony, have not scrupled to infect their master with
their own disease and by diverse crimes have seduced him into
splitting our Holy Church in twain and have brought upon him the
wrath of God and of Saint Peter. Let other advisors be given him
who care more for his advantage than their own and who place
God above all earthly profit. Let him no longer imagine that Holy
Church is his subject or his handmaid but rather let him recognize
her as his superior and his mistress. Let him not be puffed up with
the spirit of pride and defend practices invented to check the
liberty of Holy Church, but let him observe the teaching of the
holy fathers which divine power taught them for our salvation.

But if he shall have given you reliable information as to these
and other demands which may properly be made upon him, we desire that you give us immediate notice by competent messengers so
that, taking counsel together, we may with God's help decide upon
the right course of action. Above all, we forbid, in the name of St.
Peter, that any one of you should venture to absolve him from excommunication until the above-mentioned information shall have
been given to us and you shall have received the consent of the
Apostolic See and our renewed answer. We are distrustful of the
conflicting counsels of different persons and have our suspicions of
the fear and favor of men.

But now, if through the crimes of many [others] — which God
forbid! — he shall not with whole heart turn to God, let another
ruler of the kingdom be found by divine favor, such an one as
shall bind himself by unquestionable obligations to carry out the

measures we have indicated and any others that may be necessary for the safety of the Christian religion and of the whole empire. Further, in order that we may confirm your choice — if it shall be necessary to make a choice — and support the new order in our time, as we know was done by the holy fathers before us, inform us at the earliest possible moment as to the person, the character and the occupation of the candidate. Proceeding thus with pious and practical method you will deserve well of us in the present case and will merit the favor of the Apostolic See by divine grace and the blessing of St. Peter, prince of the Apostles.

As to the oath which you have taken to our best beloved daughter, the empress Agnes, in case her son should die before her, you need have no scruples, because, if she should be led by over-fondness for her son to resist the course of justice or, on the other hand, should defend justice and consent to his deposition, you will know how to do the rest. This, however, would seem to be advisable: that when you have come to a firm decision among yourselves that he shall be removed, you should take counsel with her and with us as to the person to be entrusted with the government of the kingdom. Then either she will give her assent to the common judgment of us all, or the authority of the Apostolic See will release all bonds which stand in the way of justice.

With regard to the excommunicated persons, I remind you that I have already given to those of you who defend the Christian faith as bishops should authority to absolve them, and I hereby confirm this — provided only that they truly repent and with humble hearts apply for penance.

To King William of England, Calling Attention to the Case of Juhellus, Bishop of Dol

Epistolae collectae, 16, p. 541. Sept. 27, 1076.

Gregory . . . to his most excellent son William, glorious king of the English, greeting . . .

It is doubtless known to Your Highness that the so-called bishop of Dol, the principal see of the province of Brittany, unmindful of his own welfare and trampling under foot the decrees of the sacred canons, has invaded that church by the shameless heresy of Simony and has now for a long time been oppressing it with violence. He gave numerous gifts to Count Alan, which exist openly to this day as proofs of his crime, and broke into the fold of Christ, not through the door but by another way like a thief and a robber. And not content with this infamy, he heaped up iniquity upon iniquity and, as if he thought Simony a matter of no account, he hastened to make himself also a Nicolaite. In the bishopric which he had thus wickedly assumed, he had the effrontry to introduce a wife, or rather a harlot, celebrating their nuptials publicly. By her he begot children, so that, having prostituted his spirit to the corruptor of souls by a simoniacal bargain, he devoted his body also to the Devil by foul and incestuous lust [*in contumeliam*]. Thus not a place was left in him for his Creator, which he had not completely sold out to the adversary by an inward and an outward obligation. Nor did his evil doing stop here; he added to his atrocious deed and his infamous offense an appalling sacrilege. He bestowed in marriage the daughters of his unlawful wedlock, giving them under the name of dowry estates and revenues of the Church, a most frightful crime!

Now, burdened with these iniquities, he is plotting to impose himself upon that church already torn in pieces and scattered abroad. Your Highness is aware that for these reasons he was pierced by the arrow of St. Peter thé Apostle and condemned by a fatal anathema unless he should repent of his crime. Wherefore we have taken pains to give you this fatherly admonition and briefly to explain the case lest through ignorance you might give further aid to a criminal already plunged in darkness of his own, and thus make yourself a partner in his crimes. But do you now, in humble obedience to the warnings of the Apostolic See and of ourself, cast him away from you or else by mild persuasion induce him if you can to consider his own welfare and take refuge in penitential redemption. To encourage and help men of that sort who persist in evil doing is nothing less than to kindle the wrath of God against oneself.

We on our part, being no longer able to endure the sufferings of that church, have by divine suggestion appointed and consecrated a man of approved life and well-known piety, the abbot of St. Melanius, who, coming to us upon other business which it is unnecessary to explain here, was unexpectedly obliged [by us] to accept the burden of this priestly office. Of him we confidently hope in the Lord that if — as we desire and as we have taken pains to request in numerous letters — he shall merit the favor and interest of the princes of the region and of men of good will, he will restore the church to a better estate by God's help under the patronage of St. Peter.

To Bishop Henry of Liége, in the Case of William, Bishop of Utrecht, Deceased

Book IV, 6, p. 303.   Oct. 28, 1076.

Gregory . . . to Henry, bishop of Liége, greeting . . .

The answer to your inquiry regarding the case of William, bishop of Utrecht,* Your Prudence may learn with absolute certainty not from ourself but from the unanimous opinion of the holy fathers. Whenever we have rendered judgment in church affairs we have preserved and followed their decrees, not putting forth novelties or things of our own devising but carrying out in practice what they proclaimed through the Holy Spirit.

Learn, therefore, and give diligent attention to what their authority has decreed against those who, armed with schismatic and heretical subtleties, have risen against the fathers, dividing the unity of Christ's body, which is the Church, or holding communication with excommunicated persons. Receive also, not only for this case in which Your Fraternity has made inquiry but for all similar cases, the reply of those whose footsteps we follow with God's help.

If in that schism against the Holy and Apostolic Church — which ought not to have been undertaken even against the humblest servant of the Church — he or anyone else took part of his own free will and, while he was deliberately in communication with the excommunicated king, died unrepentant, then we cannot depart from that judgment of the holy fathers: "We dare not communicate with those after death with whom we have not communicated when they were alive."

But if he took part contrary to his own wish and refrained from communication with the excommunicated king according to the order of the holy canons, then we absolve him by our apostolic authority and we not only permit but earnestly desire that prayers, sacrifice and charitable gifts be offered to the Lord in his behalf.

Further, we ask of Your Affection that you pray to God without

* William died April 27, 1076. Shortly before that date, he had signed King Henry's excommunication of Pope Gregory.

ceasing and urge your brethren and your subjects as far as you can to do the same, that he may look with pity upon his suffering Church struggling with so many and such dreadful tempests and almost crushed by them, and may snatch her out of danger and bring her safely to land for his mercy's sake.

To Countess Adela of Flanders, against Unchaste Clergy

Book IV, 10, p. 309.   Nov. 10, 1076.

Gregory . . . to Adela, countess of Flanders, greeting . . .

It has come to our knowledge that some of your people are in doubt whether or not priests and Levites and other servants of the sacred altar, if they persist in unchastity, may lawfully celebrate the office of the Mass. To these we make answer, by authority of the holy fathers, that servants of the sacred altar continuing in unchastity may on no account celebrate Mass but are to be expelled from the choir until they shall give satisfactory evidence of repentance.

Wherefore we enjoin upon you by our apostolic authority that you admit no one to the celebration of the holy mystery who persists in his criminal conduct [*scelus*], but that you bring in from whatever source you can men who will serve God in chastity. When those others have been completely removed from all church offices, pay no attention to the words of Archdeacon Hubert [of Terouanne] nor show favor to any utterances of his whatsoever, because, as I have heard, he has fallen into heresy through his wicked arguments and was publicly convicted by Hubert, legate of this Holy Roman See at Montreuil.

To the Germans, Asking Their Help in His Journey across the Alps

Epistolae collectae, 18, p. 543.   Nov., Dec., 1076.

Gregory, bishop, servant of those who serve God, to all archbishops, bishops, dukes, marquises, counts and all who defend and follow the faith and doctrine of Christ and of St. Peter, prince of the Apostles, in the whole kingdom of Germany, greeting and benediction from the blessed Apostles Peter and Paul and absolution from all their sins.

I, a priest, such as I am, and servant of the prince of the Apostles, am coming to you against the will and advice of the Romans, trusting in the mercy of Almighty God and in your Catholic faith. I am ready to suffer death for the honor of God and the salvation of your souls, as Christ offered his life for us. We are so placed that through many tribulations we make our way to the kingdom of God. And you, my dearest and best beloved brethren, pray use your utmost endeavors that with God's help I may come to you and be of use to you in every way. May he bless you by whose grace it was said to me on the day of my ordination at the tomb of St. Peter: "Whatsoever thou shalt bless shall be blessed, and whatsoever thou shalt loose upon earth shall be loosed also in Heaven." Amen. *Trying to win their favor over Henry?*

To the German Princes, Giving an Account of Canossa

Book IV, 12, p. 311. End of Jan., 1077.

Whereas, for love of justice you have made common cause with us and taken the same risks in the warfare of Christian service, we have taken special care to send you this accurate account of the king's penitential humiliation, his absolution and the course of the whole affair from his entrance into Italy to the present time.

According to the arrangement made with the legates sent to us by you we came to Lombardy about twenty days before the date at which some of your leaders were to meet us at the pass and waited for their arrival to enable us to cross over into that region. But when the time had elapsed and we were told that on account of the troublous times — as indeed we well believe — no escort could be sent to us, having no other way of coming to you we were in no little anxiety as to what was our best course to take.

Meanwhile we received certain information that the king was on the way to us. Before he entered Italy he sent us word that he would make satisfaction to God and St. Peter and offered to amend his way of life and to continue obedient to us, provided only that he should obtain from us absolution and the apostolic blessing. For a long time we delayed our reply and held long consultations, reproaching him bitterly through messengers back and forth for his outrageous conduct, until finally, of his own accord and without any show of hostility or defiance, he came with a few followers to the fortress of Canossa where we were staying. There, on three successive days, standing before the castle gate, laying aside all royal insignia, barefooted and in coarse attire, he ceased not with many tears to beseech the apostolic help and comfort until all who were present or who had heard the story were so moved by pity and compassion that they pleaded his cause with prayers and tears. All marveled at our unwonted severity, and some even cried out that we were showing, not the seriousness of apostolic authority, but rather the cruelty of a savage tyrant. *Oh man*

At last, overcome by his persistent show of penitence and the urgency of all present, we released him from the bonds of anathema and received him into the grace of Holy Mother Church, accepting from him the guarantees described below, confirmed by the signatures of the abbot of Cluny, of our daughters, the Countess Matilda and the Countess Adelaide, and other princes, bishops and laymen who seemed to be of service to us.

And now that these matters have been arranged, we desire to come over into your country at the first opportunity, that with God's help we may more fully establish all matters pertaining to the peace of the Church and the good order of the land. For we wish you clearly to understand that, as you may see in the written *reluctant* guarantees, the whole negotiation is held in suspense, so that our coming and your unanimous consent are in the highest degree necessary. Strive, therefore, all of you, as you love justice, to hold in good faith the obligations into which you have entered. Remember that we have not bound ourselves to the king in any way except by frank statement — as our custom is — that he may expect our aid for his safety and his honor, whether through justice or through mercy, and without peril to his soul or to our own.

KING HENRY'S OATH AT CANOSSA
Book IV, 12(a), p. 314.　Jan. 28, 1077.

The Oath of Henry, king of the Germans.

I, Henry, king, within the term which our lord Pope Gregory shall fix, will either give satisfaction according to his decision, in regard to the discontent and discord for which the archbishops, bishops, dukes, counts and other princes of the kingdom of Germany are accusing me, or I will make an agreement according to his advice — unless some positive hindrance shall prevent him or myself — and when this is done I will be prepared to carry it out.

Item: If the same lord Pope Gregory shall desire to go beyond the mountains or elsewhere he shall be safe, so far as I and all whom I can constrain are concerned, from all injury to life or limb and from capture — both he himself and all who are in his company or who are sent out by him or who may come to him from any place whatsoever — in coming, remaining or returning. Nor shall he with my consent suffer any hindrance contrary to his honor; and if anyone shall offer such hindrance, I will come to his assistance with all my power.

To the Germans, Explaining His Failure to Cross the Alps
Epistolae collectae, 20, p. 545. Feb., Mar., 1077.

Gregory . . . to his best beloved brethren and sons in Christ, the archbishops, bishops, dukes, counts and other princes together with all the people of Germany who are loyal to the Christian faith and practice, greeting and apostolic benediction.

As we have informed you in previous letters and by the word of our legates — knowing you to be worthy defenders of justice in true obedience and reverence toward the apostolic primacy and trusting confidently in your loyal support — we entered upon our journey to you against the will of almost all our liegemen except- ing Matilda, that most dear and faithful daughter of St. Peter, and with many difficulties and dangers. And in fact we should have gone through if we had found an escort from you at the appointed place. But when, through this interruption of our journey, the opportunity of coming to us was offered to the king, we were over- come by his display of humility and manifold penance, we received him into the grace of communion but made no further agreements with him except such as we believed to be consistent with the security and honor of you all.

Now when the bishops of Lombardy learned that the outcome of the whole transaction was reserved for a general meeting and con- ference with you and that they could not obtain absolution for their faults upon such favorable terms as they had expected, it is sad to relate and horrible to hear with what insolence and what malicious attacks they assailed us. They, who ought to be pillars in the temple of God, not only have no place in the edifice of Christ's body but are persistently attacking it and, as far as in them lies, are destroying it.

As for the king, we cannot say that he has walked so honestly and

obediently in the ways he has promised as to give us any great satisfaction, especially as by reason of his presence some of the worst
of them are encouraged rather to more hostility toward us and the
Holy See than to fear on account of their evil deeds.

Meanwhile, awaiting advices from you, we have learned through
our son Rapoto, whom we sent to you, that you are eagerly desirous
that we should come to your country and for greater security should
endeavor to do this with the king's aid and counsel. Therefore, as
we have informed you, desiring to comply with your wishes and
your judgment in all things, God willing, we are making efforts
through our messengers to accomplish this same end by agreement
and coöperation with the king. In what spirit he is likely to meet
you and us in this case we cannot ascertain in advance because of
his great distance from us; but as soon as we learn this we shall
inform you without delay.

Know, then, that it is our will and desire, with the king's consent or without it, if that is possible, to come over to you for our
mutual advantage and for the welfare of you all. But if the sins
and the efforts of evil men shall prevent this, nevertheless though
absent I shall beseech Almighty God with fervent prayers so to
guide your counsels and your deeds in every way that you may
plan and execute whatever is most pleasing to God and most ad-
vantageous to yourselves for the security and glory of your most
noble kingdom.

And may you so continue in the work of defending justice, which
you have begun for Christ's sake and for your eternal reward, that
in God's grace you may win the crown in a fight so holy and so
pleasing to him.

We should have written you at greater length were it not that we
have sent you messengers in whom you may have absolute confidence. To them we have entrusted whatever is lacking in this letter
that may show our feelings toward you and our desire for your
welfare.

To WILLIAM OF ENGLAND, IN THE CASE OF THE BISHOP OF DOL

Book IV, 17, p. 322.   March 21, 1077.

Gregory . . . to William, king of the English, greeting . . .

The case which you referred to us by letter has now, we think,
been so far settled that there is no need of further discussion about

it. After we had ordained a bishop over the church of Dol we learned not only through clerics and monks of that church but also from our legate, the monk Teuzo, that the man whose part Your Excellency had taken had completely ruined himself by his vices and finally by his disobedience. We therefore decided that there was greater danger to be feared from his crimes against the church and from his corrupt life than there was hope of recovery for the bishopric by any proclamation [of ours?].

Nevertheless, that we might not seem to have treated your intervention without due respect and attention, and in case some person might have deceived us — which we do not believe — so that we might appear too remiss in our inquiry and our decision, we determined to send thither our legates, namely our colleague Hugo, the venerable bishop of Die, and our beloved son Hubert, subdeacon of the Holy Roman Church, and also that same monk Teuzo (if his health permits), to examine carefully into the case and, if there be anything that ought to be changed or amended as justice may require, to carry this out with authority and according to reason. It seems that this affair could nowhere be more carefully or justly settled than within the church itself where both the man and his opponents can be present and your own people can give you certain evidence that reason and justice have been fully observed.

We have no doubt whatever that Your Highness will accept and concur in the decision, because, while you are endowed with many virtues by God's grace, this is your special distinction before God and men, that you admire in others that justice which you yourself are so ready to execute. Further, be it known to you that the devotion of Your Eminence to us is most welcome. We cherish in the depths of our heart both you yourself and whatever, as God wills, may avail for the glory of Your Highness. We hold you in most profound affection, and we are prepared to meet your wishes in everything you may desire of us, as far as possible, and as far as we dare to go with the divine approval. But, now that we have appointed our aforementioned son Hubert to come to you, we have not thought it necessary to write further, since in all matters which he may report to you from us we doubt not that he himself will be our most trustworthy epistle and we expect Your Excellency to receive him as such.

May Almighty God grant to you and Her Serene Highness, Queen Matilda, and to your most noble children, forgiveness,

remission and absolution for all your sins, and when he shall have
called you from the things of this world may he lead you into his
eternal kingdom, through the merits and intercession of the Apostles Peter and Paul and of all his saints.

To Bishop Josfred of Paris, regarding Complaints against Manasses of Reims *

Book IV, 20, p. 326.   March 25, 1077.

Gregory . . . to Josfred, bishop of Paris, greeting . . .

The bearer of these presents, Walter of Douai, came to us and
begged us earnestly that through the mediation of our apostolic kindness we would advise our colleague, the archbishop of Reims, to release him from the ban which he had laid upon him. He alleged that
in the case for which he had been excommunicated he had frequently, both before and after the excommunication, declared himself ready for examination and for a just decision. We, however,
did not think it prudent or reasonable to accept his story without
discussion and refused to make a final decision as to his absolution,
granting him only this favor through the pardoning grace of the
Apostles Peter and Paul, to whose shrine he had come, that he
should be permitted to receive holy communion during his journey
hither and returning until the eighth day after his arrival at home.
But now, that he may not be held too long in the bonds of excommunication through any unworthy cause, we command you on the
authority of this letter to get together with the archbishop and,
having ascertained by inquiry the precise truth of the affair, if the
man shall seem to you worthy of pardon either through innocence
or through satisfactory repentance, to direct the archbishop in our
name to grant him complete absolution. If he [the archbishop]
shall upon any pretext refuse to do this, then do you in our stead
fail not to absolve him. But if it shall be proved that he was at
fault and that he refuses to do what is right, then we decree that
he is to be held under the bond of excommunication until he shall
give due satisfaction.

[A paragraph concerning a certain Canon Azzo omitted.]

There is also another case which we desire you to take up and
carry through with the greatest care. Two brothers of the mon-

* See I, 13 and 52.

astery of S. Remi declare that they were excommunicated by the archbishop, that a lay brother of theirs was deprived of his sight and every kind of misery imposed upon them, because they had refused to obey a certain outsider, who had been foisted upon them and the monastery as abbot by means of bribery and contrary to the rule of St. Benedict, or to remain in the abbey under his rule. Nor, in the disorder of the monastery, had it been of any avail for them to appeal to the Apostolic See for a fair hearing of their case. If all this is true, you yourself can see how seriously the archbishop has involved himself in contempt for the apostolic authority. Wherefore, awaiting a more suitable place and time for conferring with him, God willing, we entrust the case to Your Fraternity for the present and enjoin upon you by our apostolic authority to warn him to lift the excommunication laid upon those monks and for the future to leave them in peace without any judicial process upon their appeal to the Apostolic See.

But if you find him in this matter disobedient and obstructive by means of his high rank and his self-will, do you absolve them yourself, relying upon our authority. Do you give warning to that abbot who is charged with having taken possession of the monastery of S. Remi through wicked ambition to present himself without fail either in that district before our colleague Hugo, venerable bishop of Die, to whom we have given this commission, or to other legates of ours if he shall find that they are to hold a synod in France, in order to render an account of his occupancy, or else to come to us at the next festival of All Saints, giving notice also to the brethren of the monastery who are bringing the charge of unlawful usurpation of the abbacy against him that they too may present themselves at the prescribed term for a discussion of the affair.

It is also reported to us that the people of Cambrai have burned a certain man because he had dared to say that priests guilty of Simony or fornication have no right to celebrate Mass and that their services should not be accepted. This seems to us terrible in the extreme and, if the report is true, it should be punished with canonical severity. We call upon you, therefore, to inquire carefully into the truth of the matter. If you find that they committed such impious cruelty, you will at once exclude the authors and their accomplices from entrance into the church and from all participation in its service. Also make every effort to inform us by letter as to the exact facts as soon as you possibly can.

On the other hand, we beg you and strongly urge upon you to send word to all your colleagues and fellow bishops throughout all France, by apostolic authority, that they are strictly to forbid all priests who refuse to give up the crime of fornication to perform the office of the holy altar, and do you yourself cease not to preach the same in every assembly. And if you find the bishops lax in this matter or that those who dare to usurp the name and function of holy orders unworthily on account of these crimes are rebellious, then in the name of St. Peter and by our apostolic authority do you prohibit every people from receiving their offices any further, so that, being put to confusion in this way, they may be compelled to reform their way of life and return to the purity of pious continence. Act, therefore, so that our holy and universal Mother Church may with God's help know you as a faithful servant and fellow worker in our apostolic care and may grant us to enjoy the fruits of your priestly office at this present and confidently to expect them in future by God's mercy.*

To Hugo of Die, concerning the Election of Gerard of Cambrai

Book IV, 22, p. 330.   May 12, 1077.

Gregory . . . to the venerable Hugo, bishop of Die, greeting . . .

Gerard, bishop-elect of Cambrai, came to us and made a frank statement and confession of the manner in which he had been appointed to the government of the church of Cambrai. He did not deny that after he had been chosen by clergy and people he had accepted the episcopate as a gift from King Henry, but he put forth as his defense and offered much evidence to us that he had not learned by any certain information of our decree against this kind of acceptance nor had he known that King Henry had been excommunicated by us. Then, after we had shown him by cogent reasoning how serious a matter it was to violate a synodal decree of the Holy and Apostolic See, even in complete ignorance, and how greatly he was defiled by taking part in this way with an excommunicated man, he promptly rejected and placed in our hands the

---

* This seems to place Gregory on record as frankly defending the doctrine that the right to administer priestly functions was dependent upon the personal character of the priest. His argument was that the evils he was attacking involved, not merely personal turpitude, but also doctrinal aberration to the point of heresy.

gift which he had received and left his whole case to our judgment, with entire subjection to our will.

In consideration of his humiliation and especially because we heard that his canonical election had had precedence, we were moved to leniency and, supported by evidence sent to us in writing by not a few of our fellow bishops petitioning in his behalf — namely that his previous life and conversation had been highly honorable and worthy of praise, we thought it not unfitting to give our consent to his promotion with a certain discretionary reserve.

However, lest this decision should be an excuse or precedent to others, whose cause and whose record for seeking indulgence might be far different from his, we made this condition: that in the presence of yourself and our colleague, the archbishop of Reims, and other bishops of the province he should make oath that before that acceptance and — as it is called — investiture with the episcopate the news of the king's excommunication and of our decree against this method of investiture or acceptance of churches had not been conveyed to him officially by any legate of ours or by any person who had been present and had heard those decrees.

Wherefore we enjoin upon you, my brother, to endeavor to assemble a council in that province, and especially to secure the consent and approval of the king of France if that can be done; but if for any reason he shall refuse his consent, then make arrangements for holding the council in the church of Langres. You may do this with the consent and assistance of our brother, the bishop of Langres, and with the knowledge that he has promised for the future to be in all matters a faithful helper and co-worker, not only with us, but with you and all our legates, and that we have great hopes and confidence in him. Count Tebaldus [of Blois] also has made us the same promise, that if the king [of France] should refuse to receive our legates he would receive them with the utmost reverence, would give them every possible convenience for holding a synod and would furnish the place and give his aid and counsel.

Make every effort, therefore, to meet with this our brother, the bishop of Langres, and arrange for a synod by mutual agreement in whatever place seems best to you. Summon thither the archbishop of Reims and as many as possible of the archbishops and bishops of France, and first of all press the discussion of the case of the bishop-elect of Cambrai, namely, that he shall publicly purge himself by the prescribed oath and by the same form of oath shall testify that he was not consenting to the death by fire of the man [referred to in the accusation]. If this shall be done we decree that his previous election shall be confirmed by apostolic direction and we desire that you and our colleague, the archbishop of Reims, shall make suitable arrangements for his consecration — unless perchance there be other obstacles of which we are ignorant and as to which we leave the inquiry to your discretion. But as to the scandal, common to almost the entire country, namely the sale of church offices — which he himself does not deny doing in his office as archdeacon — forbid it absolutely for the future as well to him as to all others.

[Two paragraphs of minor importance are here omitted.]

If, then, the grace of God shall give effect to these declarations of ours, among the articles of your program you are to lay especial stress upon this: In a general assembly of all members of the council you are to make a public and emphatic declaration that henceforth, in the appointment of bishops, canonical and apostolic authority is to be observed and, in accordance therewith, no metropolitan or other bishop shall dare to lay consecrating hands upon anyone who has received the gift of a bishopric from a lay person, under penalty of losing his own office and rank. In the same way let no [lay] power nor any person henceforth have any part in the conferring or accepting of such office. If he shall venture so to do, let him understand that he is bound by the same sentence and penalty which the blessed pope Adrian [II] in the eighth council passed upon this kind of offenders and corrupters of sacred authority. This chapter is to be read in the presence of all and you are to call upon the whole assembly to approve and confirm it. Further, you are to command by apostolic authority those who, after the renewed proclamation of this decree by us, have received investiture as bishops by the hands of secular lords or potentates or who have dared to lay the hand of ordination upon them, to come and render account of their action to us.

GREGORY ORDERS PAPAL LEGATES TO DEMAND FROM THE RIVAL KINGS
SAFE-CONDUCT TO GERMANY FOR THE POPE

Book IV, 23; p. 334.   May 31, 1077.

Gregory ... to Bernard, deacon of the Holy Roman Church, and
Bernard, abbot of Marseilles, greeting ...

It is doubtless known to you, my brethren, that relying upon
God's mercy and the help of St. Peter, we left the city of Rome to
go to Germany and there to establish peace among the people to
the honor of God and the advantage of Holy Church. But, for lack
of the promised escort and checked by the advent of the king into
Italy, we remained in Lombardy among enemies of the Christian
religion, not without great danger, and up to the present time we
have not been able to cross the mountains, as we proposed to do.

We therefore direct and, in the name of St. Peter, command you,
relying upon this our order, in our stead and fortified by the aforesaid prince of the Apostles, to enjoin upon both kings, namely,
Henry and Rudolf, to prepare a way for us to pass over in safety
and to furnish us with assistance and safe-conduct by means of
persons in whom you have confidence, so that the way may be open
to us under the guidance of Christ. It is our wish to take counsel
with clergymen and laymen of that kingdom who fear and love
God and with his aid to determine which party is the better qualified for the government of the kingdom.

You are well aware that it belongs to our office and to the function of the Apostolic See to consider the more important affairs of
churches and to settle them according to the dictates of justice.
Now this conflict which has arisen between the kings is of such
gravity and is so full of dangers that if it were to be neglected by
us for any reason, it would be a most unfortunate calamity, not
only for them and for us, but for the whole Church. Wherefore, if
either of the two kings shall refuse to bow to our will or give ear to
your admonitions, or shall proudly light the torch of his evil desire against the honor of Almighty God and seek the ruin of the
whole Roman Empire, then do you stand up against him by every
possible means, even unto death if need be, and in our stead, by
authority of St. Peter, deprive him of his royal power and exclude
both him and all his partisans from partaking of the body and
blood of our Lord Jesus Christ. Separate them from the precincts
of Holy Church, bearing always in mind that he is guilty of

idolatry who refuses to obey the Apostolic See and that the blessed Gregory, saintly and humble scholar as he was, declared that kings should lose their office if they should dare to oppose the orders of the Apostolic See.

But to the other king who shall humbly bow to our command and shall yield obedience to our universal mother as befits a Christian king, give your aid and advice in all things, first calling a council of clergymen and laymen, as many as you can bring together. Confirm him in his royal office by authority of the Apostles Peter and Paul and in our stead, and give orders in the name of Almighty God to all bishops and abbots, priests and laymen throughout the kingdom that they are to obey him and serve him faithfully as their lawful ruler.

To the German Clergy, Princes, etc., regarding a Safe-Conduct
to Germany

Book IV, 24, p. 337.   May 31, 1077.

Gregory . . . to the archbishops, bishops, dukes, counts and all faithful followers of Christ, of high or low estate, in the kingdom of Germany, greeting . . .

We desire you to know, beloved brothers, that we have given charge to our legates, Bernard, deacon and loyal son of the Holy Roman Church, and Bernard, the pious abbot of Marseilles, to admonish both the kings, Henry and Rudolf, either in person or by competent agents to provide a safe-conduct for us to come to you and by God's favor to discuss the controversy into which their sins have brought them. For our heart is tossed to and fro in grief and sorrow while so many thousands of Christian men are delivered over to temporal and eternal perdition, the Christian faith thrown into confusion and the Roman Empire brought to ruin by the pride of one man. Each of the kings is calling for our support, that is, for the help of the Apostolic See, over which we unworthily preside. And we, trusting to the mercy of God and the help of St. Peter, are prepared, with the approval of those among you who fear God and love the Christian faith, to try the justice of the case impartially and give our support to the one whose government of the kingdom is decided to be the more according to right.

Wherefore, if either of them, puffed up with pride, shall oppose our coming to you by any device and, [not] fearing the judgment of the Holy Spirit for his evil doing, shall disobediently resist our holy and universal Mother Church, do you hold him in contempt as a member of Antichrist and destroyer of the Christian religion, and do you carry out the decision which our legates shall pronounce against him in our stead, remembering that "God resisteth the proud, but giveth grace unto the humble." But to the other, who carries himself humbly and does not despise the judgment declared by the Holy Spirit through you — for we believe beyond a doubt that where two or three are gathered together in the Lord's name, they are enlightened by his presence — to him, I say, show reverence and service according as our legates shall decree, giving him your obedient support in every way so that he may honorably receive the royal dignity and bring aid to the almost ruined Church. Never forget that he who refuses obedience to the Apostolic See is guilty of idolatry, and that the blessed Gregory, a holy and most humble scholar, decreed that kings should forfeit their dignities and be denied participation in the body and blood of our Lord Jesus Christ if they should dare to disregard the decrees of the Apostolic See. For if the See of St. Peter decides and gives judgment in heavenly and spiritual things, how much more in things earthly and secular?

You are aware, best beloved brethren, that ever since we left Rome we have been in great peril in the midst of enemies of the Christian faith and yet have not been moved by either fear or favor to promise any aid to either of the kings contrary to what is right. We would rather face death, if need were, than suffer the Church of God to fall into ruin through our own will. For we know that we were ordained and set in the seat of the Apostles to the end that we might seek in this life not our own but the things that are of Jesus Christ, and that, following in the footsteps of the fathers, we might through much labor attain to eternal peace by the mercy of God.

PASTORAL LETTER TO THE RULERS OF SPAIN

Book IV, 28, p. 343. June 28, 1077.

Gregory . . . to the kings, counts and other princes of Spain, greeting . . .

We trust that Your Prudence is well aware that the Holy and Apostolic See is the chief and universal mother of all the churches and peoples whom divine mercy foreordained to have knowledge of

his name in the faith of our Lord and Savior Jesus Christ through
the teaching of the Gospels and the Apostles. She is therefore
bound to unremitting care that the truth of the Catholic faith may
be preserved and that wholesome instruction and warning may be
applied to the perception and maintenance of justice. But since by
divine dispensation we have been given the duty of this administration — unworthy and reluctant though we be — we stand in
holy awe of this our service, seeing that we are debtors both to
those near us and those who are far away and that we can have
no excuse before the supreme judge if their welfare is neglected or
their faults encouraged by our silence. Of this there are many
proofs and examples given us in the pages of prophets and evan-
gelists together with terrible threats, as that great preacher and
Apostle says: "Necessity to preach the Gospel is laid upon me;
for woe is unto me if I preach not the Gospel!" Wherefore, best
beloved, since we cannot address you face to face, as we could wish,
we have taken pains to admonish you in writing in token of our
affectionate devotion to you.

[Here follows a long conventional exhortation to the Christian
life, and then comes the gist of Gregory's appeal:]

Further, we desire you to know, what we are bound not to pass
over in silence and what is most necessary for you at present as
well as for the future, that the kingdom of Spain belongs to St.
Peter and the Holy Roman Church, as handed down in ancient
grants. Down to the present time this fact has certainly been obscured, partly by the disturbances of former times and partly by a
certain indifference on the part of our predecessors. After that
kingdom had been invaded by pagan Saracens and the tribute
[servitium] formerly paid to St. Peter had so long been withheld
from us on account of their lack of faith and their tyranny, the
very memory of the facts and of our proprietorship began to slip
away. But now, since by divine mercy a permanent conquest of the
land has been granted to you, we are unwilling any longer to over-
look the matter. The supreme arbiter and founder of justice has
conferred upon Your Eminences great merit for the recovery and
restoration of the rights and dignity of St. Peter and of the Apostolic See, and we must see to it that nothing occurs to obstruct this
divinely offered recompense through culpable negligence on our
part, or ignorance — which God forbid — on yours. We have confidence in the mercy of God, who has given you power and victory

and that good will by which, when you know the truth, you choose to follow the statutes and the example of truly Christian princes rather than the impiety of those who would rather persecute the Christian name than show reverence to it.

We are sending to you our colleague Amatus, the venerable bishop of Oleron, whom we make our personal representative in those parts, and have joined with him the abbot of St. Pons, a venerable man of approved piety and honorable character, so that if need be they can explain in greater detail what we have written you in outline regarding these matters and, so far as circumstances require, may give you personal and authoritative declarations of the truth. By their counsel you may establish beyond a doubt your faith in the things that are of God and such as are necessary for the salvation of your souls — as we have proved by their zeal for religion and for well-doing and as you can judge from your dealings with them.

We have thus by God's grace done what belonged to us to do in fulfillment of our official duty and for the satisfaction of the right. What your own welfare demands of you and how great is your debt to St. Peter, chief of the Apostles, we have made plain to you, lest ignorance should prevent you or with the lapse of time negligence — which God forbid! — should steal upon you in a vain security. And now do you take heed of what belongs to you. Consider, determine and enact with prudent counsel what a loyal and Christian devotion to your princely duty requires in imitation of the most pious princes. Show yourselves so ready and so high-minded toward the honor of St. Peter and your holy mother, the Roman Church, that your glorious valor, already strong and splendidly victorious, may become loftier and more illustrious by apostolic intercession. And may their blessing ever strengthen you, their authority absolve you from your sins, their protection keep you safe and unharmed in every peril, by whose power divinely granted to them the whole race of man is bound and loosed in Heaven and upon earth and the doors of the heavenly kingdom opened and closed for all.

THE FIFTH BOOK

TO THE PEOPLE OF CORSICA, CLAIMING TEMPORAL JURISDICTION OVER THAT ISLAND

Book V, 4, p. 351.   Sept. 16, 1077.

Gregory . . . to all bishops and nobles and to all the inhabitants of Corsica of high and low estate, greeting . . .

You are aware, brethren and best beloved sons in Christ, that it is a matter of common knowledge not only to you but to many peoples that the island which you inhabit belongs by right of legal proprietorship to no mortal person and to no power but that of the Holy Roman Church and that those who have hitherto held it by force without paying tribute or fealty or any kind of subjection or obedience to St. Peter have made themselves guilty of the crime of sacrilege, to the great peril of their souls.

Having learned, therefore, through certain liegemen of ours, who are also friends of yours, that you desire to return to the honor and the jurisdiction of the apostolic sovereignty, as you know you ought to do, and give back to St. Peter in your own time and through your own efforts the rights so long withheld by usurpers, we have rejoiced greatly in the knowledge that this will redound to your advantage and your glory in the future as well as at the present time. You need have no doubt or hesitation upon this point, if only your will stands firm and your loyalty to St. Peter remains unchanged; for we have, by God's grace, a strong force of noble men-at-arms in Tuscany ready to come to your defense if occasion should arise. Wherefore we are taking advantage of a most fortunate situation to send to you our brother Landulf, of the church of Pisa, to be your bishop, and are entrusting to him our authority in spiritual matters, so that he may receive your land in the name of St. Peter, and in our stead, may govern it with all diligence and may take part in all business and in all causes pertaining to St. Peter and through him to us. It is our wish and our apostolic admonition that you render him obedience and faithful service in all respects for the sake of your love and reverence for St. Peter, chief of the

Apostles. And, in order that he may be the more secure in his administration of all your affairs, in case he shall call for your fealty [*fidelitatem*] you are not to deny him nor refuse to pay it upon any pretext — saving, however, your loyalty to St. Peter and to ourself and to our successors.

To the Bishops of Sens and Bourges, regarding the Bishop of Orleans

Book V, 8, p. 358. Oct. 6, 1077.

Gregory . . . to Richer, archbishop of Sens, and Richard, archbishop of Bourges, and their suffragans, greeting . . .

Some of you are aware that we have labored in many urgent letters that the church of Orleans might be restored to its former noble position. But up to the present time, partly as I believe through the sins of the people, it has been so burdened with usurping pseudo-bishops that we have been unable to root out the thorns of its disorders. We have no doubt that you know with what a disobedient spirit their so-called bishop Rainerius has fought against the authority of the Apostolic See and what confusion and injury he has brought upon that church; but we have arranged to send men to you who will explain his outrages to you in detail.

It is said that before he had reached the canonical age and contrary to the decrees of the holy fathers he made his way into the church without formal election by the clergy and people. It is said that he added to this iniquity the further one that in the promotion of the clergy he bargained for the sale of archdeaconries and abbacies regardless of his honor or the fear of God. Furthermore, after he had been twice and thrice summoned by us, not only did he fail to come, but he refused to send anyone to present his reply to the charges against him. Placed by us under the ban and separated from participation in the body and blood of the Lord, he dared to perform the office of a bishop. He allowed our messenger Benedict, bearer of our letters, to be held captive by his people, in contempt of the Apostolic See.

Wherefore, no longer able to bear with his wrongdoing, we direct you by apostolic authority to arrange a conference at a suitable place for an inquiry into his actions, first sending him a summons in writing, that he may give you an answer to the above charges and may, if possible, prove his innocence. But if, persisting in his haughtiness, he shall refuse to present himself within forty days after the summons, or if he shall come and fail to clear himself by canonical process, then by the judgment of the Holy Spirit and by apostolic authority we pronounce against him sentence of condemnation and deposition without hope of restitution. This sentence you will publish in suitable ways to the assembled people and will install Sanzo, about whom you wrote to us and who has sought our counsel with that of St. Peter, in place of the deposed bishop.

GREGORY SUMMONS WIBERT OF RAVENNA TO THE LENTEN SYNOD AT ROME

Book V, 13, p. 366.　Jan. 28, 1078.

Gregory . . . to Wibert, archbishop of Ravenna, to all his suffragans and to all bishops and abbots in the March of Fermo and Camerino, in the Pentapolis, Emilia and Lombardy.

Gladly would we send you greeting and the apostolic blessing had not the authority of the holy fathers been opposed to your audacity. For God and the rule of the holy fathers and your own conscience bear witness how gravely and in what unchristian ways you have offended St. Peter the Apostle and his Holy Church of Rome, mother of you as of all believers. But, since to err is human and it is God's will to pardon repentant sinners, the Church founded upon the blood of that same God and Lord has like a mother awaited until now your return to her bosom, for she desires not to persecute you to your destruction — nay, rather, to further your salvation.

Wherefore, for the welfare, not of you alone but of the whole flock of Christ committed to your charge, in the name of Almighty God and of our universal mother, the Church of Rome, we summon you by our apostolic authority to a synod which with God's help we are to hold in the first week of the next Lenten season. You shall be given safe-conduct against injury to life or limb or to your property so far as our control extends. For you are to understand that on our part no personal enmity nor anyone's wishes or base clamor shall in any way prejudice your case — nay, rather, that we are prepared to temper the rigor of justice as far as we can without injury to your soul or danger to us. For we desire, as God is our witness, your welfare and that of your people rather than any temporal advantage whatsoever to ourself.

FROM THE DECREE OF THE LENTEN SYNOD AT ROME

Book V, 14(a), p. 369. Feb. 27 to March 3, 1078.

§1. Tedaldus, so-called archbishop of Milan, and Wibert of Ravenna, who have risen against this holy Catholic Church with unexampled heresy and pride, we suspend absolutely from the episcopal and priestly office and renew the anathema already laid upon them.

TO THE GERMAN PRINCES, ASKING THEIR COÖPERATION IN A GERMAN COUNCIL

Book V, 15, pp. 374-375. March 9, 1078.

Gregory . . . to the archbishops, bishops, clergy, dukes, princes, marquises and all officials, higher and lower, in the kingdom of Germany, excepting those who lie under canonical excommunication, greeting and apostolic benediction, provided they be obedient to the decrees of the Roman Church.

We beg to inform you, beloved brethren, that at the synod which we recently held at Rome, among many other things accomplished by God's help for the welfare of Holy Church, we took into careful consideration the ruin and confusion of your most noble country. It seemed to us the most fitting and practical way to restore peace among you that pious legates of the Apostolic See should be sent into your country and should summon your archbishops, bishops and clergy, together with laymen qualified for this purpose, to assemble in a place accessible and agreeable to both parties and either, with God's help, to make peace among you or to ascertain surely to which side the scales of justice incline.

At that synod it was determined that we would proceed under the power of St. Peter in every way and with the utmost energy against that party which should reject peace insolently and unjustly. And now that we have learned that not a few in your country prefer discord and controversy rather than peace, we ordain in the name of Almighty God and the blessed Apostles Peter and Paul that no one shall hinder those men by any device or plot or violence from coming together for the restoration of peace in your kingdom, so that by this convention they may bring the present discord to a just and lawful conclusion. Furthermore, to check all evil schemes and unlawful attempts, and acting under the judgment of the Holy

Spirit and the authority of the Apostolic See, we have anathematized and do now anathematize everyone, be he king, archbishop, bishop, duke or marquis or of whatever rank or station, who shall venture to interfere with this salutary proclamation — whosoever, that is to say, shall use any means to prevent the assembling of this convention or the conclusion of peace after such great disorders.

We add further to this anathema that whoever shall take the lead in this evil deed shall suffer the vengeance of Almighty God, not only in his soul but also in his person and his estate. Never in his life shall he find support or enjoy a triumph at arms, but he shall be crushed by twofold pressure and be brought ever lower and lower until finally he shall be taught to turn and repent.

We are sending the bearer of these presents to you that he together with our venerable brother the archbishop of Trier, who is on the side of Henry, and another from the party of Rudolf, who shall be a bishop suited to this task, may fix the place and date for the convention, so that our aforementioned legates may come to you more securely and with your coöperation and with God's help may bring about what is pleasing to him.

THE SIXTH BOOK

Book VI, 3, p. 394.   Aug. 22, 1078.

Gregory . . . to Bishop Hugo of Die and Hugo, abbot of Cluny,
greeting . . .

It is our duty to keep careful watch upon the administration of
Holy Church over which by God's will we preside, and therefore
we require of you that you seek the divine aid for us by your
earnest prayers.

Wherefore we now command you to make most diligent inquiry
and pronounce a final judgment according to law upon the complaints which our colleague, the archbishop of Reims, has submitted
to us by letter. He charges that our colleague Warmond, archbishop
of Vienne, has deposed and reinstated priests within the archbishopric of Reims. He complains further that two suffragans of
Reims, namely the bishops of Laon and Soissons, have disregarded
the sanctions of the canon law and have ventured to consecrate a
bishop of Amiens while he himself was with us at Rome humbly
awaiting our decision regarding him. Do you now make every
effort to investigate these charges with the utmost care and determine whether the case stands as we have understood from his letters. Make an especial effort, in case the bishop of Amiens has
dared with impious ambition and audacious boldness to receive his
investiture at the hands of a layman, contrary to the decree of a
Roman synod and of the Apostolic See, to prove this against him
and to punish him with canonical severity so that others may be
afraid to follow his example.

In the case of Manasses [provost of Reims] about whom the
archbishop makes a similar complaint and who is continually har-
assing him and the Church by giving aid and protection to [Count]
Evulus, strive to reconcile him and cause him to cease from disturbing the Church and annoying the archbishop. But if he persists in
his obstinacy and refuses to obey, then, unless you find that he has
a valid excuse, you are to take such action as seems to you right.

As to other obligations, if the archbishop shall show due obedience give him your support and by authority of St. Peter defend
the church entrusted to his care as you are bound to do with other
churches. He himself, as we have learned from his letters which we
have sent on to you, is seeking for delay as a means of escape, and
you may see from the copy how we replied to him.

And now, my beloved brethren, act wisely and manfully; do all
things in charity, so that the oppressed may find you cautious defenders and oppressors may learn that you are lovers of justice.
May Almighty God fill your hearts with the Holy Spirit; may he
lead you in the way that pleases him and bring you into the company of the holy fathers.

To the Bishop of Liége, Rebuking Him for Lack of Respect
to the Holy See

Book VI, 4, p. 396. Oct. 9, 1078.

Gregory . . . to Henry, bishop of Liége, greeting and apostolic
benediction — provided he has no dealings with those who do not
respect the [decrees of] the last Lenten synod at Rome.

As we read your letter, my brother, we were greatly surprised
that you should write without due respect for the Apostolic See
and should so bitterly have reproached us because we gave absolution to that parishioner of yours who came to us a while ago — as
if the Apostolic See had not the right to bind and to loose whom-
ever and wherever it please! Understand me, I should have been
greatly disturbed by your audacity were I not restrained by the
leniency of the Apostolic See and had I not been in some doubt regarding the letter which I had sent you some time before about
this matter. For we had some fear that that letter might have been
changed by someone's fraud and therefore we thought a copy of it
should be shown to you in order that you might understand our
intentions. If, then, it should appear that the letter had not been
changed, you will understand that either through presumption or
ignorance you have used language toward the Holy Roman Church
as if you were imitating the Easterners who dared to slander the
blessed pope Julius [I] because he gave absolution to the most holy
patriarch Athanasius without their consent. And be careful that
you do not reply to us with like audacity, but rather go back humbly to the writings of the holy fathers, which will show you what to

say and what to write. So, in accordance with the letter, a copy of which we are sending you, bring the case of that man to a settlement.

A certain man named Werembold has complained to us that he and his wife have been unjustly excommunicated by you. I find it hard to believe this, but nevertheless we direct you to bring the case to the notice of our colleagues, the archbishop of Trier and the bishop of Metz, and to see that it is settled according to their advice and judgment. As to the monastic dress and veil required and the money collected, you will not refuse to do what is right and give a just account in accordance with the evidence of the same prelates, so that you may avoid the necessity of making proclamation and may protect yourself against any accusation, by thus preserving in all respects the integrity of justice and the authority of the canon law.

In the greeting at the beginning of this letter we have described as contemners of the [Lenten] synod those who have attempted by any trick or violence to prevent the holding of a council or conference in Germany at which may be determined by careful inquiry which of the two, Henry or Rudolf, is the better fitted to govern the kingdom.

Further we desire you to know that the bearer of this has been absolved by us from excommunication *timore mortis* and has promised in our hand to do everything according to your order under advice of the aforementioned bishops.

FROM THE ACTS OF THE ROMAN SYNOD
Book VI, 5(b), p. 403(3). Nov. 19, 1078.

§3. Whereas we have learned that investiture into benefices by laymen is practiced in many places and that in consequence great confusion has arisen in the Church, whereby the Christian faith is being trampled under foot, we ordain that no cleric shall receive the investiture of a bishopric, an abbey or a church from the hand of an emperor, or a king, or any lay person, man or woman. If he shall presume to do this, let him know that such investiture is invalid according to apostolic authority, and that he is subject to excommunication until he shall have made due satisfaction.

NOTIFICATION TO THE RAVENNESE OF THE DEPOSITION OF WIBERT

Book VI, 10, p. 411.   Nov. 26, 1078.

Gregory . . . to all those citizens of Ravenna, of both high and low estate, who reverence St. Peter and his son Apollinaris, martyr and bishop, as Christians should, greeting . . .

With what fidelity and humility the church of Ravenna has always clung to St. Peter, prince of the Apostles, and what obedience it has shown toward the Holy Roman Church, you, my brethren, best know. But he who is now called bishop of that church, once rich as it was pious — how he has ruined it by his tyrannical plunderings and corrupted it by the example of his impious life you have seen and felt through your sufferings and we have learned by reliable investigation. Since, however, entangled in these and many other crimes and polluted by them, he could not be brought to reason, but puffed up with haughty conceit persisted in his disobedience, a sin comparable to that of idolatry, be it known to you now that in a holy synod at Rome, by the judgment of the Holy Spirit and by authority of the Apostolic See, he was deposed from his office without hope of restoration.

Wherefore we ordain by authority of St. Peter, prince of the Apostles, that no one of you shall henceforth show toward him the obedience due to a bishop. But if any of you, infected by the contagion of excommunication, shall reject these wholesome precepts, we cut them off with the sword of anathema as foul members from Christ's body which is the Church Catholic, and cast them out. To you, however, who love God and obey St. Peter, we grant remission of all your sins by authority of the same prince of the Apostles.

PRIVILEGE FOR THE ARCHBISHOP OF PISA, CONFIRMING HIM AS
APOSTOLIC VICAR IN CORSICA

Book VI, 12, p. 413.   Nov. 30, 1078.

Gregory . . . to his beloved brother in Christ, Landulf, bishop of Pisa, and his successors:

In the sight of the Supreme Mercy we have accepted the charge of the Church Universal and we bear the burden of apostolic rule to this end: that we may show favor with earnest beneficence toward the just requests of our suppliants and may, so far as God shall grant, hold the scales of justice for all who are in need.

Wherefore, brother Landulf, at your request we are favoring your just petition that we should defend by our apostolic authority the church over which you preside by God's will, together with all its belongings, from the assaults of its enemies, and by grant of this present privilege we confirm to you the bishopric of the church of Pisa, together with all the rights thereunto appertaining. And because the church of Pisa, having strayed from the decrees of the holy fathers in its selection of pastors, has at length accepted the wholesome counsel of the Holy Roman Church for the restoration of its former liberties and has joyfully received you as its pastor by our ordinance, you who enter by the door — which is Christ — and not by any other way, we therefore grant, allow and confirm to that church all those rights which were formerly conveyed to it. Further, we confirm in like manner those rights which the divine favor deigned to grant through Her Serene Highness, our daughter Matilda, for the repose of the soul of her mother, who is buried in that same church, — namely, a place called Scanello, with its castles and other belongings — and also whatever properties may in future be legally granted, with God's favor, by loyal friends.

Furthermore, recognizing that the acceptable fruits of religious faith abound in you, we have granted to you and your successors our vicariate in the island of Corsica, provided, however, that they shall enter thereon canonically with the consent of the Roman pontiff and by the choice of the people of Pisa, as it is evident that you have done. So that, as God shall instruct you, you may teach the bishops, clergy and people of that island what belongs to the Christian religion and may confirm them in honorable living according to the word of the prophet: "To destroy and to overthrow; to build and to plant."

And since that island, withdrawn from the jurisdiction and sovereignty of the Holy Roman Church by the usurpation of certain evil men, has by your energy been restored to the lordship of the Roman Church according to the ancient custom and the invaders driven out, we grant to you, through whom the church of Pisa has been brought back to its former splendor and who have been the prime mover in the restoration of the aforesaid island, one-half of all the revenues and one-half of the fees derived from the courts. To your next two successors a fourth part of the revenues and of the court fees — provided however that castles and fortresses acquired by you shall remain in our possession and in that of our successors, but with the reservation that in case of necessity the wardens of such places shall be subject to your orders and to those of your successors, saving the rights and the honor of the Roman Church.

It is certainly fitting that, as they have accepted the pastoral office subject to the rule and by consent of the Roman Church — under God — they should receive from the generosity of the Roman See a dignified maintenance in their secular affairs.

We think proper to add that in the sessions of your courts a nuncio of ours should always be present.

PASTORAL LETTER TO THE KING OF NORWAY
Book VI, 13, p. 415.   Dec. 15, 1078.

Gregory . . . to Olaf, king of Norway, greeting . . .

Although we are under obligation to extend to all who accept the faith of Christ the protection of the Holy and Apostolic See, over which we preside by the mercy of God, nevertheless as regards you, placed as you are at the farthest end of the earth, we feel the greater need and reason for especial care because you have fewer persons who can instruct you in the Christian religion and a lesser share in its necessary services.

Wherefore, as opportunity offered we have written to confirm Your Highness in the faith which is in Christ Jesus, who was made man by the will of God, the everlasting Father, the Holy Spirit working with him, was born of a virgin, reconciling the world to God by his death, wiping away all our sins through his redeeming blood and, overcoming death in himself, restored us also to a living hope and to an heritage unfailing, undefiled and incorruptible. In him, as we firmly believe, there is prepared for you by his mercy salvation and life eternal — provided, however, that you keep your hope fixed upon him unto the end, because as the Apostle Paul says: "In him dwelleth all the fullness of the Godhead bodily." Wherefore serve him in all fear and humility, bearing in mind what the Psalmist says: [Quotations from Ps. 21: 29, 31.]

We desire you to know that it is our purpose, if it be possible in any way, to send to you certain of our brethren, men of sound faith and learning, to instruct you in the whole knowledge and doctrine of Christ Jesus. Thus properly taught the evangelical and apostolic doctrine, you will be in no wise uncertain, but, being rooted and grounded in that foundation which is Christ Jesus, you will increase the more abundantly and more perfectly in divine virtue and according to the operation of faith will bear fruits worthy of eternal reward. Such a legation, however, is very difficult for us on account both of the great distance and of the difference of language, and we therefore ask you, as we have asked the king of Denmark, to send to the apostolic court some of your young men of good family, so that they may be carefully educated in the sacred law and may be able to carry to you the orders of the Apostolic See not as ignorant, but as well-informed persons; to preach worthily, not as rude or uneducated men, but as those trained in languages, in learning and in behavior, and so with God's help effectually to promote culture among you.

It is reported to us that the brothers of the king of Denmark have applied to Your Excellency for help in compelling him to divide the kingdom with them. Now, what an injury this may bring to the kingdom, what confusion to a Christian people, what destruction to churches continually exposed to the cruelty of neighboring heathen, we are taught by the Truth itself which is Christ, saying: ''Every kingdom divided against itself is brought to desolation; and a house divided against a house falleth.'' Wherefore we earnestly counsel Your Highness not to lend your aid or countenance to either side in this controversy lest such wrong action may be turned against you and that through the division of that kingdom the wrath of God may be kindled against you or your kingdom. This, however, we do desire and recommend: that you persuade the king of Denmark to receive his brothers into the kingdom with affection and make such distribution to them of goods and honors, wherever possible, that they shall not suffer deprivation, and that the welfare and dignity of the realm shall be preserved. . . .

TO THE MONKS OF ST. VICTOR OF MARSEILLES, ON THE PROPOSED
UNION WITH THE CHURCH OF ST. PAUL (ROME)

Book VI, 15, p. 419. Jan. 2, 1079.

Gregory . . . to his very dear brethren of the monastery at Marseilles, greeting . . .

I have been a cause of grief to you — nay, it was the blessed Peter who afflicted you and who will make you well again. For his son, your abbot [Bernard], came to us and out of love for him became devoted to us even to the point of being made a prisoner.* And, being ready to die if need were, for this also he shall have his reward. But as you know, my brethren, few are those who serve God even in peace, and fewer still those who for love of him fear not persecution and withstand his enemies without hesitation. Wherefore the religion of Christ, alas! has all but perished and the insolence of the wicked has grown far too great.

But your father, being truly devoted to the prince of the Apostles, has stood by us in his line of battle and given his support to us, lending an attentive ear to the words of the Apostle: "As ye are partakers of the sufferings, so shall ye be also of the consolation."

But since it is love, though reason finds excuses, which causes your grief at being so long separated from so precious a father, we beg you in the name of Almighty God and for the love of St. Peter to bear patiently with us because with God's help we shall soon send him back to you rejoicing, and so by the authority of St. Peter, prince of the Apostles, committed to us, all unworthy as we are, we promise you indulgence and absolution for all your sins with our benediction. For we have faith to believe that by the exceeding clemency of the Most High and the unspeakable mercy of the Queen of Heaven, the blessed Peter and Paul will guard your House more carefully than ever since you have suffered injury and inconvenience in their service.

It is our wish to join your House so closely with that of St. Paul [at Rome] that, as has long been the case with Cluny, it may be especially united with the Apostolic See and may enjoy the special protection and blessing of that church. . . .

To Hugo of Cluny, Chiding Him for Admitting the Duke of Burgundy into the Monastery

Book VI, 17, p. 423.   Jan. 2, 1079.

Gregory . . . to Hugo, venerable abbot of Cluny, and his best beloved brother, greeting . . .

If there were more frequent intercourse between your people and the Romans, we could give you more detailed information by letter or by word of mouth how things are going with us as well in spirit-

* By order of King Henry during Bernard's legation in Germany.

ual as in temporal affairs. But, while you are eager to give support to courtiers, you care little for common people. You ought to remember that our lowly and pious Redeemer gave food to the angels in heaven just as he did not despise sinners upon the earth but took food with them also.

Why, my dearest brother, do you not consider in what misery and danger our Holy Church is involved? Where are those who of their own free will and for the love of God set themselves against dangers, resist the wicked and fear not to die for the sake of the right and true? Behold, those who seem to fear and love God desert from the warfare of Christ, neglect the welfare of their brethren and, caring only for themselves, seek their own peace and quietness. The shepherds and the dogs, defenders of the flocks, desert them, and ravening wolves attack the sheep with no one to resist them.

Now you have received a duke into the repose of Cluny and have caused a hundred thousand Christians to be without a guardian. And if our urgency had no weight with you and the command of the Apostolic See met no response from you as it should have done, why did not the groans of the poor, the tears of widows, the ruin of churches, the cries of orphans and the complaints of priests and monks move you to respect the words of the Apostle, "Charity seeketh not her own," and to keep in mind, as you are wont to do that "he who loves his neighbor fulfills the law"? . . .

We say these things in sorrow that scarce a single good prince is to be found. By the mercy of God, however, there are monks and priests and gentlefolk and not a few of low estate to be discovered in many places who fear God. But princes who fear and love God are almost entirely wanting throughout the whole western world.

We will write no further on this matter because I have confidence that by God's grace the love of Christ, which is wont to dwell in you, may pierce your heart in my defense and may show you how greatly I regret that a good prince should be taken away from his mother. If only a worse one do not succeed him, it will be some consolation.

Further, we admonish you, our brother, that you proceed cautiously in such affairs and place the love of God and your neighbor before all other virtues. . . .

140   **THE SIXTH BOOK**

FROM THE PROTOCOL OF THE ROMAN LENTEN SYNOD OF FEBRUARY 11, 1079

Book VI, 17(a), p. 425.

Oath of Berengar, a presbyter of Tours:

"I, Berengar, believe with my heart and confess with my lips that the bread and the wine which are laid upon the altar are, through the mystery of the sacred prayer and words of our Redeemer, in substance [*substantialiter*] converted into the true and actual and life-giving body and blood of Jesus Christ our Lord, and after consecration are the true body of Christ which was born of a virgin, was hung upon a cross for the salvation of the world and is seated at the right hand of the Father; and the true blood which flowed from his side — not merely as the symbol and agent of a sacrament, but in the essence [*proprietate*] of nature and the reality [*veritate*] of substance. As is contained in this writing, as I have read it and as you understand it, so I believe and in future I will teach nothing contrary to this belief. So help me God and these Holy Gospels."

Then the lord Pope commanded Berengar by authority of Almighty God and the holy Apostles Peter and Paul never again to dispute with anyone concerning the body and blood of the Lord, or to give instruction to anyone, excepting for the purpose of bringing back to the true faith those who had departed from it on account of his teaching.

TO ALL WHOM IT MAY CONCERN, FORBIDDING INJURY TO BERENGAR

Epistolae collectae, 24, p. 550. Feb., 1079.

Gregory ... to all faithful followers of St. Peter, greeting ...

Be it known to you all that by authority of God Almighty, Father, Son and Holy Spirit, and of the blessed Apostles Peter and Paul we have declared anathema upon all who shall dare to cause any harm to Berengar, a son of the Roman Church, either in his person or his property or who shall call him "heretic." After a long visit with us, staying as long as we wished, we are sending him home under the escort of Fulco, one of our own liegemen.

To Rudolf, Archbishop of Tours, and Eusebius, Bishop of
Angers, Enjoining Aid to Berengar

Epistolae collectae, 36, p. 564. About 1080.

Gregory . . . to Rudolf, archbishop of Tours, and Eusebius,
bishop of Angers, greeting . . .

We have learned that Fulco, count of Anjou, at the instigation
of certain enemies of our very dear son, the priest Berengar, has
been hotly pursuing him. Wherefore we enjoin upon Your Fraternity that you charge the said count in our name not to disturb this
man any further. And not only this but we also enjoin upon you
in the name of the blessed Apostles Peter and Paul that you act as
our agent in helping him against all his enemies and spoilers of his
goods. Farewell, and under no consideration do you fail to carry
out my orders!

To Lanfranc, Urging an Immediate Visit to Rome

Book VI, 30, p. 443. March 25, 1079.

Gregory . . . to Lanfranc, archbishop of Canterbury, greeting . . .

Since we took upon our shoulders, unworthy as we are, the burden of the supreme priestly office, you, our brother, have given
little thought to the matter of a visit to us. This has caused us to
wonder greatly, because we had a right to expect a different treatment from your devotion to us, and were it not for our apostolic
forbearance and your early pledges of affection we should long
since have been gravely offended against you.

We have most certain information that we have been deprived of
this visit either by your fear of the king — a king whom we have
specially favored above others of the same rank — or else through
your own fault. But if the memory of your former affection still
survives or if the devotion due to your mother, the Roman Church,
still remains in your heart, no fear of any earthly power and no
superstitious loyalty to any person whomsoever ought to hold you
back from our presence. And if some new attack of arrogance has
now roused him [the king] against the Apostolic See or any ambition or wantonness has stirred him against us, we shall be the more
aggrieved because this will show him to be unworthy of our favor.

To avoid this, we desire Your Reverence to make plain to him by
your constant advice that he may not venture to commit any injus-

HIERARCHY

tice against the Roman Church, mother of us all; that he dare not follow any policy hostile to religion; and that he no longer attempt to hinder your journey to the Apostolic See. It is your duty to check by your wisdom the excesses of his negligence, to hasten to the Apostolic See as soon as you can and to place yourself under our protection according to our often repeated desire, so that we may confer in person upon this and other affairs and the welfare of the Church may be promoted by our discussions.

To the Archbishops of Rouen, Tours and Sens, on the Church Hierarchy

Book VI, 35, p. 450.   April 20, 1079.

Gregory . . . to his brethren and fellow bishops of Rouen, Tours and Sens, greeting . . .

As you are aware, my brethren, the Apostolic See, over which we — unworthy as we are — preside by the grace of God and the inspiration of the Holy Spirit, has established archbishops as prelates over the several provinces and kingdoms. In accordance with this arrangement the church of Lyons has had the primacy over four provinces, namely, Lyons, Rouen, Tours and Sens, during a long period of years. Wherefore we, desiring to follow the example of the holy fathers as far as God's favor permits, and relying upon their authority, propose to confirm the primacy of the aforesaid church which they established and sanctioned by their decrees. For to this end the dispensation of Divine Providence ordained that there should be diverse grades and orders, that through the reverence of the lower for the higher and the affectionate care of the higher for the lower, there should be concord in diversity, and a harmonious administration of the several offices. The whole could not exist were it not supported by this wide system of diversities. The example of the heavenly host teaches us that the universe cannot exist or be governed by one and the same kind of equality. There are angels and archangels and it is obvious that these are not equals, but differ one from the other in power and in rank, as you well know. If, then, there is this distinction among sinless beings, what man can refuse to submit himself freely to this same order? For thus peace and mutual love are inwrought together and there remains a firm confidence and affection pleasing to God, and each fulfills his office the more efficiently because there is one superior to whom he may refer his action.

[A long paragraph, taken from the *Pseudo-Isidorean Decretals,* is here omitted.]

Wherefore we enjoin upon you by apostolic authority that you show toward the church of Lyons the same honor and reverence, prescribed by our predecessors for your churches, which you do not scruple to demand from your own suffragans.

May Almighty and Merciful God, the calm searcher of peace and justice, deign so to inspire your hearts that you may walk with firm step in the way of equity and concord in this world, may take on eternal things in place of the things that are temporal and may be worthy to attain to the realm of the heavenly Jerusalem.

To BISHOP RAINALD OF COMO, REGARDING ORDINATION BY SIMONIACAL BISHOPS

Book VI, 39, p. 457.   June 21, 1079.

Gregory . . . to Rainald, bishop of Como, greeting . . .

[Final paragraph:] In reply to the inquiry made by our son, the presbyter M., as to the merciful judgment of the Apostolic See in the case of men ordained by simoniacs unknowingly and without payment, we desire you to observe the following rule: that those who were promoted to any rank by simoniacs before the time of Pope Nicholas [II] without bribery, and provided they are shown to be of blameless life, are to be confirmed by laying on of hands and are to retain their orders and perform their services.

THE SEVENTH BOOK

To Baron Wezelin, in Defense of King Demetrius of Dalmatia

Book VII, 4, p. 463.   No date.

Gregory . . . to Baron Wezelin, greeting . . .

Be it known to you that we are greatly surprised that you, who but lately promised fealty to St. Peter and to ourself, are now trying to take up arms against the king of Dalmatia, whom the apostolic authority has constituted.

Wherefore we warn Your Excellency and in the name of St. Peter command you that you presume not to proceed against that king, knowing that whatever you may adventure against him is also beyond a doubt against the Apostolic See. If, however, you have perchance any grievance against him, you should ask a judgment from us and await our just decision rather than go to war with him to the injury of the Apostolic See. And if you shall not repent of your rash conduct and shall attempt to act in rebellion against our commands, understand that we will most certainly unsheathe the sword of St. Peter against your audacity and will punish therewith the obstinacy of yourself and of all who stand with you in this undertaking, unless you shall come to your senses. If, however, you shall wisely obey as becomes a Christian, you will receive the favor of St. Peter and the blessing of the Apostolic See as an obedient son.

Pastoral Letter to King Alfonso VI of Leon

Book VII, 6, p. 465.   Oct. 15, 1079.

Gregory . . . to his best beloved son in Christ, Alfonso, glorious king of the Spanish, greeting . . .

We give thanks and praise to God Almighty who has enlightened Your Majesty by the grace of his visitation and has bound you in faithful devotion to St. Peter, chief of the Apostles, to whom he has made subject all principalities and powers of the earth and has granted him the power of binding and loosing in Heaven and upon the earth. To you also this should be cause for rejoicing, since greater rewards are awaiting you, in that divine counsel has reserved for your time the reformation of your kingdom so long bound in error, in order that your sublime humility and loyal obedience might worthily receive the truth and righteousness of God, in which, as well through the blindness of ignorance as through their insolent obstinacy, your predecessors — rulers, princes and the whole people — were lacking for so many years.

But, since all good works have their due reward not from their beginnings but from their conclusion, we warn Your Excellency in fatherly love to hold fast what you have received from our legates concerning doctrine and order in the Church and also what you may receive in future by God's will. For as those who stand fast in the observance of the faith and teaching of this Holy Apostolic See have a sure hope of salvation, so those who depart from unity and concord with it are without a doubt threatened with the terrors of condemnation.

Indeed, we have great hopes of you, since we have learned from the report of our beloved son Richard, cardinal-priest of the Holy Roman Church, whom we are sending to you for the second time, that you are well disposed towards us. But since loyal hearts always welcome admonition and even virtues require exercise, we exhort Your Highness to lift up your heart from these earthly and fleeting honors to that which is eternal in the heavens; that you make use of the former as temporary and quickly perishable, but strive for the latter as for a glorious eternity. You ought seriously to consider that you are hastening daily, whether you will or not, toward the end of your life, and while riches, honor and power now smile upon you, death, coming when you are least aware, will snatch you away and all will be wrapped in bitter darkness. What hope or glory or pleasure or enjoyment, therefore, can there be in things which deceive those who love them, escape those who pursue them and fail those who have them? The less one rejoices in these, and the less one is carried away by joy in them, the more surely is one led to things that are good in reality.

The example in this was clearly shown to us by our Lord and Savior Jesus Christ when he refused in pious humility the kingdom offered him by men. He who came into this world to lead us into the Kingdom of Heaven was unwilling to wear even the appearance of earthly splendor before the eyes of men. Wherefore we admonish you as a beloved son to ponder well these things and humble yourself before him who has set you in a high place and, striving in all things and above all things to please God, so with God's help to administer the government of the kingdom entrusted to you that Your Highness may suffer no decline of fortune, but may pass on to the crown of a kingdom beyond compare and to a throne of everlasting glory.

Furthermore, in order that our exhortations may be more deeply impressed upon your heart, we are sending you, after the custom of holy men [? our holy predecessors], a golden key in which is enclosed a blessing from the chains of St. Peter, that through his ever present patronage you may feel richer benefits from him to you and that Almighty God, who through his wondrous power delivered him from bands of iron, may through his merits and intercessions set you free from every sinful bondage and lead you into everlasting joy.

To this end we commend to you this our beloved son whom, as we have said above, we are sending to you now for the second time. May you listen to him as to ourself and show him favor in all respects that his journey and his labors in your country may not be in vain, but that in accordance with his commission he may be able to carry through the church reforms which awaited his action and, with God's help, bring them into permanent order.

Whatever else is not contained in this writing we have committed to him verbally. Have no hesitation whatsoever in giving full credit to him, knowing as you do that our authority is represented to you through him.

To the Bishops of Upper Italy, on the Subject of a Marriage with a Brother's Betrothed

Book VII, 9, p. 470.   Nov. 3, 1079.

Gregory . . . to his brethren and fellow bishops of Asti and Turin and the bishop-elect of Acqui, greeting . . .

It has come to our knowledge that the marquis Boniface [del Vasto], brother of Manfred and Anselm, who were recently murdered, is proposing to take as his wife the betrothed of that same Anselm. How dreadful a crime this is and how contrary to the laws of the Christian religion, no one who knows the sacred canons can have any doubt. Wherefore we enjoin upon you to summon him in our stead and warn him not to enter upon such an iniquitous marriage contrary to the statutes of the holy fathers. But if he thinks himself bound by an oath to commit this sin, we decree that the obligation of so wicked an agreement is not to be observed but is to be canceled as invalid and is so to be regarded by you. But if he shall harden his heart to his own salvation and persist in this criminal contract and refuse to listen to wholesome warnings as a Christian should, do you first proclaim the canonical judgment which we will then by God's help confirm and support by our apostolic authority, so that others may not be led astray by this example or fall into more evil ways or think that similar conduct is permitted to them.

To the Bishops and Barons of Brittany, on Reform of Penitential Practice

Book VII, 10, p. 471. Nov. 25, 1079.

Gregory . . . to the bishops, clergy, princes and all other inhabitants of Brittany, greeting and apostolic benediction, if they shall be obedient.

As Your Loyalty is aware, the highest office of the Church has for a long time been in a state of collapse by reason of sin, partly through the inexperience, partly through the negligence of the clergy. In consequence countless evils have sprung up, as it were from a corrupt root. So that down to the present time, among other ills that have cropped out, a false system of penance has become established. Wherefore, since it belongs to us in virtue of our office and the abundance of our anxious care to set right these and similar evils by God's aid, we desire and command that Your Fraternity summon reverently our legate Amatus, bishop of Oleron, to whom we have entrusted our representation in your region, and that through his agency a local council may be brought together at which, among other questions pertaining to the salvation of souls, the subject of penance may be thoroughly discussed.

In this matter you should yourselves take especial care and give warning to others that if anyone having become involved in murder, adultery, perjury or any similar crime shall persist in the same; or shall take part in any transaction which can hardly be carried through without sin; or shall take up arms except in defense of his own rights or those of his lord or of a friend or of the poor, or in defense of churches and with the advice of men of religion who know how to counsel wisely in view of their eternal welfare; or shall illegally hold the goods of others; or shall have shown hatred against his neighbor — such an one can in no wise bring forth the fruits of a true penance. We mean by a "fruitless penance" one that is accepted in such a way that the sinner may remain in the same or worse or only slightly less wicked sin.

So that, if anyone desires to perform a proper penance, he must needs go back to the origins of his faith and with watchful care keep the promise made at his baptism, namely, to renounce the Devil and all his works and to believe in God, that is, to have the right idea of him, and to obey his commandments.

Whoever, therefore, shall do penance in this manner, since to do otherwise is a pretense and not penance, to him we, relying upon our apostolic power, grant remission of his sins and moreover, trusting in the mercy of Almighty God, we promise him the enjoyment of everlasting bliss.

To Wratislaw, Duke of Bohemia, Forbidding Use of the Vernacular in Divine Service

Book VII, 11, p. 474.   Jan. 2, 1080.

[Paragraph 2.] In reply to the request of Your Excellency that we would sanction the celebration of the sacred offices in your country in the Slavic tongue, let it be known that we cannot in any way grant this petition. It is evident to those who consider the matter carefully that it has pleased God to make Holy Scripture obscure in certain places lest, if it were perfectly clear to all, it might be vulgarized and subjected to disrespect or be so misunderstood by people of limited intelligence as to lead them into error. Nor can it be said in excuse that some pious persons have yielded patiently to this demand of simple souls or let it go without reproof, since the primitive church passed over many things which later, when Christianity had become established and religious observances had increased, were corrected by the holy fathers after close examination.

We, therefore, by authority of St. Peter, forbid this practice unwisely requested by your people and command you to oppose this foolish rashness by every possible means.

ABSOLUTION OF BISHOP HENRY OF LIÉGE FROM AN OATH TAKEN
UNDER COMPULSION

Epistolae collectae, 34, p. 562.   Jan. 30, 1080.

[No greeting.]

It has come to our knowledge that you, our brother and colleague, Henry, bishop of Liége, while on your way to the shrine of the Apostles, were despoiled of your goods by Count Arnulf and, to make the offense still worse, were compelled to swear upon [his] sword that you would never reclaim the stolen property and would demand of us pardon for this outrageous crime. When we heard of this insult to you — nay to St. Peter — we were deeply moved and declared that Your Fraternity could not possibly be held by the obligation of an oath taken under such an infamous compulsion. We therefore absolve you by our apostolic authority, that you may not seem to be bound by your own conscience or that of anyone else on this account.

Furthermore, relying upon the same authority and to prevent this from being a precedent to other evildoers for worse actions in the future, we order our brother, the bishop of Verdun, and others in that country who are loyal to St. Peter to attack the count with weapons both carnal and spiritual as a tyrant and an oppressor of the Christian religion and to bring every possible pressure to bear upon him until he shall duly repent. We desire also that the aforesaid bishop shall call together as many bishops and other clergy as he can and shall summon that enemy of God to give due satisfaction. But if he shall refuse to repent and to restore the stolen property, then after a period of fifteen days let him be forbidden to enter a church. Thus shall the insult to St. Peter be duly punished.

EXCOMMUNICATION OF KING HENRY IV

Book VII, 14(a), p. 483.   March 7, 1080.

O blessed Peter, chief of the Apostles, and thou, Paul, teacher of the Gentiles, deign, I pray, to incline your ears to me and mercifully to hear my prayer. Ye who are disciples and lovers of the truth, aid me to tell the truth to you, freed from all falsehood so hateful to you, that my brethren may be more united with me and may know and understand that through faith in you, next to God and his mother Mary, ever virgin, I resist the wicked and give aid to those who are loyal to you. For you know that I entered holy orders not of my own pleasure, and that I accompanied the lord Pope Gregory [VI] unwillingly beyond the mountains, but still more unwillingly returned with my master Pope Leo [IX] to your special church, where I have served you as best I could; and then most unwillingly and unworthy as I was, to my great grief and with groans and lamentations I was set upon your throne.

I say this because it is not I that have chosen you, but you that have chosen me and laid upon me the heavy burden of your Church. And because you have commanded me to go up into a high mountain and denounce their crimes to the people of God and their sins to the sons of the Church, those limbs of the Devil have begun to rise up against me and have dared to lay hands upon me even unto blood.

The kings of the earth, and the princes, both secular and clerical, have risen up, courtiers and commons have taken counsel together against the Lord, and against you, his anointed, saying, "Let us burst their chains and throw off their yoke," and they have striven utterly to overwhelm me with death or banishment.

Among these especially Henry, whom they call "king," son of the emperor Henry, has raised his heel against your Church in conspiracy with many bishops,. as well ultramontanes as Italians, striving to bring it under his control by overturning me. Your authority withstood his insolence and your power defeated it. In confusion and humiliation he came to me in Lombardy begging for release from his excommunication. And when I had witnessed his humiliation and after he had given many promises to reform his way of life, I restored him to communion only, but did not reinstate him in the royal power from which I had deposed him in a Roman synod. Nor did I order that the allegiance of all who had taken oath to him or should do so in future, from which I had released them all at that same synod, should be renewed. I held this subject in reserve in order that I might do justice as between him and the ultramontane bishops and princes, who in obedience to your Church had stood out against him, and that I might establish peace amongst them, as Henry himself had promised me to do on his oath and by the word of two bishops.

The above-mentioned ultramontane bishops and princes, hearing that he had not kept faith with me, and, as it were, in despair about him, chose Duke Rudolf for their king, without my approval as you will bear witness. Then King Rudolf immediately sent an envoy to me declaring that he had assumed the government of the kingdom under compulsion, but nevertheless was prepared to obey me in every way. And to make this the more acceptable, from that time on he repeatedly sent me the same declaration, adding that he would confirm his promise by sending as hostages his own son and the son of his liegeman Bertaldus [of Zähringen].

Meanwhile Henry was beginning to beg for my help against Rudolf. I replied that I would gladly take action after I had heard both sides in order that I might learn which was the more in accord with what was right. But he, thinking himself strong enough to overcome his opponent, paid no attention to my reply. Later, however, as he saw that he could not do as he had hoped, the two bishops of Verdun and Osnabrück came to Rome on the part of his followers and at a synod requested me in behalf of Henry to do what was right by him. The envoys of Rudolf made the same request. Finally, by divine inspiration as I believe, I decreed at the same synod that a conference should be held beyond the mountains that peace might be restored there, or else that he should be recognized as king whose cause seemed to be the more just. For I, as you, my fathers and my lords, will bear me witness, have never to the present day taken either side except as justice required. And because I reckoned that the wrong side would not be willing to have a conference in which justice was to prevail, I excommunicated and placed under the bonds of anathema all persons, whether of a king or a duke or a bishop or of any vassal, who should try by any device to prevent the holding of a conference. But the aforesaid Henry together with his supporters, not fearing the perils of disobedience — which is the crime of idolatry — incurred excommunication by preventing a conference and bound himself in the bonds of anathema and caused a great multitude of Christians to be delivered to death, churches to be scattered abroad and almost the whole kingdom of the Germans to be desolated.

Wherefore, trusting in the justice and mercy of God and of his most worshipful mother Mary, ever virgin, and relying upon your authority, I place the aforesaid Henry, whom they call "king," and all his supporters under excommunication and bind them with the chains of anathema. And again forbidding him in the name of Almighty God and of yourselves to govern in Germany and Italy, I take from him all royal power and state. I forbid all Christians

to obey him as king, and I release all who have made or shall make
oath to him as king from the obligation of their oath. May Henry
and his supporters never, so long as they may live, be able to win
victory in any encounter of arms. But that Rudolf, whom the
Germans have chosen for their king in loyalty to you, may rule and
protect the kingdom of the Germans, I grant and allow in your
name. And relying upon your assurance, I grant also to all his
faithful adherents absolution of all their sins and your blessing in
this life and the life to come. For as Henry is justly cast down
from the royal dignity for his insolence, his disobedience and his
deceit, so Rudolf, for his humility, his obedience and his truthful-
ness is granted the power and the dignity of kingship.

And now, most holy fathers and princes, I pray you to take such
action that the whole world may know and understand that if you
are able to bind and loose in Heaven, you are able also on earth to
grant and to take away from everyone according to his deserts
empires, kingdoms, principalities, dukedoms, marquisates, earl-
doms and the property of all men. You have often taken patriarch-
ates, primacies, archbishoprics and bishoprics away from wicked
and unworthy men and have granted them to pious holders. And
if you can give judgment in spiritual things, what may we not believe as to your power over secular things? Or, if you can judge
the angels who guide all haughty princes, what can you [not] do to
their servants? Now let kings and all princes of the earth learn how
great is your power, and let them fear to neglect the commands of
your Church. And against the aforesaid Henry send forth your
judgment so swiftly that all men may know that he falls and is
overwhelmed, not by chance but by your power — and would that
it were to repentance, that his soul be saved in the day of the Lord!

PASTORAL LETTER TO KING HAAKON OF DENMARK AGAINST HEATHEN PRACTICES

Book VII, 21, p. 497.   April 19, 1080.

Gregory . . . to King Haakon and the bishops, princes, clergy and
laity of the Danes, greeting . . .

So far as we have been able to learn, you have shown up to the
present time absolute obedience and all due reverence to God and
St. Peter, and we have no doubt whatever that on this account divine grace has conferred glory and triumph upon you above others.

And if you shall persevere in this same devoted effort even unto the end, you will be able to keep the glory you now enjoy and with God's help will acquire still greater in future.

We enjoin upon you especially, beloved son, to whom Divine Providence has entrusted the care of a kingdom, that you strive to imitate the kingly virtues of your most admirable father. His commanding qualities so greatly excelled those of other kings, that setting aside all others, not excepting even the emperor Henry [III], who was a most zealous adherent of the Holy Roman Church, we felt that we ought to hold him in especial affection. His death was a great grief to us, and we desire, exhort and warn you to take him as your model, so that you may trace the brilliancy of your virtues to the same source from which you derive the lineage of your blood.

Finally, you should consider and carefully reflect how vain and transient are the things of this world; how all are hastening to their end, so that no permanence can persuade us to put our trust in them, but dreadful fear lurks in the possession of them. If, then, you clearly perceive these passing things and wisely ponder them you will be able to apply your mind to those fixed and permanent aims which invite your attention and which the example of good men encourages you to desire. Among the virtues which you ought to imitate, we hope the protection of churches will be prominent in your mind, that reverence for the priestly order will hold the next place and that justice and mercy will be wisely observed in all your judgments.

Meanwhile there is one matter which has come to our knowledge and which cannot be passed over but must be sternly repressed by apostolic prohibition, namely, that you ascribe to your priests the inclemency of the weather, foulness of the air and certain ills of the body. How grave an offense this is, you may clearly perceive from the fact that our Savior himself paid honor to the Jewish priests by sending to them men who had been cured of leprosy and charged others to observe what the priests commanded. But your priests, whatever you may think of them, are far superior to those. We therefore direct you by apostolic authority to abolish this pestilent practice absolutely from your kingdom and no longer presume to inflict such disgrace upon priests and clerics, who deserve honor and reverence, by ascribing to them the hidden causes of divine judgments.

Further, think not that you have a right to proceed by any

impious method against women who are condemned by any similar barbarity of heathen practices. Learn rather to avert the divine vengeance by suitable penance than to bring down the wrath of God still more heavily by treating those innocent women with useless severity. If you persist in these crimes, there is no doubt that your prosperity will be changed to ruin and that you will be conquered by those over whom you have been wont to rule and will be compelled to come under their yoke. If, however, you shall be obedient in this to us — nay, to St. Peter — as we trust in divine mercy you will, then you will be able to obtain both pardon for your sins and the apostolic blessing.

Pastoral Letter to King William of England, Giving Assurances of Friendship and Exhortations to Loyalty to Rome

Book VII, 23, p. 499. April 24, 1080.

Gregory . . . to William, king of the English, greeting . . .

I am sure that you know how devoted I was to your interests before I was raised to the summit of priestly rule, how useful I showed myself to you and with what zeal I labored to advance you to your royal state. So much so that I had to bear from certain of my brethren the almost infamous charge of having lent my aid in bringing about so great a sacrifice of human life. But God was my witness how conscientiously I acted, trusting as I did in your excellent qualities and believing that the higher you might rise the more useful you would be to God and to Holy Church, as has now — thanks be to God! — been proved.

And now I will declare to you briefly and familiarly as to a best-beloved son and liegeman of St. Peter and of ourself what your present duty is. When it pleased him who exalteth the lowly that our Holy Mother, the Church, should seize upon me as ruler of the Apostolic See, unwilling and reluctant enough as I was, God knows, I could not hide the abominable wrongs which she suffers from the worst of her sons. In this I was bound by the obligations of my office and actuated alike by love and fear: by love, because St. Peter had tenderly brought me up from a child in his own house and because the love of the Lord our God had chosen me, as if I were of some account, to be the vicar of so great a shepherd in the government of our Holy Mother Church; then also by fear, because the divine law declares with terrible emphasis: "Cursed be the man who withholds his sword from blood," that is to say, who withholds his preaching from destruction of the carnal life.

Now therefore, best-beloved son in Christ, since you see your mother in such tribulation and see also the pressing need of succor for us, I desire and adjure you by your own honor and your hope of salvation, in sincere affection, that you render us complete obedience. As you have earned with God's help the place of a jewel among princes, so may you be the standard of justice and the model of obedience to all the princes of the earth. So may you be chief among the princes of the future and may princes find salvation to the end of time by the example of your obedience. And if any of them shall refuse salvation, your reward shall in no wise be diminished — and thus not only [in Heaven], but in this world also victory, honor, glory and power shall be granted to you and to your heirs.

Set yourself as an example to yourself. As you would wish to be duly honored by one whom you had raised from a poor, miserable slave to be a mighty king, so do you, whom God's grace has made from a poor, wretched slave of sin — for such are we all born — to be a mighty king, hasten to do honor to your helper and protector, Jesus the all-powerful. And let not the mob of evil princes deter you from this; for the wickedness of the many is the virtue of the few. It is the glory of the well-proved soldier to stand firm in the fight when the many flee; the more precious the jewel, the more rarely is it found. So, the more the mighty of this world, blinded by their pride and their impious deeds, are plunged into the depths, so much the more fitting is it that you, who have been proved to be beloved of God before them, shall be raised by humility and obedience, that it may be fulfilled as is written: "He that is wicked, let him be wicked still; and he who is filthy, let him be filthy still; and the righteous, let him be righteous still."

I would have written you many things by way of exhortation, but since you have given such satisfaction both to myself and to our son Hubert with your messages, I have thought that for a wise man enough had been said, hoping that Almighty God would deign to work upon you and through you to his glory beyond what we have said. Whatever is lacking in our letters we have entrusted to your legates to be communicated to you by word of mouth.

May Almighty God our Father graciously deign so to implant these things in your heart by his Holy Spirit that he may increase your kingdom and power in this world, and in the world to come may lead you amongst the sainted kings into the inexpressibly greater felicity of the heavenly kingdom. Amen.

THE EIGHTH BOOK

To the Archbishop of Sivas in Armenia, Admonishing Him in Certain Matters of Faith and Practice

Book VIII, 1, p. 510. June 6, 1080.

Gregory . . . to his beloved brother in Christ, G[regory], archbishop of Sivas, greeting . . .

The guardianship of the Supreme See, over which we, unworthy as we are, preside by the grace of God, and the care of the Church Universal, entrusted to us by his Providence, compel us not only to mourn exceedingly over the ruin of those who separate themselves from the body of Christ, but also to wish happiness with joy unspeakable to those who hold the right doctrine and are known to preserve the unity of the faith. When, therefore, it was reported to us that your church, namely that of the Armenians, had wandered from the true faith of the Church Universal, handed down by the Apostles and holy fathers, into certain vicious opinions, we were grieved with a truly fatherly compassion.

We have learned by the reports of several persons that in the celebration of the healing sacrament of sacrifice among you no water whatsoever is mixed with the wine, whereas no Christian who knows the Holy Gospels can doubt that blood together with water flowed from the Lord's side. We have heard also that contrary to the practice of Holy Church your church prepares the sacred ointment not from balsam but from butter, and that it reveres and approves the archheretic Dioscorus of Alexandria, who was condemned and deposed by the Council of Chalcedon for persistent lack of faith.

Now although the bearer of this, your own legate, has denied the truth of these reports in our presence, nevertheless we desire more precise information from you, our brother, and request you to make answer to us under your own seal and by this same Johannes, presbyter, as to your belief on the points above mentioned and on any others about which you may be in doubt; also that you will henceforth send frequent letters to the Apostolic See. We desire further that you will inform us in writing whether your church accepts, as does the Church Universal, the faith of the Four Councils as approved by the holy fathers and confirmed with apostolic authority by the Roman pontiffs Silvester, Leo and others. Among these, the most blessed pope Gregory, an eminent scholar, writing to the elder churches of Alexandria, Antioch and others, bore witness that he held this faith in these words: [Here follows a long quotation.]

And now that these declarations of a most holy man and distinguished scholar have been carefully set forth, we have decided to recommend to your good judgment and in all charity that in future the phrase "who was crucified for us" which you add to the laud: "Sanctus Deus, sanctus fortis, sanctus immortalis," be omitted, since neither the Holy Roman Church nor any of the eastern churches except yours uses it, so that you may avoid all occasion for offense or for suspicion of a false interpretation. For if that chosen vessel, the most blessed Paul, speaking of food, declared that it was better neither to eat nor drink than that a brother should be offended, you ought to consider how serious a risk it is to cause offense to brethren in a matter of faith when it may be avoided by a clearer understanding. Wherefore, my brother, believe that it is sufficient for the church committed to your care to hold the doctrine which the Catholic Church throughout all the world, taught and enlightened by the Holy Spirit, is known to believe and has been declared to hold.

[Here follow two paragraphs of further admonitions.]

FEUDAL OATH OF DUKE ROBERT GUISCARD TO POPE GREGORY VII

Book VIII, 1(a), p. 514. June 29, 1080.

I, Robert, by the grace of God and St. Peter duke of Apulia, Calabria and Sicily, henceforth from this hour will be the vassal [*fidelis*] of the Holy Roman Church and of the Apostolic See and of you, my lord Gregory, universal pope. I will have no part in any plot or action whereby you might lose life or limb or be taken captive unlawfully. Confidence which you may place in me, requesting me not to share it, I will not wittingly betray to your injury. I will aid you and the Holy Roman Church to hold, to acquire and to protect the revenues [*regalia*] and the property of St. Peter to the best of my ability against all comers — excepting Salerno, Amalfi and a part of the marquisate of Fermo, concerning which no agreement has as yet been made. I will aid you to hold the Roman Papacy in security and honor.

The lands of St. Peter which you may hold now or in future, when I know them to be in your possession, I will not seek to trespass upon or to acquire, nor will I commit any depredation there without a special license from you or your successors who may be duly ordained to the service of St. Peter, excepting such land as you or your successors may grant to me. The tribute from the lands of St. Peter which I hold or may hold in future I will endeavor in good faith and according to agreement to pay annually to the Holy Roman Church. All churches remaining under my control, together with their possessions, I will hand over into your power and will be their protector in loyalty to the Holy Roman Church. And if you or your successors shall depart from this life before me, I will lend my aid according to the advice of the higher Roman cardinals and laymen in the election of a pope and his ordination to the office of St. Peter.

All the above obligations I will keep to the Holy Roman Church and to you in good faith, and I will keep the same faith with your successors who may be ordained to the office of St. Peter and who shall have confirmed to me, if no fault of mine remains, the investiture granted to me by you.

THE INVESTITURE OF DUKE ROBERT BY POPE GREGORY VII

Book VIII, 1(b), p. 515.   June 29, 1080.

I, Pope Gregory, invest you, Duke Robert, with the lands granted to you by my predecessors of blessed memory, Nicholas [II] and Alexander [II]. As to the lands which you unjustly hold, namely, Salerno, Amalfi and a part of the marquisate of Fermo, I will bear with you in patience for the present, trusting in God and your own rectitude that you will in future so govern yourself to the honor of God and of St. Peter as is fitting for you to do and for me to accept, without peril to your soul or to mine.

AGREEMENT OF ROBERT GUISCARD TO PAY TRIBUTE TO ROME

Book VIII, 1(c), p. 516.   June 29, 1080.

I, Robert, by the grace of God and of St. Peter, duke of Apulia, Calabria and Sicily, in confirmation of the grant and in acknowledgment of vassalage, do promise to pay annually to St. Peter and to you, my lord Pope Gregory, and to all your successors, or to your agents or those of your successors, from all lands which I hold in my own right and which I have not up to the present time conveyed in fee to any person from beyond the Alps, for every yoke of oxen twelve *denarii* in currency of Pavia. The date of this payment shall always be in each year the Sunday of the Holy Resurrection, and I bind myself, my heirs and successors to you, my lord Pope Gregory, and your successors under the obligation of this tribute.

To Hugh of Cluny, against the Monk Robert
Book VIII, 2, p. 517.   June 27, 1080.

Gregory . . . to Hugh, venerable abbot of Cluny, greeting . . .

How great an evil has gone forth from your cloister through the bold assurance of your monk Robert, you may judge from the report of our legate Richard, abbot of Marseilles. This Robert, following the example of Simon Magus, with all the malignant cunning he could employ, dared to rebel against the authority of St. Peter and lead back into error a hundred thousand persons who had begun to find the way of truth through our exertions. We believe, not that you were consenting to this iniquity, but rather that you share our grief at the enormity of the crime and are intending to impose a due penalty, especially since experience has shown that you are of one mind with us as to the honor of the Holy Roman Church and that you have preserved your freedom to execute righteousness which has almost disappeared from the earth with the decline of charity. From this conviction no rumors and no insinuations can turn us. Not even those who on many accounts were murmuring against you could raise suspicion in our mind before the time of [our] fraternal conference. Not to mention other things, almost all our friends would have changed their affection for those men into extreme hostility had they not been restrained by the check of our persuasion.

Wherefore, out of regard for your welfare as for our own, we warn you to discipline your subordinates and give to us who love you no further occasion for such murmurings. Especially we order you to exclude that Robert, who was the author of the aforementioned scandal and who has caused such peril to the Spanish church by the prompting of the Devil, from all access to the church and from all share in your affairs, until he shall return to you and accept a penance worthy of his offense. You will also give the king, who was deceived by his misrepresentations, to understand by letter that he has roused the anger of St. Peter and, unless he shall repent, will bring severe punishment upon himself and his kingdom. He has treated the envoy of the Roman Church unbecomingly, giving credit to falsehoods rather than to the truth, and for this he will have to give satisfaction to God and St. Peter and, as he has dishonored our legate, he must commend himself to him by humble devotion and praiseworthy reverence.

Let him know further that unless he shall amend his fault we shall proceed to excommunicate him and to rouse against him all the faithful followers of St. Peter who are in Spain. If then he shall not obey our orders, we shall not consider it a serious undertaking to go over to Spain and to take severe measures against him as an enemy of the Christian faith. Let it be your care also that the monks who are irregularly scattered through those parts shall return to their own Houses and that no ordinations there shall be considered valid except those approved by our legate. We desire also that you should order our enclosed letter to be transmitted to the king.

To the Bishops of Southern Italy, against Henry IV and Wibert of Ravenna

Book VIII, 5, p. 521.   July 21, 1080.

Gregory . . . to his beloved brethren in Christ, his fellow bishops of the Principates [Salerno, Benevento,] Apulia and Calabria, greeting . . .

We suppose that you, my brothers, are aware that many disciples of Satan falsely called bishops in various regions, excited by a devilish pride, have sought to throw the Holy Roman Church into confusion, but that by the help of Almighty God and the authority of St. Peter their wicked presumption has brought shame and confusion upon them, but glory and honor to the Apostolic See. In fact, from the lowest to the highest, that is to say, King Henry, who was proved to be the head and author of their pestilent undertaking, they were made to feel, through many perils to soul and body, the power of the blessed Peter to punish their wrongdoing.

You know what injury that same Henry sought to inflict upon the Church of St. Peter in the time of our lord Pope Alexander

[II] by means of [the antipope] Cadalus and into what a pit of destruction he was doomed to fall together with the same Cadalus, and with what a glorious triumph our Roman pontificate came out of that conflict. You know also with what detestable intrigues the bishops, especially of Lombardy, took up arms against us under the lead of the same Henry and how we remained safe and unhurt through the protection of St. Peter and with great honor and glory to ourselves and our faithful adherents. But, because they thought their first defeat was not enough, the sword of apostolic vengeance smote them so mightily from the sole of their feet to the crown of their heads that the wounds remain unhealed to this day.

But through all this, carrying themselves with the effrontery of harlots and laying up against themselves the wrath of a righteous judgment, these men, who in view of their disgrace ought to have come back to their senses, have followed the example of their sire when he said, "I will fix my seat in the North and will become like unto the Most High," and have striven to renew their former conspiracy against the Lord and the Holy Universal Church and to set up a robber of temples, a perjurer against the Holy Roman Church, notorious throughout the whole Roman world for the basest of crimes, namely, Wibert, plunderer of the holy church of Ravenna, Antichrist and archheretic. In this compact with Satan those men have taken part whose lives were shameful and whose ordinations were heretical by reason of their great and manifold crimes. To this madness they were driven by despair, because they could not gain our forgiveness for their wrongdoing by entreaty or by promises of service or of gifts unless they would submit themselves to our judgment and our discipline with such conditions of mercy as befit our office.

These utterly abandoned men, therefore, who have no reasonable support, we hold of less account the higher they imagine themselves to have climbed. By the grace of God and the prayers of St. Peter which miraculously overthrew Simon the Magician when he was climbing to higher things, we hope that the downfall of these men will not long be delayed and that the peace of Holy Church will be gloriously spread abroad and its enemies put to flight as they ever have been.

Do you, then, my beloved brethren, bearing in mind the innocence of your common mother, the Holy Roman Church, and considering how the Devil urges his members to disturb her peace, put forth all

your energies, by prayer and every other means by which help can
be given to your struggling mother, as the duty of your office requires, that you may show yourselves to be her true sons and share
with us both in diligence of labor and in our sense of humiliation.
Surely, if you shall be our companions in sorrow you shall also,
with God's help, be partners in our joy.

Other matters not here contained we have entrusted to our
legates, in whom you may have the same confidence as in ourself.

To the Liegemen of St. Peter, Summoning Them to War
Book VIII, 7, p. 525. Summer, 1080.

Gregory . . . to his brethren and fellow bishops, defenders of the
Christian religion, and to other liegemen [*fideles*] of St. Peter, both
lay and clerical, greeting . . .

Be it known to you, my beloved, that we have held conference,
both in person and by legates, with Duke Robert [Guiscard] and
Jordanes [prince of Capua] and other chiefs of the Normans. All,
without exception, have given their promise under oath to defend
the honor of the Holy Roman Church and of ourselves and to give
their help against all opponents. The same promise has been made
to us by all the princes far and wide around the City, in Tuscany
and other districts.

Accordingly we are proposing early in September, as soon as cool
weather sets in, to enter the territory of Ravenna with an armed
force, to rescue that holy church from impious hands and restore
it to its father, the blessed Peter, trusting beyond all doubt by
God's help to deliver it. Wherefore we hold of no account the audacity of the ungodly and the devices of those who have risen
against us — nay, against St. Peter — and we desire and exhort
you to look down upon their insolence and their undertakings
equally with us and to be the more certain of their destruction, the
higher you see their aims to be. For of such men thus saith the
prophet, "The tumult of those that rise up against thee ascendeth
continually," thus openly declaring that rash ungodliness is nearer
a fall the higher it imagines itself to have climbed.

Do you, therefore, who fear God and stand fast in your loyalty
to St. Peter, doubt not at all of God's mercy but have faith that the
disorders of the wicked shall quickly be quieted by their well-
deserved destruction, and that the peace and safety of Holy Church

shall soon be established as we promise, trusting in the grace of God.

To Orzocco, Judex of Cagliari, Urging Assistance in Reforms and Promising Help against Invaders

Book VIII, 10, p. 528.   Oct. 5, 1080.

Gregory . . . to the glorious judge Orzocco of Cagliari, greeting . . .

We render thanks to Almighty God that Your Highness has paid due honor and reverence to our legate William, bishop of Populonia, in recognition of St. Peter. We accept your devotion as paid to ourself, that is, to St. Peter, according to the word of the Lord: "Whosoever receiveth you, receiveth me." We therefore warn you by this loyalty to keep fresh in your memory whatever you have heard from our legate and from that wise person Azo, if you wish your memory to remain with us before God. For at the request of that bishop, who reports that he has been received with respect and honorably treated by you, we desire to bear you especially in mind before him whose unworthy agent we are.

We hope that Your Excellency will not be offended that we have required your archbishop James to follow the custom of the Holy Roman Church, mother of all churches and especially of yours — namely, that he, our brother, your archbishop, should observe the practice of the whole Western Church from the very beginning and should shave his beard. We also require of Your Highness that you receive him as your pastor and spiritual father and in accordance with his advice compel the whole clergy under your control to shave their beards. You will also confiscate the property of those who refuse, will turn it over to the church of Cagliari and will prevent them from any further concern with it. You will give the archbishop every assistance in maintaining the dignity of the churches.

We desire you to understand that your country is being sought for by many peoples. We have been promised very high rewards if we would allow it to be invaded — one half the land to be handed over to our use and the other half to be held in fealty to us. This has been repeatedly proposed to us, not only by Normans, Tuscans and Lombards, but also by certain persons from beyond the Alps, but we determined never to give our consent to anyone until we could send a legate to you and ascertain your wishes. And now, therefore, since you have shown your devotion to St. Peter in the person of his messenger, not only shall no sanction be given to anyone for a forcible invasion of your territory, but if anyone shall attempt this he shall be forbidden and repelled by us with both corporal and spiritual weapons. If you will continue in your loyalty to St. Peter, we promise you that his help will not fail you either now or in time to come.

To the Clergy and People of the Archbishopric of Ravenna, Urging Them to Support Richard, Newly Appointed Archbishop

Book VIII, 14, p. 534. Dec. 11, 1080.

Gregory, bishop and servant of those who serve God, . . . to all bishops, abbots, counts and knights [milites] in the parishes of Ravenna, the Pentapolis, the march of Fermo, and the duchy of Spoleto — such, that is, as reverence St. Peter and are not bound by the fetters of excommunication — greeting and apostolic benediction.

We trust you understand that, by the grace of God throughout the world, men of religion, whether clerks or laymen, hold us in reverence and freely approve and obediently accept our words and commands — we mean such men as know what is right and who recognize our good intentions. On the other hand, those who are enemies of the cross of Christ — nay, enemies of their own souls — rise up against us and, in their mad blindness and against their own salvation, strive to beat down our Holy Church. And we rejoice greatly at this when we see those who love God taking our side and those who hate their own souls coming out as our enemies. We have incurred their hatred, as you well know, chiefly because we have tried to snatch them from the snares of the Devil and bring them back to the bosom of Mother Church.

But now it is time, we think, for you, whom we believe to be far removed from their treachery and utterly strangers to it, to show what your feeling is toward us — that is, toward St. Peter, whom we unworthily represent — and if, as we believe, you are loyal to us, to declare this openly when the time comes and the cause demands it.

The way in which you can especially show your devotion is by striving to further to the utmost of your power the decrees and statutes of the Apostolic See. Wherefore use every effort to assist our brother Richard, archbishop of Ravenna, who, after long hindrance by usurping rivals, has recently been found worthy to receive Ravenna from the Roman Church as long ago Apollinaris received it from St. Peter. For the love of the most holy martyr, whose chair and whose relics adorn that church, and for the sake of the reverence due to the Apostolic See, give him your support and your aid in every way against that sacrilegious condemned usurper Wibert.

We order that according to the directions of our legate who brings you this message you pledge your aid and counsel to our brother, the archbishop, so that when his enemies hear of it they may be confounded and our loyal friends may understand that they may most certainly rely upon your promises.

To Hermann of Metz, in Defense of the Papal Policy toward Henry IV

Book VIII, 21, p. 547.   March 15, 1081.

Gregory . . . to his beloved brother in Christ, Hermann, bishop of Metz, greeting . . .

We know you to be ever ready to bear labor and peril in defense of the truth, and doubt not that this is a gift from God. It is a part of his unspeakable grace and his marvelous mercy that he never permits his chosen ones to wander far or to be completely cast down; but rather, after a time of persecution and wholesome probation, makes them stronger than they were before. On the other hand, just as among cowards one who is worse than the rest is broken down by fear, so among the brave one who acts more bravely than the rest is stirred thereby to new activity. We remind you of this by way of exhortation that you may stand more joyfully in the front ranks of the Christian host, the more confident you are that they are the nearest to God the conqueror.

You ask us to fortify you against the madness of those who babble with accursed tongues about the authority of the Holy Apostolic See not being able to excommunicate King Henry as one who despises the law of Christ, a destroyer of churches and of the empire, a promoter and partner of heresies, nor to release anyone from his oath of fidelity to him; but it has not seemed necessary to reply to this request, seeing that so many and such convincing proofs are to be found in Holy Scripture. Nor do we believe that those who abuse and contradict the truth to their utter damnation do this as much from ignorance as from wretched and desperate folly. And no wonder! It is ever the way of the wicked to protect their own iniquities by calling upon others like themselves; for they think it of no account to incur the penalty of falsehood.

To cite but a few out of the multitude of proofs: Who does not remember the words of our Lord and Savior Jesus Christ: "Thou art Peter and on this rock I will build my Church, and the gates of hell shall not prevail against it. And I will give thee the keys of the kingdom of heaven and whatsoever thou shalt bind on earth shall be bound in heaven and whatsoever thou shalt loose on earth shall be loosed in heaven." Are kings excepted here? Or are they not of the sheep which the Son of God committed to St. Peter? Who, I ask, thinks himself excluded from this universal grant of the power of binding and loosing to St. Peter unless, perchance, that unhappy man who, being unwilling to bear the yoke of the Lord, subjects himself to the burden of the Devil and refuses to be numbered in the flock of Christ? His wretched liberty shall profit him nothing; for if he shakes off from his proud neck the power divinely granted to Peter, so much the heavier shall it be for him in the day of judgment.

This institution of the divine will, this foundation of the rule of the Church, this privilege granted and sealed especially by a heavenly decree to St. Peter, chief of the Apostles, has been accepted and maintained with great reverence by the holy fathers, and they have given to the Holy Roman Church, as well in general councils as in their other acts and writings, the name of "universal mother." They have not only accepted her expositions of doctrine and her instructions in [our] holy religion, but they have also recognized her judicial decisions. They have agreed as with one spirit and one voice that all major cases, all especially important affairs and the judgments of all churches ought to be referred to her as to their head and mother, that from her there shall be no appeal, that her judgments may not and cannot be reviewed or reversed by anyone.

Thus Pope Gelasius, writing to the emperor Anastasius, gave him these instructions as to the right theory of the principate of the Holy and Apostolic See, based upon divine authority:

Although it is fitting that all the faithful should submit themselves to all priests who perform their sacred functions properly, how much the more should they accept the judgment of that prelate who has been appointed by the supreme divine ruler to be superior to all priests and whom the loyalty of the whole later Church has recognized as such. Your Wisdom sees plainly that no human capacity [*concilium*] whatsoever can equal that of him whom the word of Christ raised above all others and whom the reverend Church has always confessed and still devotedly holds as its Head.

So also Pope Julius, writing to the eastern bishops in regard to the powers of the same Holy and Apostolic See, says:

You ought, my brethren, to have spoken carefully and not ironically of the Holy Roman and Apostolic Church, seeing that our Lord Jesus Christ addressed her respectfully [*decenter*], saying, "Thou art Peter and upon this rock I will build my church, and the gates of hell shall not prevail against it; and I will give thee the keys of the kingdom of heaven." For it has the power, granted by a unique privilege, of opening and shutting the gates of the celestial kingdom to whom it will.

To whom, then, the power of opening and closing Heaven is given, shall he not be able to judge the earth? God forbid! Do you remember what the most blessed Apostle Paul says: "Know ye not that we shall judge angels? How much more things that pertain to this life?"

So Pope Gregory declared that kings who dared to disobey the orders of the Apostolic See should forfeit their office. He wrote to a certain senator and abbot in these words:

If any king, priest, judge or secular person shall disregard this decree of ours and act contrary to it, he shall be deprived of his power and his office and shall learn that he stands condemned at the bar of God for the wrong that he has done. And unless he shall restore what he has wrongfully taken and shall have done fitting penance for his unlawful acts he shall be excluded from the sacred body and blood of our Lord and Savior Jesus Christ and at the last judgment shall receive condign punishment.

Now then, if the blessed Gregory, most gentle of doctors, decreed that kings who should disobey his orders about a hospital for strangers should be not only deposed but excommunicated and condemned in the last judgment, how can anyone blame us for deposing and excommunicating Henry, who not only disregards apostolic judgments, but so far as in him lies tramples upon his mother the Church, basely plunders the whole kingdom and destroys its churches — unless indeed it were one who is a man of his own kind?

As we know also through the teaching of St. Peter in his letter touching the ordination of Clement, where he says: "If any one were friend to those with whom he [Clement] is not on speaking terms, that man is among those who would like to destroy the Church of God and, while he seems to be with us in the body, he is against us in mind and heart, and he is a far worse enemy than those who are without and are openly hostile. For he, under the forms of friendship, acts as an enemy and scatters and lays waste the Church." Consider then, my best beloved, if he passes so severe a judgment upon him who associates himself with those whom the pope opposes on account of their actions, with what severity he condemns the man himself to whom the pope is thus opposed.

But now, to return to our point: Is not a sovereignty invented by men of this world who were ignorant of God subject to that which the providence of Almighty God established for his own glory and graciously bestowed upon the world? The Son of God we believe to be God and man, sitting at the right hand of the Father as High Priest, head of all priests and ever making intercession for us. He despised the kingdom of this world wherein the sons of this world puff themselves up and offered himself as a sacrifice upon the cross.

Who does not know that kings and princes derive their origin from men ignorant of God who raised themselves above their fellows by pride, plunder, treachery, murder — in short, by every kind of crime — at the instigation of the Devil, the prince of this world, men blind with greed and intolerable in their audacity? If, then, they strive to bend the priests of God to their will, to whom may they more properly be compared than to him who is chief over all the sons of pride? For he, tempting our High Priest, head of all priests, son of the Most High, offering him all the kingdoms of this world, said: "All these will I give thee if thou wilt fall down and worship me."

Does anyone doubt that the priests of Christ are to be considered as fathers and masters of kings and princes and of all believers? Would it not be regarded as pitiable madness if a son should try to rule his father or a pupil his master and to bind with unjust obligations the one through whom he expects to be bound or loosed, not only on earth but also in heaven? Evidently recognizing this the emperor Constantine the Great, lord over all kings and princes throughout almost the entire earth, as St. Gregory relates in his letter to the emperor Mauritius, at the holy synod of Nicaea took his place below all the bishops and did not venture to pass any judgment upon them but, even addressing them as gods, felt that they ought not to be subject to his judgment but that he ought to be bound by their decisions.

Pope Gelasius, urging upon the emperor Anastasius not to feel himself wronged by the truth that was called to his attention said: "There are two powers, O august Emperor, by which the world is governed, the sacred authority of the priesthood and the power of kings. Of these the priestly is by so much the greater as they will have to answer for kings themselves in the day of divine judgment;" and a little further: "Know that you are subject to their judgment, not that they are to be subjected to your will."

In reliance upon such declarations and such authorities, many prelates have excommunicated kings or emperors. If you ask for illustrations: Pope Innocent excommunicated the emperor Arcadius because he consented to the expulsion of St. John Chrysostom from his office. Another Roman pontiff deposed a king of the Franks, not so much on account of his evil deeds as because he was not equal to so great an office, and set in his place Pippin, father of the emperor Charles the Great, releasing all the Franks from the oath of fealty which they had sworn to him. And this is often done by Holy Church when it absolves fighting men from their oaths to bishops who have been deposed by apostolic authority. So St. Ambrose, a holy man but not bishop of the whole Church, excommunicated the emperor Theodosius the Great for a fault which did not seem to other prelates so very grave and excluded him from the Church. He also shows in his writings that the priestly office is as much superior to royal power as gold is more precious than lead. He says: "The honor and dignity of bishops admit of no comparison. If you liken them to the splendor of kings and the diadem of princes, these are as lead compared to the glitter of gold. You see the necks of kings and princes bowed to the knees of priests, and by the kissing of hands they believe that they share the benefit of their prayers." And again: "Know that we have said all this in order to show that there is nothing in this world more excellent than a priest or more lofty than a bishop."

Your Fraternity should remember also that greater power is granted to an exorcist when he is made a spiritual emperor for the casting out of devils, than can be conferred upon any layman for the purpose of earthly dominion. All kings and princes of this earth who live not piously and in their deeds show not a becoming fear of God are ruled by demons and are sunk in miserable slavery. Such men desire to rule, not guided by the love of God, as priests are, for the glory of God and the profit of human souls, but to display their intolerable pride and to satisfy the lusts of their mind. Of these St. Augustine says in the first book of his Christian doctrine: "He who tries to rule over men — who are by nature equal to him — acts with intolerable pride." Now if exorcists have power over demons, as we have said, how much more over those who are subject to demons and are limbs of demons! And if exorcists are superior to these, how much more are priests superior to them!

Furthermore, every Christian king when he approaches his end asks the aid of a priest as a miserable suppliant that he may escape the prison of hell, may pass from darkness into light and may appear at the judgment seat of God freed from the bonds of sin. But who, layman or priest, in his last moments has ever asked the help of any earthly king for the safety of his soul? And what king or emperor has power through his office to snatch any Christian from the might of the Devil by the sacred rite of baptism, to confirm him among the sons of God and to fortify him by the holy chrism? Or — and this is the greatest thing in the Christian religion — who among them is able by his own word to create the body and blood of the Lord? or to whom among them is given the power to bind and loose in Heaven and upon earth? From this it is apparent how greatly superior in power is the priestly dignity.

Or who of them is able to ordain any clergyman in the Holy Church — much less to depose him for any fault? For bishops, while they may ordain other bishops, may in no wise depose them except by authority of the Apostolic See. How, then, can even the most slightly informed person doubt that priests are higher than kings? But if kings are to be judged by priests for their sins, by whom can they more properly be judged than by the Roman pontiff?

In short, all good Christians, whosoever they may be, are more properly to be called kings than are evil princes; for the former, seeking the glory of God, rule themselves rigorously; but the latter, seeking their own rather than the things that are of God, being enemies to themselves, oppress others tyrannically. The former are the body of the true Christ; the latter, the body of the Devil. The former rule themselves that they may reign forever with the supreme ruler. The power of the latter brings it to pass that they perish in eternal damnation with the prince of darkness who is king over all the sons of pride.

It is no great wonder that evil priests take the part of a king whom they love and fear on account of honors received from him. By ordaining any person whomsoever, they are selling their God at a bargain price. For as the elect are inseparably united to their Head, so the wicked are firmly bound to him who is head of all evil — especially against the good. But against these it is of no use to argue, but rather to pray God with tears and groans that he may deliver them from the snares of Satan, in which they are caught, and after trial may lead them at last into knowledge of the truth.

So much for kings and emperors who, swollen with the pride of this world, rule not for God but for themselves. But since it is our duty to exhort everyone according to his station, it is our care with God's help to furnish emperors, kings and other princes with the weapons of humility that thus they may be strong to keep down the floods and waves of pride. We know that earthly glory and the cares of this world are wont especially to cause rulers to be exalted, to forget humility and, seeking their own glory, strive to excel their fellows. It seems therefore especially useful for emperors and kings, while their hearts are lifted up in the strife for glory, to learn how to humble themselves and to know fear rather than joy. Let them therefore consider carefully how dangerous, even awesome is the office of emperor or king, how very few find salvation therein, and how those who are saved through God's mercy have become far less famous in the Church by divine judgment than many humble persons. From the beginning of the world to the present day we do not find in all authentic records [seven] emperors or kings whose lives were as distinguished for virtue and piety as were those of a countless multitude of men who despised the world — although we believe that many of them were saved by the mercy of God. Not to speak of Apostles and Martyrs, who among emperors and kings was famed for his miracles as were St.

Martin, St. Antony and St. Benedict? What emperor or king ever raised the dead, cleansed lepers or opened the eyes of the blind? True, Holy Church praises and honors the emperor Constantine, of pious memory, Theodosius and Honorius, Charles and Louis, as lovers of justice, champions of the Christian faith and protectors of churches, but she does not claim that they were illustrious for the splendor of their wonderful works. Or to how many names of kings or emperors has Holy Church ordered churches or altars to be dedicated or masses to be celebrated?

Let kings and princes fear lest the higher they are raised above their fellows in this life, the deeper they may be plunged in everlasting fire. Wherefore it is written: "The mighty shall suffer mighty torments." They shall render unto God an account for all men subject to their rule. But if it is no small labor for the pious individual to guard his own soul, what a task is laid upon princes in the care of so many thousands of souls! And if Holy Church imposes a heavy penalty upon him who takes a single human life, what shall be done to those who send many thousands to death for the glory of this world? These, although they say with their lips, *mea culpa*, for the slaughter of many, yet in their hearts they rejoice at the increase of their glory and neither repent of what they have done nor regret that they have sent their brothers into the world below. So that, since they do not repent with all their hearts and will not restore what they have gained by human bloodshed, their penitence before God remains without the fruits of a true repentance.

Wherefore they ought greatly to fear, and they should frequently be reminded that, as we have said, since the beginning of the world and throughout the kingdoms of the earth very few kings of saintly life can be found out of an innumerable multitude, whereas in one single chair of successive bishops — the Roman — from the time of the blessed Apostle Peter nearly a hundred are counted among the holiest of men. How can this be, except because the kings and princes of the earth, seduced by empty glory, prefer their own interests to the things of the Spirit, whereas pious pontiffs, despising vainglory, set the things of God above the things of the flesh. The former readily punish offenses against themselves but are not troubled by offenses against God; the latter quickly forgive those who sin against them but do not easily pardon offenders against God. The former, far too much given to worldly affairs, think little of spiritual things; the latter, dwelling eagerly upon heavenly subjects, despise the things of this world.

All Christians, therefore, who desire to reign with Christ are to be warned not to reign through ambition for wordly power. They are to keep in mind the admonition of that most holy pope Gregory in his book on the pastoral office: "Of all these things what is to be followed, what held fast, except that the man strong in virtue shall come to his office under compulsion? Let him who is without virtue not come to it even though he be urged thereto." If, then, men who fear God come under compulsion with fear and trembling to the Apostolic See where those who are properly ordained become stronger through the merits of the blessed Apostle Peter, with what awe and hesitation should men ascend the throne of a king where even good and humble men like Saul and David become worse! What we have said above is thus stated in the decrees of the blessed pope Symmachus — though we have learned it by experience: "He, that is St. Peter, transmitted to his successors an unfailing endowment of merit together with an inheritance of innocence;" and again: "For who can doubt that he is holy who is raised to the height of such an office, in which if he is lacking in virtue acquired by his own merits, that which is handed down from his predecessor is sufficient. For either he [Peter] raises men of distinction to bear this burden or he glorifies them after they are raised up."

Wherefore let those whom Holy Church, of its own will and with deliberate judgment, not for fleeting glory but for the welfare of multitudes, has called to royal or imperial rule — let them be obedient and ever mindful of the blessed Gregory's declaration in that same pastoral treatise: "When a man disdains to be the equal of his fellow men, he becomes like an apostate angel. Thus Saul, after his period of humility, swollen with pride, ran into excess of power. He was raised in humility, but rejected in his pride, as God bore witness, saying: 'Though thou wast little in thine own sight, wast thou not made the head of the tribes of Israel?' " and again: "I marvel how, when he was little to himself he was great before God, but when he seemed great to himself he was little before God." Let them watch and remember what God says in the Gospel: "I seek not my own glory," and, "He who would be first among you, let him be the servant of all." Let them ever place the honor of God above their own; let them embrace justice and maintain it by preserving to everyone his right; let them not enter into the counsels of the ungodly, but cling to those of religion with all their hearts. Let them not seek to make Holy Church their maidservant or their subject, but recognizing priests, the eyes of God, as their masters and fathers, strive to do them becoming honor.

If we are commanded to honor our fathers and mothers in the flesh, how much more our spiritual parents! If he that curseth his father or his mother shall be put to death, what does he deserve who curses his spiritual father or mother? Let not princes, led astray by carnal affection, set their own sons over that flock for whom Christ shed his blood if a better and more suitable man can be found. By thus loving their own son more than God they bring the greatest evils upon the Church. For it is evident that he who fails to provide to the best of his ability so great and necessary an advantage for our holy mother, the Church, does not love God and his neighbor as befits a Christian man. If this one virtue of charity be wanting, then whatever of good the man may do will lack all saving grace.

But if they do these things in humility, keeping their love for God and their neighbor as they ought, they may count upon the mercy of him who said: "Learn of me, for I am meek and lowly of heart." If they humbly imitate him, they shall pass from their servile and transient reign into the kingdom of eternal liberty.

THE NINTH BOOK

To King Alfonso VI of Castile and Leon, Defending Himself and Urging Conformity to Roman Practice in Those Kingdoms

Book IX, 2, p. 569. 1081.

Gregory . . . to Alfonso, glorious king of Spain, greeting . . .

Your Prudence is well aware that falsehood is a sin, and that for every idle word we must give account in the Day of Judgment. But not even that falsehood which is told with good intention for the sake of peace can be regarded as wholly free from blame. We say this by way of preface that while you have no doubts as to this sin in others you may understand that in priests it is little less than sacrilege and may recognize what we send you as the veritable truth.

It has not escaped our notice that many things regarding our acts and words have come to your ears with false interpretation. Wherefore we have thought it not improper to reply to our detractors in our own defense and bring it to the attention of Your Devotion. I have no hesitation in confessing myself a sinner, for that is the truth. But if the reasons for the hatred and abuse of those who are raging against us be carefully studied, it will appear that their anger is excited not so much by any wrongdoing on my part as by my declarations of the truth and my opposition to their offenses. We might have commanded their services and their gifts more abundantly than many of our predecessors if we had been willing to suppress the truth and to hide their evil purposes. We, on the other hand, considering that, owing to the brevity of this life and the nature of temporal goods, no one can ever be a better bishop than when he is persecuted for righteousness' sake, have determined rather to incur the hatred of the wicked by obeying the commands of God than to provoke the wrath of God by making an evil compromise with them.

And now, beloved son, let us turn to your affairs. Your Excellency knows that this one thing is wholly pleasing to us — nay, to the divine mercy — namely, that in the churches of your kingdom you have caused the order of the Roman Church, mother of them all, to be received and celebrated according to the ancient custom. But then, as we learn from the reports of pious men, in the order which you seem to have followed up to the present time certain things contrary to the Catholic faith are proved to have been inserted. If you shall decide to give these up and return to the ancient custom, namely, that of this Church, you will have demonstrated that you choose St. Peter for your patron and that under divine inspiration you have the welfare of your subjects at heart as becomes a king. And still more do we rejoice in your wisdom when we bring to memory the glorious reputation of your humility and consider that that virtue, so seldom found dwelling in the same house with royal power, rules in your heart.

As to your inquiries regarding your wife and the abbey of St. Secundus, we have thought best to reply through our son and legate Richard, cardinal of the Holy Roman Church, and our brother, Bishop Simeon [of Burgos].

In regard to the person who was to be chosen as archbishop [of Toledo], we say that although he seems to be sufficiently practical and liberal-minded, still, as we know and as your letter does not deny, he is lacking in the foundations of discipline, namely, in literary training. You yourself well know how necessary that is, not merely for bishops but for priests as well, for without it no one can teach others or defend himself. Your Serenity should, therefore, take counsel with our legate Richard, abbot of Marseilles, and other pious men, and procure the election of some person whose piety and learning will bring honor and prosperity to your church and your kingdom — one from that diocese if possible; if not, from elsewhere. Have no hesitation or shame in choosing a stranger or a man of humble origin, if only he be a suitable person, for the government of your church, which demands the very best. The Roman state, as well in pagan times as under Christian rule, grew great under divine favor because it believed that greater weight should be given to virtue of mind and body than to nobility of family or of race.

But since we are bound not only to congratulate you upon the glories of your welldoing but also sorrowfully to restrain you from unworthy actions, we have to enjoin upon you no longer to permit Jews in your country to rule over Christians or have power over them. For to place Christians under Jews or to subject them to their jurisdiction — what is that but to oppress the Church of God, to exalt the synagogue of Satan, and in aiming to please the enemies of Christ to throw contempt upon Christ himself? Beware then, my son, of acting toward your lord and creator as you would not permit a servant of yours to act toward yourself with impunity. Bear in mind the honor and glory vouchsafed to you beyond all kings of Spain by the mercy of Christ; set his will before you as a pattern for your actions, strive to balance your account with him in all respects and remember always so to subject yourself to him in everything that you may be worthy to be exalted both here and hereafter. Most unfair would it be not completely to subject one man — namely, yourself — to him who has subjected thousands upon thousands to you and entrusted them to your judgment.

[A paragraph acknowledging a gift is omitted.]

Now may Almighty God, creator and ruler of all things and ineffable dispenser of all honors, who giveth salvation unto kings, by the merits of our supreme mistress, Mary, Mother of God, and by authority of the blessed Apostles Peter and Paul granted by them to our unworthy self, absolve you and your faithful subjects from all your sins and grant you victory over your enemies seen and unseen; may he ever enlighten your mind, so that you may realize his goodness and your own human frailty, may despise the glories of this world and attain unto everlasting glory under the guidance of St. Peter.

To Bishop Altmann of Passau and Abbot William of Hirschau, on the State of Politics in Germany

Book IX, 3, p. 573.   March, 1081.

Gregory . . . to his beloved brother in God and fellow bishop, Altmann of Passau, and to William, reverend abbot of Hirschau, greeting . . .

We send you our hearty thanks for your zeal in writing to us a true report, especially when so many and so diverse accounts are brought to us from your country. We desire to inform you that, upon the death of King Rudolf of blessed memory, almost all our loyal supporters exhorted us repeatedly to receive Henry again into our favor, he being already prepared to meet our wishes at many points and being supported by nearly all Italians. They said further, that if he should invade Italy as an enemy of the Church and should not be able to make peace with us on his own terms, we could not expect any aid from you. This does not seem to us a very serious matter, since we consider his insolence to be of small account. But if you do not support our daughter Matilda, the loyalty of whose soldiers you have to consider, what else can she do, if her people refuse to resist him, but to accept his terms of peace or lose all her possessions? Wherefore it is of the utmost importance that you give her certain information whether she may confidently look to you for protection.

If perchance Henry should enter Lombardy, we desire you, dear brother, to advise Duke Welf to swear fealty to St. Peter, as he promised me to do in the presence of the empress Agnes and the bishop of Como when his fief was granted him after his father's death. For we wish to establish him completely in the bosom of St. Peter and to win him over to his especial service. If you find him or other men of rank inclined to seek absolution for their sins through devotion to St. Peter, labor to make them carry this through and take all pains to give us reliable information about it. Relying upon this, we believe that the Italians, if they are separated from Henry, will cling devotedly to us, that is, to St. Peter.

Furthermore, all those in your country who fear God and desire the freedom of the Bride of Christ are to be warned not to be persuaded by any fear or favor rashly or hastily to elect any man whose personal character or the lack of any of those qualities which a king ought to have might stand in the way of his undertaking to protect the religion of Christ. In fact, we think it would be better to allow some delay in procuring a suitable king according to God's will and to the honor of Holy Church, rather than to raise an unworthy person to kingly power through too great haste. We quite understand that our brethren are worn out by the long contest and the manifold confusions. But still we hold it to be far nobler to fight on for a long time for the freedom of Holy Church than to sink into a miserable and devilish servitude. For the wretched fight as limbs of the Devil, and are crushed down into miserable slavery to him. The members of Christ, on the other hand, fight to bring back those same wretches into Christian freedom.

Wherefore continual prayers are to be poured forth and abundant gifts of charity are to be made, and our Redeemer is to be exhorted in every way, that our enemies, whom we love as he com-

manded, may see the error of their ways and return to the bosom
of Holy Church, and that he may give to his bride, for whom he
deigned to lay down his life, a ruler and protector such as she
ought to have. But if the one chosen shall not be thus humbly devoted and a useful servant to Holy Church, as befits a Christian
king and as we expected from Rudolf, then beyond a doubt Holy
Church will not only not support him, but will directly oppose him.
What Holy Church expected of Rudolf and what he himself promised, you, dear brother, know perfectly well. Provision must be
made, then, that we may expect no less from him who shall be
chosen king in the midst of such great toils and dangers.

We therefore proclaim the conditions which the Holy Roman
Church will require of him under oath as follows:

From this hour onward I will be the liegeman [*fidelis*] of the holy Apostle
Peter and of his vicar Gregory now living. And whatever he shall command me with the words, "by [your] strict obedience," I will faithfully
perform as befits a Christian man. As regards the regulation of churches
and the lands or revenues given to St. Peter by the emperors Constantine
and Charles, also all churches or estates granted to the Apostolic See by
any man or woman at any time and which are or may be in my power, I
will make such arrangements with the pope that I shall not incur the
danger of sacrilege or imperil my soul. I will, with Christ's help, pay to
God and St. Peter all due honor and service. And on the day when I shall
first come into his [the pope's] presence I will faithfully give my hand as
the vassal [*miles*] of him and of St. Peter.

Since, however, we have entire confidence in your loyal devotion
to the Apostolic See both from experience and from your promises,
if you think that anything here contained should be enlarged or
diminished, saving always the absolute formula of vassalage and the
promise of obedience — we entrust this to your ability and the
loyalty which you owe to St. Peter. In reply to your inquiry about
priests: It is our decision that at present, considering the popular
disturbances, the lack of good men and the very small number of
those who serve the offices of religion for faithful Christians, you
ought for the time being to relax the strictness of canonical rules.
These matters can be more suitably discussed in a time of peace
and quietness, which in the mercy of God we trust will soon come,
and then the canonical rules can be observed.

In regard to Buggo [*sic* — Bishop Burkhard of Halberstadt?],
whose evil conduct you have reported to us, we have no recollection

of having entrusted him with so great an office, namely that of granting absolution, or of having seen him or having had speech with
him.

At the holy synod which we held recently by divine inspiration
we again placed under the ban those who had been excommunicated
until they should give due satisfaction. We begged also the multitude of brethren present to beseech the mercy of God daily that he
may lead them back into the bosom of our Holy Mother Church
with sincere penitence and may grant them the gift of perseverance
in well-doing. For we seek not the ruin of any man, but desire the
salvation of all in Christ.

To Desiderius, Abbot of Monte Cassino, regarding Negotiations with the Normans

Book IX, 4, p. 577. Feb., 1081.

Gregory . . . to the venerable Desiderius, abbot of Monte Cassino,
greeting . . .

Your Affection is well aware what great advantages the Holy
Roman Church expected from the pacification of Duke Robert and
what fear it inspired in his enemies, nor do we suppose it has
escaped your notice how valuable it has been to this Apostolic See
on that side.

Since, therefore, the expectations of many of [our] liegemen in
this matter are evidently not progressing, we desire you to ascertain precisely what his attitude is toward the Roman Church. Especially we ask you to find out his intentions upon this point:
whether, if we should need to prepare an expedition after Easter,
he will promise to aid us faithfully either in person or through his
son, or, if this is impracticable, how many soldiers he will promise
without reserve to detail after Easter for service with the house
troops of St. Peter.

Further, you will carefully inquire whether on those days of
Lent, on which the Normans are wont to abstain from fighting, the
duke will agree to make a sacrifice to God by sending a competent
commission into certain lands of St. Peter to make arrangements
with us or with our agent, so that by this display of his loyalty
he may confirm the good in their apostolic fidelity and may recall
the rebellious and the obstinate to their due reverence and service

toward the Holy Roman Church by fear or force, and by this use of his soldiery may offer a voluntary gift to God.

Furthermore, in regard to his nephew, Robert of Loritello, remind the duke of the assurance he gave us that the count [Robert] had promised no longer to trespass upon the lands of the Apostolic See — except those which he held in possession. We now hear, however, that he has not desisted from such trespass whenever it was possible. Do you, therefore, urge and command the duke to suppress the sacrilegious boldness of this nephew and to persuade him that, both by making good his past offenses and by refraining from such in future, he may win the favor of St. Peter, in whose anger he will find ruin and by whose favor he will obtain everlasting life and happiness.

We have no definite news from beyond the Alps, except that almost all who come from there report that Henry was never in worse condition.

GREGORY ORDERS HIS LEGATES IN NORMANDY TO DEAL GENTLY WITH OFFENDERS

Book IX, 5, p. 579. 1081.

Gregory . . . to his beloved brethren in Christ, Hugo, bishop of Die, and Amatus, bishop of Oleron, greeting . . .

It has been brought to our attention that you have suspended all the prelates of Normandy who were summoned to your council excepting the bishop of Rouen and the abbot of St. Pierre de la Couture [at Le Mans], whom we have restored. It is, however, indicated that they absented themselves not so much through disobedience as from fear of the king of France, so that they could not attend safely. Hear, therefore, what we recommend to Your Prudence.

The king of England, though in certain respects he is not as scrupulous about religion as we could wish, nevertheless shows himself to be more acceptable and more to be honored than other kings in this: that he neither wastes nor sells the churches of God, that he causes peace and justice to prevail among his subjects, that when he was asked by certain enemies of the cross of Christ to enter into a plot against the Apostolic See he refused his consent and that he bound priests by oath to dismiss their wives and laymen to give up the tithes which they were withholding. Therefore it is not unfitting that his power should be dealt with more leniently and that out of respect for his upright conduct the shortcomings of his subjects and his favorites should be borne with indulgence. Moreover, you may remember how the blessed Pope Leo [I] supported the neophytes and the blessed Gregory [I] the ex-patrician Venantius, who had been justly corrected by his bishop, and how the mercy of God pardoned Jehoshaphat, king of Judah, who had incurred the wrath of God by giving aid to the impious Ahab.

We desire, then, my brother, that you send by the bearer of this a letter of restitution to the bishops and abbots — including the abbot of la Couture — whom you have suspended, and in future avoid all offense against the king [of England] without our approval. It seems to us far better and easier to win him to God and bring him to enduring loyalty to St. Peter by gentleness and leniency and open reasoning rather than by severity and stern justice.

Furthermore it has come to our knowledge that you have greatly disturbed many gentlemen, who formerly aided you in disciplining simoniac and immoral priests, by excommunicating them because they refused to pay their tithes, whereas we have postponed bringing such persons under the ban of anathema by synodal decision as a matter of prudence. We therefore advise and desire you for the time being to temper the severity of the law in your discretion and moderate this storm of discontent, excusing some things and overlooking others. In this way they will not be led to worse conduct by the severity of justice, but if sentence be suspended for the moment and they be given time to recognize what is just, they may afterward the more easily come to terms, or finally, in a time of peace — which we hope with God's favor may soon come — a decisive judgment may restore to its normal condition what the discretion of the Apostolic See patiently postpones in the present crisis.

To Abbot Desiderius of Monte Cassino, concerning Negotiations with Robert Guiscard

Book IX, 11, p. 588. May, 1081.

Gregory . . . to Desiderius, venerable cardinal of St. Peter and abbot of Monte Cassino, greeting . . .

We desire you to know, best-beloved brother, that as we are certainly informed, Henry, so-called king, is lingering in the neighborhood of Ravenna and is proposing, if he is able, to come to Rome about Pentecost. We know for certain that he has there a small troop of ultramontanes and Lombards. We have heard also that he hopes to get together an army from around Ravenna and the March [of Ancona] for this expedition. We have little fear of his doing this, because he could not obtain supplies from the territory through which he would pass.

You know well, beloved brother, that if we were not restrained by our love of justice and the honor of Holy Church and were willing to compromise with the ill will and the wickedness of the king and his followers, not one of our predecessors could ever have had such complete and devoted service from any king or archbishop as we could now have from this king and this archbishop [Wibert]. But we care nothing for either their threats or their offers of service and are prepared rather to face death than yield to their iniquities or abandon the cause of righteousness. Wherefore we beg you to stand by us in every fitting way, so that the honor of your holy mother, the Roman Church, which has great confidence in you, may be strengthened now and for all time.

We desire you also to know that Countess Matilda has written us that she has certain information from some of his intimates that the king has made a compact with Duke Robert [Guiscard] by which a son of the king is to marry a daughter of the duke and the king is to hand over the March [of Fermo] to the duke. The Romans will readily believe this if they see the duke withdrawing the aid which he promised us in his oath of fealty. May Your Prudence keep careful watch and find out by close inquiry what is being done in this matter, and pray come to us as soon as ever you can.

I want you also to understand that the Romans and all who are about us are ready with prompt and loyal service to God and ourself.

PASTORAL LETTER TO THE KINGS OF SWEDEN

Book IX, 14, p. 592. 1081(?).

Gregory . . . to the glorious kings of the Visigoths, Inge and Alsten, and to their peoples, greeting . . .

Your bishop, our brother, coming to the shrine of the Apostles told us of the recent conversion of your people: how they had abandoned the errors of the Gentiles and had come to the truths of the Christian faith. Rejoicing greatly in the Lord, we gave profound thanks to him who has compassion for all, who has enlightened your minds and has deigned to lead you out from darkness

[of their] subjects or even slaves abandon their iniquities at [our] command and strive to take the lives of their masters.

And yet, up to the present time very few of us have withstood the wicked to blood, and but few have suffered death for Christ's sake, as was greatly to be desired. Consider, beloved, consider how many soldiers of this world, enlisted for filthy lucre, give their lives daily for their lords! And we, what do we do or suffer for the Supreme King and for our eternal glory? What shame and disgrace and what ridicule are put upon us because they fear not to suffer death for a mere trifle while we avoid suffering persecution for a treasure in heaven and eternal blessedness. Lift up your hearts then with strength; keep your hope alive, having ever before your eyes, the banner of our leader, the King Eternal, with his device: "In patience possess your souls."

And if we desire to break our ancient enemy swiftly and mightily, with God's help, and to make light of all his craftiness, let us strive not only not to avoid the persecutions he sends upon us and death for righteousness' sake but even to seek them for the love of God and the defense of the Christian religion. Thus shall we trample under foot all waves of the sea and the pride of this world and think them of no account, and shall reign together with our Head who sits at the right hand of the Father. For our Master calls: "If we suffer together we shall also reign together."

Meanwhile we declare to you, my brethren, who, like myself, are unequal to the harder battles of the conflict, that our blessed Redeemer will straightway grant us a happy issue out of our temptations, lest we might be overcome by our frailty and not be able to hold out. But, among whomsoever of his followers we may be placed, may we learn to serve him *in prosperitate* [*perpetuitate*].

GREGORY WARNS AN UNKNOWN COUNT C — TO REPENT OF HIS SIN

Book IX, 23, p. 603. 1082.

Gregory . . . to the noble count C.*

It is a great grief to us that, as reported to the Apostolic See, the craft of the Devil has been strong enough to prevail over your previous high reputation known through every part of France.

---

* The identity of the person to whom this letter is addressed is uncertain, but circumstances point to Fulco, Count of Anjou, in spite of the initial C. The next letter seems to confirm this conjecture.

For as we once rejoiced in you and used to refer to you in our discourse as a man of quite exceptional zeal in well-doing, excelling not only princes but kings in integrity and honor, so now it seems grievous to us that Your Prudence should have so fallen from grace and from such a height of virtue.

We perceive that the ancient deceit of the enemy of man has here wrought most infamously. For as he drove Adam out of Paradise by means of a woman, so now through that same sex he has deprived you of your fair fame in this life and brought your many good deeds to naught by that same kind of deception. For this offense you were reprimanded and excommunicated by your bishop, that you might redeem yourself and your companion from so great peril and free your house from eternal disgrace. You, however, not only refused satisfaction to God for your crime but, contrary to your usual fairness, cruelly persecuted the bishop himself, whom you were bound to obey even if he had passed an unjust sentence against you; for it is evident that no man can have any love for God who is proved to have lost the favor and affection of his spiritual father through the sin of disobedience.

When we heard this news we were influenced by our love for you and our memory of your good qualities, which had been reported to us by pious men, to bear with you until now, hoping that you might be touched by light from above and return to wiser counsels, striving to present yourself purified before the Eternal King, whose judgment seat you are daily approaching. But since you have set the love of this world above the safety of your soul, we are afraid that divine wrath may severely punish your long-continued and uncorrected offense.

Wherefore we admonish you in fatherly love to rise above this sin which completely destroys the fruit of your well-doing and, following wiser counsels, to rescue yourself from bondage to the Devil. If you have confidence that your innocence in this matter can be proved, it seems to us highly advisable that a synod be held at which our legates, Hugo, bishop of Die, and Richard [abbot of Marseilles], or either of them, may be present, so that in the hearing of men of religion inquiry may be made whether or in what way the sentence passed upon you should be modified.

God knows and our conscience bears us witness that our heart would rejoice greatly in you as one whom we once sincerely loved, if in any way you could free yourself from this disgrace and shut the door against the ancient enemy by means of your reformation, so that he may do you no further injury. The gifts you offer we do not think we can receive, because it is clear that they are not acceptable in the sight of God so long as you are not freed from your sin and have not returned to the favor of Almighty God as befits a Christian prince. But, though we may not receive your gifts on account of this sin, still we do not cease to implore the mercy of God for you.

Further, we warn and command Your Excellency to restore to your bishop the goods you have taken from him, to give him due compensation and presume not to annoy him in future.

TO THE CLERGY AND PEOPLE OF TOURS AND ANGERS, IN THE AFFAIR OF COUNT FULCO

Book IX, 24, p. 605. 1082-1083.

Gregory . . . to those abbots, clergy and laity of the archbishopric of Tours and the bishopric of Angers who are obedient to God and St. Peter and the Apostolic See, greeting . . .

You are doubtless aware that the Count of Anjou has been excommunicated for his sins, and this ban is extended also to those who aid and abet him, as is evident to all who are versed in Holy Scripture. After long delay he has not only refused to depart from his evil ways and return to God as becomes a Christian man but has added to his misdeeds by plotting with other excommunicated persons to drive out our brother, the archbishop of Tours, from his see and to plunder the goods of the Church.

Therefore, by our apostolic authority, we command you to avoid with the greatest care all associations and all dealings with the count and all his followers and accomplices. But as to our brother, the archbishop, who has suffered blows and persecution for righteousness' sake, we enjoin upon you with equal earnestness to obey him loyally and devotedly and do your best to assist him generously as faithful sons. For as those who favor the count will surely call down upon themselves the wrath of God, so surely will those who are helpful to our brother in his necessity merit the favor of St. Peter and absolution for their sins.

We direct B., venerable abbot of St. Mary [?], to carry to the canons of St. Martin the letters which we are addressing to them.

A General Apologia to All Clerics and Laymen Not under Ban

Book IX, 29, p. 612. Summer, 1083.

Gregory . . . to all, clergymen or laymen, who are not under excommunication, greeting . . .

This will inform you, beloved brethren and sons, that we greatly desire under sanction of our apostolic authority to summon a general council in a place of security and so accessible that friends and enemies, lay or clerical, from all quarters of the earth may gather there without fear. We propose to hold an inquiry and after careful discussion drag forth out of the caverns of his evasions into the sight of all the world the author and cause of the multitude of evils that are now pressing upon the Christian faith. It is his disloyalty and unheard-of audacity that have thus far prevented a peace of God and a sincere reconciliation between Papacy and Empire, and such a peace as Christian fidelity desires and demands we hope to accomplish at this council.

There also we shall be ready, with God's help and to the honor of St. Peter, according to the decrees of the holy fathers, to lay bare the iniquities of the evil-minded and to make plain the innocence of the Apostolic See of the charges made against it, which have caused certain of our brethren to murmur in secret — and this in such a way that, above all, the property of the Holy Roman Church which, as everyone knows, has been confiscated may be duly restored.

We think it worth while to call your loyal attention to the fact that, as God is our witness, it was not by our advice or command that Rudolf was made king by the Germans; furthermore, that we proclaimed by a synodal decree that unless the archbishops and bishops who consecrated him could lawfully defend this action they should be deprived of their offices and Rudolf deposed from his kingdom. Meanwhile, who it was that interfered with this declaration of ours many of you know, and it could not escape our knowledge. For if Henry, so-called king, had preserved the obedience which he had vowed to us — nay, to St. Peter — I say with confidence that by God's help so many evils, murder, perjury, sacrilege, simony and treason would never have happened.

And so now do you, who are moved by such misfortunes or by the fear of God toward a peace worthy of his approval, labor and strive that a council such as we have proposed may come to pass, so that Holy Church, both head and members, now tossed about by tempests of wicked fraud, may find rest and be established forever by the common consent and power of all good men.

A Call to the Faithful to Protect the Church from Her Enemies

Epistolae collectae, 46, p. 572.   1084.

Gregory . . . to all the faithful in Christ who truly love the Apostolic See, greeting . . .

You are aware, beloved brethren, that in our day the question arises which was asked in the Psalm: "Why do the nations rage and the peoples imagine a vain thing? The kings of the earth set themselves and the rulers take counsel together against the Lord and against his anointed."

The rulers of the people and the rulers of the priests have taken counsel together against Christ, son of Almighty God, and against Peter, his Apostle, to crush the Christian faith and to spread abroad the iniquity of heresy. But, by the grace of God, they have not been able to turn those who trust in the Lord to their impious ways by any fear or cruelty or by any promise of earthly glory. These evil conspirators have lifted up their hands against us for no other reason except that we would not let the peril of Holy Church pass in silence and those . . .* who are not ashamed to reduce the bride of Christ to slavery. In every country even the poorest of women is permitted to take a lawful husband according to the law of the land and by her own choice; but, through the desires and evil practices of the wicked, Holy Church, the bride of God and mother of us all, is not permitted lawfully to cling to her spouse on earth in accordance with divine law and her own will. We ought not to suffer the sons of the Church to be subjected to heretical adulterers and usurpers as to their fathers and to be branded by these with the mark of adultery.

How many evils, what diverse perils and unheard-of criminal cruelties have arisen from this cause you may see as plain as day from the true reports of our legates. If you are truly grieved at the ruinous confusions of the Christian faith and desire to lend a helping hand, you may receive ample instruction from them. For they are most loyal to St. Peter and are numbered, each in his own

* Hiatus in the manuscript.

order, among the chief members of his House. No promises and no
earthly rewards have been able to turn them from their loyal defense of him or to separate them from the bosom of Holy Mother
Church. But because, as you my brethren know, the divine voice
speaks to the unworthy and the sinful by the Prophet: "Upon a
high and lofty mountain . . . ," and again, "Cry aloud, spare not!"
therefore, setting aside all false shame or fear or any earthly affection, I preach the Gospel, whether I will or no. I cry aloud again
and again, and I declare to you that the true Christian faith, as
taught to us by our fathers through the son of God descending
from Heaven, is turned over to the evil fashions of this world and
is alas! alas! almost annihilated. Its ancient colors are changed,
and it has become the laughingstock, not only of the Devil, but of
Jews, Saracens and pagans.

For these obey their own laws, though they are now of no avail
for the salvation of souls and are not, like our law, set forth and
sanctioned by repeated declarations of the Eternal King. Whereas
we, intoxicated by worldly desire and setting greed and pride
above all religion and honor, appear like outlaws and simpletons.
We do not regard our welfare and dignity in this life or in the
future as our fathers did, nor have we their hope as we ought to
have. Or if there be some — and very few they are — who fear
God, they are willing enough to fight for themselves but not for the
common welfare of their brethren. Who is there, or how many are
there who, in the fear and love of Almighty God in whom we live
and move and have our being, strive and labor even unto death as
do soldiers of this world for their masters or even for their subordinates? Behold thousands of these rushing into death daily for
their masters, but for the true God of Heaven and for our Redeemer they will not only not meet death, but will not even brave
the enmity of a few men.

And if there be those — for by God's mercy there are some,
though few indeed — who stand up and face the wicked even unto
death for love of the Christian law, not only are they not supported
by their brethren as they should be, but they are looked upon as
weak and reckless madmen. But now, since these and other evils
are threatening us, that we may be able, by God's grace, to root out
vice from the hearts of our brethren and plant virtue in its place,
we beg and beseech you in the name of our Lord Jesus, who re-

deemed us by his death, to inform yourselves by careful inquiry what trials and oppressions we suffer from the enemies of the Christian faith and why we suffer them. From the moment when by divine inspiration Mother Church raised me, unworthy and God knows unwilling, to the apostolic throne, I have labored with all my power that Holy Church, the bride of God, our Lady Mother, might come again to her own splendor and might remain free, pure, and Catholic. But because this was not pleasing to our ancient enemy, he stirred up his members against us to bring it to nought. Thus he accomplished against us — nay, against the Apostolic See — what he had not been able to do since the time of Constantine the Great. And no wonder! for the nearer the day of Antichrist approaches, the harder he fights to crush out the Christian faith.

And now, beloved brethren, give attentive ear to what I say. Throughout the world all who own the Christian name and truly understand the Christian faith know and confess: that St. Peter, chief of the Apostles, is the father of all Christians and, under Christ, their chief pastor; and that the Holy Roman Church is the mother and mistress of all churches. If, therefore, you believe and hold this without a doubt, I ask and command you, by Almighty God, to aid and rescue these your father and mother if you wish to gain through them absolution for all your sins and grace and blessing in this world and the world to come.

May Almighty God, from whom all good things do proceed, enlighten your minds forever and fill them with love for him and for your neighbor. So that you may be worthy to have your father and your mother as your debtors and may enter without shame into their fellowship. Amen.

BIBLIOGRAPHY

Bernheim, E., Quellen zur Geschichte des Investiturstreits. 2 vols., 1913.

Blaul, Otto, Studien zum Register Gregors VII. *Archiv für Urkundenforschung*, IV (1912), 113-228.

Carlyle, R. W. and A. J., A History of Mediaeval Political Theory in the West. 4 vols., 1903-1922.

Caspar, Erich, Das Register Gregors VII. "Monumenta Germaniae historica . . . Epistolae selectae," t. II, pts. 1, 2, 1920-1923.

—— Gregor VII in seinen Briefen. *Historische Zeitschrift*, CXXX (1924).

—— Studien zum Register Gregors VII. *Neues Archiv*, XXXVIII (1913), 143-226.

Chalandon, D., Histoire de la domination normande en Italie et en Sicile. 2 vols., 1907.

Delarc, O., Saint Grégoire VII et la réforme de l'Église au XIᵉ siècle. 3 vols., 1889-1890.

Ewald, Paul, "Das Registrum Gregorii VII." Historische Untersuchungen A. Schaefer gewidmet. 1881.

Fliche, Augustin, La Réforme Grégorienne. 2 vols., 1924. With an extended bibliography.

Gay, J., Les Papes du XIᵉ siècle et la Chrétienté. 1926.

Hammler, R., Gregors VII Stellung zu Frieden und Krieg. Diss. Greifswald, 1912.

Heinlein, E., Die Bedeutung der Begriffe "superbia" und "humilitas" bei Papst Gregor VII im Sinne Augustins. Diss. Greifswald, 1921.

Herzfeld, J., Papst Gregors VII Begriff der bösen Obrigkeit im Sinne der Anschauungen Augustins und Papst Gregor des Grossen. Diss. Greifswald, 1914.

Jaffé, Philip, Registrum Gregorii VII. "Bibliotheca rerum Germanicarum," t. II (Monumenta Gregoriana). Berlin, 1865.

—— Gregorii VII, epistolae collectae, *ibid.*, pp. 520-576.

Koch, B., Manegold von Lautenbach und die Lehre von der Volkssouveränität unter Heinrich IV. 1902.

Koeniger, A. M., "Prima sedes a nemine judicatur." Beiträge zur Geschichte des christlichen Alterthums. 1922, pp. 273-300.

Krüger, H., Was versteht Gregor VII unter "justitia" und wie wendet er diesen Begriff im einzelnen praktisch an? Diss. Greifswald, 1910.

Lange, J., Das Staatensystem Gregors VII auf Grund des augustinischen Begriffs von der "libertas ecclesiae." Diss. Greifswald, 1915.

Letters of King Henry IV. "Monumenta Germaniae historica. . . Constitutiones et Acta," I. Also in Bruno, De bello saxonico, c. 66-67, "Monumenta Germaniae historica . . . Scriptores," V, 351; and in Jaffé, "Bibliotheca rerum Germanicarum," V, 498.

Libelli de lite imperatorum et pontificum. "Monumenta Germaniae historica," 3 t., 1891-1897. A collection of the most important controversial writings.

Martens, W., Gregor VII, sein Leben und Wirken. 2 vols., 1894.

Massino, J., Gregor VII im Verhältniss zu seinen Legaten. Diss. Griefswald, 1907.

Mathew, A. H., The Life and Times of Hildebrand. 1910.

Meine, Otto, Gregors VII Auffassung vom Fürstenamt im Verhältniss zu den Fürsten seiner Zeit. Diss. Griefswald, 1907.

Meyer von Knonau, Gerold, Jahrbücher des deutschen Reichs unter Heinrich IV und V. 7 vols., 1890-1909.

Mirbt, Karl, Die Publizistik im Zeitalter Gregors VII. Leipzig, 1894.

———— Quellen zur Geschichte des Papstthums und des römischen Katholicismus. 4th ed., 1924.

Oestreich, Rev. Th., The Personality and Character of Gregory VII in Recent Historical Research. *Catholic Historical Review*, New Series I (1921), 35-43.

Richard, P., La Monarchie pontificale jusqu'au concile de Trente. *Revue d'histoire ecclésiastique*, t. XX (1924), 413-456.

Rivière, J., Le Problème de l'Église et de l'État au temps de Philippe le Bel. Paris, 1926.

Scharnagl, A., Der Begriff der Investitur in den Quellen und der Literatur des Investiturstreits. Stuttgart, 1908.

Schneider, W., Papst Gregor und das Kirchengut. Griefswald, 1919.

Schumann, O., Die päpstlichen Legaten in Deutschland zur Zeit Heinrichs IV und Heinrichs V. Diss. Marburg, 1912.

Peitz, W. M., S. J., Das Originalregister Gregors VII im Vatikanischen Archiv, nebst Beiträgen zur Kenntniss der Originalregister Innozenz' III und Honorius' III. *Sitzungsberichte der kaiserlichen Akademie der Wissenschaften in Wien, philosophisch-historische Klasse*, Bd. 165, Abth. 5 (1911).

Seckel, E., Die Anfänge der europäischen Jurisprudenz im 11^n und 12^n Jahrhundert. *Zeitschrift der Savigny-Stiftung für Rechtsgeschichte*, Röm. Abth. XLV (1925), 391-395.

Stutz, U., Zur Geschichte des Königswahlrechtes im Mittelalter. *Zeitschrift der Savigny-Stiftung für Rechtsgeschichte*, Germ. Abth. XLIV (1924), 263-288.

Voosen, Élie, Papauté et pouvoir civil à l'époque de Grégoire VII. 1927. With an extended bibliography.

Weinert, E., Die Bedeutung der superbia und humilitas in den Briefen Gregors VII. Diss. Greifswald, 1920.

THE CORRESPONDENCE OF
POPE GREGORY VII

INDEX

INDEX

The abbreviations f. and ff. indicate that the reference is to the page designated and, respectively, to that next following or to the two next following.

Vassalage, 126 f., 134 ff., 158 ff., 180
Venantius, 183
Venice, letter of Gregory to the doge and people of, 61 f.
Vernacular, use of, forbidden in divine service, 148
Victor II, pope (1054-57), 16
Vineyard, parable of the, applied to Sweden, 185
Visigoths, 184
Visitatio liminum, xxvi, 5, 13 f., 16, 20, 22, 25, 28, 30, 33 f., 43, 52, 53, 56, 59, 60, 70, 74, 75, 78 f., 80, 85, 86, 116, 117, 128, 141 f., 149, 185

Walter of Douai, 116
Warmond, archbishop of Vienne, 131
Welf IV, duke of Bavaria, 179
Werembold, complaint of, 133
Werner II, bishop of Strasbourg, 33 f., 56, 82; letter of Gregory to, 49 f.
Wezelin, letter of Gregory to, 144
Wibert, archbishop of Ravenna, xviii; letters of Gregory to, xx, 3 f., 128 f.; decree of suspension against, 129. *See* Clement III, antipope
Wilfred of Milan, letter of Gregory to, 91 f.
William I (the Conqueror), king of

England, 20, 141 f.; letters of Gregory to, 30 ff., 107 ff., 114 ff., 154 ff.; called *gemma principum*, 155; to be dealt with leniently, 182 f.
William, count of Poitou and duke of Aquitaine, letters of Gregory to, 38 f., 50 f.
William, count of Upper Burgundy (Franche-Comté), letter of Gregory to, 22 f.
William, archbishop of Auch, 13 f.
William, archbishop of Rouen, 182
William, bishop of Pavia, 46; letter of Gregory to, 59
William, bishop of Populonia, papal legate, 164
William, bishop of Utrecht, 109
William, abbot of Hirschau, letter of Gregory to, 178-181
Wine, unmixed, used in the sacrament, 157
Worms, concordat of (1122), xii
Wratislaw, duke of Bohemia, 43; letters of Gregory to, 14 f., 44 f.

Yoke of oxen, unit in reckoning tribute, 160

Zachary, pope (741-752), 103, 170

The Art of Courtly Love, by Andreas Capellanus. Translated with an introduction and notes by John Jay Parry.

Medieval Handbooks of Penance: The Principal Libri Poenitentiales and Selections from Related Documents. Translated by John T. McNeill and Helena M. G. Editingamer.

Macrobius: Commentary on The Dream of Scipio. Translated with an introduction by William Harris Stahl.

Medieval Trade in the Mediterranean World: Illustrative Documents. Translated with introductions and notes by Robert S. Lopez and Irving W. Raymond, with a foreword and bibliography by Olivia Remie Constable.

The Cosmographia *of Bernardus Silvestris.* Translated with an introduction by Winthrop Wetherbee.

Heresies of the High Middle Ages. Translated and annotated by Walker L. Wakefield and Austin P. Evans.

Martianus Capella and the Seven Liberal Arts.

> Vol. I: *The Quadrivium of Martianus Capella: Latin Traditions in the Mathematical Sciences,* by William Harris Stahl with Richard Johnson and E. L. Burge.

> Vol. II: *The Marriage of Philology and Mercury,* by Martianus Capella. Translated by William Harris Stahl and Richard Johnson with E. L. Burge.

The See of Peter, by James T. Shotwell and Louise Ropes Loomis.

Two Renaissance Book Hunters: The Letters of Poggius Bracciolini to Nicolaus de Niccolis. Translated and annotated by Phyllis Walter Goodhart Gordan.

Guillaume d'Orange: Four Twelfth-Century Epics. Translated with an introduction by Joan M. Ferrante.

Visions of the End: Apocalyptic Traditions in the Middle Ages, by Bernard McGinn, with a new preface and expanded bibliography.

The Letters of Saint Boniface. Translated by Ephraim Emerton, with a new introduction and bibliography by Thomas F. X. Noble.

Imperial Lives and Letters of the Eleventh Century. Translated by Theodor E. Mommsen and Karl F. Morrison, with a historical introduction and new suggested readings by Karl F. Morrison.

An Arab-Syrian Gentleman and Warrior in the Period of the Crusades: Memoirs of Usāmah ibn-Munqidh. Translated by Philip K. Hitti, with a new foreword by Richard W. Bulliet.

De expugnatione Lyxbonensi (The Conquest of Lisbon). Edited and translated by Charles Wendell David, with a new foreword and bibliography by Jonathan Phillips.

Defensor pacis. Translated with an introduction by Alan Gewirth, with an afterword and updated bibliography by Cary J. Nederman.

History of the Archbishops of Hamburg-Bremen. Translated with an introduction and notes by Francis J. Tschan, with a new introduction and bibliography by Timothy Reuter.

The Two Cities: A Chronicle of Universal History to the Year 1146, by Otto, Bishop of Freising. Translated in full with an introduction and notes by Charles Christopher Mierow, with a foreword and updated bibliography by Karl F. Morrison.

$\mathcal{R}$ECORDS OF WESTERN CIVILIZATION is a series published under the auspices of the Interdepartmental Committee on Medieval and Renaissance Studies of the Columbia University Graduate School. The Western Records are, in fact, a new incarnation of a venerable series, the Columbia Records of Civilization, which, for more than half a century, published sources and studies concerning great literary and historical landmarks. Many of the volumes of that series retain value, especially for their translations into English of primary sources, and the Medieval and Renaissance Studies Committee is pleased to cooperate with Columbia University Press in reissuing a selection of those works in paperback editions, especially suited for classroom use, and in limited clothbound editions.

CPSIA information can be obtained at www.ICGtesting.com
Printed in the USA
LVOW06s2123020116

468774LV00005B/32/P